Cost of Capital Fourth Edition Workbook and Technical Supplement

Cost of Capital Fourth Edition Workbook and Technical Supplement

SHANNON P. PRATT
ROGER J. GRABOWSKI

WILEY

John Wiley & Sons, Inc.

For general information on our other products and services or for technical support, please contact our Customer Care Department within the United States at (800) 762-2974, outside the United States at (317) 572-3993 or fax (317) 572-4002.

Wiley also publishes its books in a variety of electronic formats. Some content that appears in print may not be available in electronic books. For more information about Wiley products, visit our web site at www.wiley.com.

Library of Congress Cataloging-in-Publication Data:

ISBN 978-0-470-47606-2; ISBN 978-0-470-94492-9 (ebk); ISBN 978-0-470-94934-4 (ebk); ISBN 978-0-470-94935-1 (ebk)

Printed in the United States of America

10 9 8 7 6 5 4 3 2 1

Contents

Preface

Why did we add the *Workbook and Technical Supplement* to the *Cost of Capital: Applications and Examples*, 4th ed.? We wanted to further assist practitioners in better understanding how to estimate the cost of capital. This text adds more detailed examples to the *Cost of Capital: Applications and Examples*, 4th ed. It also contains questions and problems covering the material contained in the *Cost of Capital: Applications and Examples*, 4th ed. designed to help the reader better grasp that material.

This book uses the identical notation and abbreviations as those used in the text. Those can be referenced either in *Cost of Capital: Applications and Examples*, 4th ed. or on the companion web site (see later).

Part One contains technical supplements to several chapters. These will help the reader to be better able to implement the methods of analyses discussed in the main book.

Part Two contains an example of specific applications of applying the theory to the cost of capital for private investment companies, including one approach to incorporating the discount for lack of control and lack of marketability into the cost of capital. It also contains chapters extending the general concepts of developing cost of capital to real estate properties and real estate entities. These investments have their own set of terminologies unique to the industry, and we cover the terminology and methods of analysis commonly used in the industry in detail.

Part Three contains learning objectives, questions, and problems to help the practitioner better understand the content of the first 34 chapters of the *Cost of Capital: Applications and Examples*, 4th ed.

Part Four contains the answers to the questions and solutions to the problems presented in Part Three.

Finally, this book includes a companion web site, which can be found at www .wiley.com/go/coc4e. The web site includes the following:

1. The notation system and abbreviations used in this book.
2. The worksheets that are presented as exhibits in Chapters 5, Iterative Process Using CAPM to Calculate the Cost of Equity Component of the Weighted Average Cost of Capital When Capital Structure Is Constant; in Chapter 6, Iterative Process Using CAPM to Calculate the Cost of Equity Component of the Weighted Average Cost of Capital When Capital Structure Is Changing; and in Chapter 8, Cost of Capital of Private Investment Company Interests. These exhibits are provided for your reference so that you can track the methodologies discussed in the book and see how they are implemented through the Microsoft *Excel* worksheets. This will assist you in building models of your own using the worksheets as templates. Note that each file, however, typically contains additional information in different worksheets within that file.

3. Three appendices:
   - Appendix I: Sample Report Submitted to U.S. Tax Court (Supplement to Chapters 7 and 17) is an example of a report submitted to the U.S. Tax Court to help readers communicate the cost of capital methods in a straightforward way to the nontechnical reader.
   - Appendix II discusses the *ValuSource* Valuation Software, which is a helpful tool for the practitioner.
   - Appendix III contains a comprehensive review of the statistics discussed in the *Cost of Capital: Applications and Examples,* 4th ed. and used in developing the cost of capital. We included this appendix so practitioners who may need a refresher in basic statistics do not need to try to locate their statistics books from college. It covers many topics including probability theory (important for understanding and measuring risk), the statistics (e.g., mean, mode, standard deviation, beta, etc.) that are used to summarize return and risk data, and basic concepts of risk neutral payoffs and probabilities. It also includes formulas, terminology, and the statistical tools of the Microsoft *Excel* Analysis Toolpak.
4. PowerPoints that accompany the chapters of *Cost of Capital: Applications and Examples,* 4th ed. to assist those that want to use the book in seminars.

About the Authors

Dr. Shannon P. Pratt, CFA, FASA, ARM, MCBA, ABAR, CM&AA, is the chairman and CEO of Shannon Pratt Valuations, Inc., a nationally recognized business valuation firm headquartered in Portland, Oregon. He is also the founder and editor emeritus of Business Valuation Resources, LLC, and one of the founders of Willamette Management Associates, for which he was a managing director for almost 35 years.

He has performed valuation assignments for these purposes: transaction (acquisition, divestiture, reorganization, public offerings, public companies going private), taxation (federal income, gift, and estate and local ad valorem), financing (securitization, recapitalization, restructuring), litigation support and dispute resolution (including dissenting stockholder suits, damage cases, and corporate and marital dissolution cases), and management information and planning. He has also managed a variety of fairness opinion and solvency opinion engagements. He regularly reviews business valuation reports for attorneys in litigation matters.

Dr. Pratt has testified on hundreds of occasions in such litigated matters as dissenting stockholder suits, various types of damage cases (including breach of contract, antitrust, and breach of fiduciary duty), divorces, and estate and gift tax cases. Among the cases in which he has testified are *Estate of Mark S. Gallo v. Commissioner, Charles S. Foltz, et al. v. U.S. News & World Report et al., Estate of Martha Watts v. Commissioner,* and *Okerlund v. United States.* He has also served as appointed arbitrator in numerous cases.

Previous Experience

Before founding Willamette Management Associates in 1969, Dr. Pratt was a professor of business administration at Portland State University. During this time, he directed a research center known as the Investment Analysis Center, which worked closely with the University of Chicago's Center for Research in Security Prices.

Education

Doctor of Business Administration, Finance, Indiana University.
Bachelor of Arts, Business Administration, University of Washington.

Professional Affiliations

Dr. Pratt is an Accredited Senior Appraiser and Fellow (FASA), Certified in Business Valuation, of the American Society of Appraisers (their highest designation) and is also accredited in Appraisal Review and Management (ARM). He is a Chartered Financial Analyst (CFA), a Master Certified Business Appraiser

(MCBA) and Accredited in Business Appraisal Review (ABAR) by the Institute of Business Appraisers, a Master Certified Business Counselor (MCBC), and is Certified in Mergers and Acquisitions (CM&AA) with the Alliance of Merger and Acquisition Advisors.

Dr. Pratt is a life member of the American Society of Appraisers, a life member of the Business Valuation Committee of that organization, and a teacher of courses for the organization. He is also a lifetime member emeritus of the Advisory Committee on Valuations of the ESOP Association. He is a recipient of the magna cum laude award of the National Association of Certified Valuation Analysts for service to the business valuation profession. He is also the first life member of the Institute of Business Appraisers. He is a member and a past president of the Portland Society of Financial Analysts, the recipient of the 2002 Distinguished Achievement Award, and a member of the Association for Corporate Growth. Dr. Pratt is a past trustee of the Appraisal Foundation and is currently an outside director and chair of the audit committee of Paulson Capital Corp., a NASDAQ-listed investment banking firm specializing in small initial public offerings (usually under $50 million).

Publications

Dr. Pratt is the author of *Valuing a Business: The Analysis and Appraisal of Closely Held Companies*, 5th ed. (New York: McGraw-Hill, 2008); co-author, *Valuing Small Businesses and Professional Practices*, 3rd ed., with Robert Schweihs and Robert Reilly (New York: McGraw-Hill, 1998); co-author, *Guide to Business Valuations*, 20th ed., with Jay Fishman, Cliff Griffith, and Jim Hitchner (Fort Worth, TX: Practitioners Publishing Company, 2010); co-author, *Standards of Value*, with William Morrison and Jay Fishman (Hoboken, NJ: John Wiley & Sons, 2007); co-author, *Business Valuation and Taxes: Procedure, Law, and Perspective*, 2nd ed., with Judge David Laro (Hoboken, NJ: John Wiley & Sons, 2010); and author, *Business Valuation Discounts and Premiums*, 2nd ed. (Hoboken, NJ: John Wiley & Sons, 2009); *Business Valuation Body of Knowledge: Exam Review and Professional Reference*, 2nd ed. (Hoboken, NJ: John Wiley & Sons, 2003); *The Market Approach to Valuing Businesses*, 2nd ed. (Hoboken, NJ: John Wiley & Sons, 2005); and *The Lawyer's Business Valuation Handbook*, 2nd ed. (Chicago: American Bar Association, 2010). He has also published nearly 200 articles on business valuation topics.

Roger Grabowski, ASA, is a managing director of Duff & Phelps, LLC.

Mr. Grabowski has directed valuations of businesses, partial interests in businesses, intellectual property, intangible assets, real property, and machinery and equipment for various purposes, including tax (income and ad valorem) and financial reporting; mergers, acquisitions, formation of joint ventures, divestitures, and financing. He developed methodologies and statistical programs for analyzing useful lives of tangible and intangible assets, such as customers and subscribers. His experience includes work in a wide range of industries, including sports, movies, recording, broadcast and other entertainment businesses; newspapers, magazines, music, and other publishing businesses; retail; banking, insurance, consumer credit, and other financial services businesses; railroads and other transportation companies; mining ventures; software and electronic component businesses; and a variety of manufacturing businesses.

Mr. Grabowski has testified in court as an expert witness on the value of closely held businesses and business interests; matters of solvency, valuation, and amortization of intangible assets; and other valuation issues. His testimony in U.S. District Court was referenced in the U.S. Supreme Court opinion decided in his client's favor in the landmark *Newark Morning Ledger* income tax case. Among other cases in which he has testified are *Herbert V. Kohler Jr., et al. v. Comm.* (value of stock of The Kohler Company); *The Northern Trust Company, et al. v. Comm.* (the first U.S. Tax Court case that recognized the use of the discounted cash flow method for valuing a closely held business); *Oakland Raiders v. Oakland–Alameda County Coliseum Inc. et al.* (valuation of the Oakland Raiders); *In re: Louisiana Riverboat Gaming Partnership, et al. Debtors* (valuation of business enterprise owning two riverboat casinos and feasibility of plan of reorganization); *ABC-NACO, Inc. et al., Debtors, and The Official Committee of Unsecured Creditors of ABC-NACO v. Bank of America, N.A.* (valuation of collateral); *Wisniewski and Walsh v. Walsh* (oppressed shareholder action); and *TMR Energy Limited v. The State Property Fund of Ukraine* (arbitration on behalf of world's largest private company in Stockholm, Sweden, on cost of capital for oil refinery in Ukraine in a contract dispute).

Previous Experience

Mr. Grabowski was formerly managing director of the Standard & Poor's Corporate Value Consulting practice and a partner of PricewaterhouseCoopers, LLP, and one of its predecessor firms, Price Waterhouse (where he founded its U.S. Valuation Services practice and managed the real estate appraisal practice). Prior to Price Waterhouse, he was a finance instructor at Loyola University of Chicago, a cofounder of Valtec Associates, and a vice president of American Valuation Consultants.

Education

Mr. Grabowski received his BBA–Finance from Loyola University of Chicago and completed all coursework in the doctoral program, Finance, at Northwestern University, Chicago.

Professional Affiliations

He serves on the Loyola University School of Business Administration Dean's Board of Advisors. Mr. Grabowski is an Accredited Senior Appraiser of the American Society of Appraisers (ASA) certified in business valuation. He serves as Editor of the *Business Valuation Review*, the quarterly journal of the Business Valuation Committee of the American Society of Appraisers.

Publications

Mr. Grabowski authors the annual Duff & Phelps *Risk Premium Report*. He lectures and publishes regularly. Recent articles include "The Cost of Capital," *Journal of Business Valuation*, the Canadian Institute of Chartered Business Valuators, August 2009; "Problemas relacionados con el cálculo del coste de capital en el entorno actual: actualizaciòn," co-authored with Mathias Schumacher, *Análisis Financiero Internactional*, Sumario N° 137 Tercer trimestre 2009; "Cost of Capital Estimation in the Current Distressed Environment," *The Journal of Applied Research in Accounting and Finance*, July 2009; "Cost of Capital in Valuation of Stock by the Income Approach: Updated for an Economy in Crisis," with Shannon P. Pratt, *Jahreskonferenz der NACVA, Bewertungs Praktiker*, January 2009; "Problems with Cost of Capital Estimation in the Current Environment—2008 Update," *Business Valuation Review*, Winter 2008 and *Business Valuation E-Letter*, February 2009; and "Cost of Capital in Valuation of Stock by the Income Approach: Updated for Economy in Crisis," *The Value Examiner*, January–February 2009.

He is the co-author *Cost of Capital: Applications and Examples*, 3rd ed., with Shannon P. Pratt (Hoboken, NJ: John Wiley & Sons, 2008) and co-author of three chapters (on equity risk premium, valuing pass-through entities, and valuing sports teams) in Robert Reilly and Robert P. Schweihs, *The Handbook of Business Valuation and Intellectual Property Analysis* (New York: McGraw-Hill, 2004).

He teaches courses for the American Society of Appraisers including *Cost of Capital*, a course he developed.

Joanne Fong, CFA, CPA, is a Senior Manager in the Transaction Advisory Services–Valuation & Business Modeling practice in the Chicago office of Ernst & Young LLP. Ms. Fong holds a Master of Business Administration and a Bachelor of Business Administration, both from the University of Michigan, Ross School of Business.

Ms. Fong co-authored Chapter 7 of the *Cost of Capital: Applications and Examples*, 4th ed. *Workbook and Technical Supplement.*

William H. Frazier, ASA, is a principal and founder of the firm of Howard Frazier Barker Elliott, Inc, and manages its Dallas office. He has 30 years of experience in business valuation and corporate finance. Mr. Frazier has been an Accredited Senior Appraiser of the American Society of Appraisers (ASA) since 1987 and serves on the ASA's Government Relations Committee. He has participated as an appraiser and/or expert witness in numerous U.S. Tax Court cases, including testimony in *Jelke, McCord, Dunn,* and *Gladys Cook.* Mr. Frazier has written numerous articles on the subject of business valuation for tax purposes, appearing in such publications as the *Business Valuation Review, Valuation Strategies, BV E-Letter, Shannon Pratt's Business Valuation Update,* and *Estate Planning.* He is the co-author of the chapter on valuing family limited partnerships in Robert Reilly and Robert P. Schweihs, eds., *The Handbook of Business Valuation and Intellectual Property Analysis* (New York: McGraw-Hill, 2004). Mr. Frazier serves on the IRS Advisory Council (IRSAC) and the Valuation Advisory Board of *Trusts & Estates Journal.*

Mr. Frazier contributed Chapter 8 of the *Cost of Capital: Applications and Examples*, 4th ed. *Workbook and Technical Supplement* and the companion *Excel* worksheets that appear on the John Wiley & Sons web site.

Terry V. Grissom, PhD, CRE, MAI, serves on the faculty at the University of Washington. He just completed a faculty assignment at the University of Ulster, Built Environment Research Institute. He received his PhD in Business from the University of Wisconsin, Madison, majoring in Real Estate and Urban Land Economics, with minors in Finance/Risk Management and Civil-Environmental Engineering. He received an MS in Real Estate Appraisal and Investment Analysis, also from the University of Wisconsin, and an MBA in Finance, Real Estate, and Urban Affairs from Georgia State University. He did postdoctoral work at Texas A&M University in Econometrics and Statistics.

Dr. Grissom was formerly Professor of Real Estate and Urban Land Economics at Georgia State University, Atlanta, in the Robinson College of Business. Prior to his tenure at GSU, he was Vice-President of Investment Research for Equitable Real Estate Investment Management, an institutional investment advisory for pension funds, insurance companies, and other financial institutions. From 1992 through October 1994, he was the National Research Director for Price Waterhouse's Financial Services Industry Practice.

Dr. Grissom has published more than 100 academic and professional articles, monographs, and working papers in his career to this point. He has also authored, co-authored, and edited four books concerning real estate appraisal and investment analysis, market analysis, and real estate development and land economics. He has also authored chapters in books on real estate development, investment analysis, business and property valuation techniques, and education theory and practice for both academics and practitioners and for both domestic and international audiences.

Dr. Grissom co-authored Chapters 9 and 10 of the *Cost of Capital: Applications and Examples*, 4th ed. *Workbook and Technical Supplement*.

Jim MacCrate, MAI, CRE, ASA, owns his own boutique real estate valuation and consulting company, MacCrate Associates, LLC, located in the New York City metropolitan area, concentrating on complex real estate valuation issues. Formerly, he was the Northeast regional practice leader and director of the Real Estate Valuation/ Advisory Services Group at Price Waterhouse LLP and Pricewaterhouse Coopers LLP. He received a BS degree from Cornell University and an MBA from Long Island University, C. W. Post Center.

Mr. MacCrate has written numerous articles for Price Waterhouse LLP, "The Counselors of Real Estate," and has contributed to the *Appraisal Journal*. He initiated the *Land Investment Survey* that has been incorporated into the PricewaterhouseCoopers *Korpacz Real Estate Investor Survey*. He is on the national faculty for the Appraisal Institute and adjunct professor at New York University.

Mr. MacCrate co-authored Chapters 9 and 10 in the *Cost of Capital: Applications and Examples*, 4th ed. *Workbook and Technical Supplement*.

Harold G. Martin Jr., CPA/ABV/CFF, ASA, CFE, is the Principal-in-Charge of the Business Valuation, Forensic, and Litigation Services Group for Keiter, Stephens, Hurst, Gary & Shreaves, P.C., in Richmond and Charlottesville, Virginia. He has more than 25 years of experience in financial consulting, public accounting, and financial services. He has appeared as an expert witness in federal and state courts, served as a court-appointed neutral business appraiser, and also served as a federal court–appointed accountant for receiverships. He is an adjunct faculty member of the College of William and Mary Mason Graduate School of Business and teaches forensic accounting and valuation in the Master of Accounting program. He is also a guest lecturer on valuation in the MBA program.

Prior to joining Keiter Stephens, he served as a Senior Manager in Management Consulting Services for Price Waterhouse and as a Director in Financial Advisory

Services for Coopers & Lybrand. He currently serves as an instructor for the American Institute of Certified Public Accountants National Business Valuation School and ABV Exam Review Course and also as an editorial advisor and contributing author for the *AICPA CPA Expert*. He is a former member of the AICPA Business Valuation Committee, former editor of the *AICPA ABV e-Alert*, and a two-time recipient of the AICPA Business Valuation Volunteer of the Year Award. He is a frequent speaker and author on valuation topics and is a co-author of *Financial Valuation: Applications and Models*, 2nd ed. (Hoboken, NJ: John Wiley & Sons, 2006).

Mr. Martin received his AB degree in English in 1979 from the College of William and Mary and his MBA degree in 1991 from Virginia Commonwealth University.

Mr. Martin contributed Chapter 10 of the companion *Cost of Capital: Applications and Examples*, 4th ed. *Workbook and Technical Supplement* and the companion *Excel* worksheets that appear on the John Wiley & Sons web site.

James Morris, PhD, AM, received his PhD in Finance from University of California, Berkeley. He is a professor of finance at the University of Colorado at Denver, where he teaches courses in business valuation, financial modeling, and financial management, and he has also served on the finance faculties at the Wharton School of University of Pennsylvania and at the University of Houston and taught finance courses at business schools in England, France, and Germany.

Dr. Morris's recent publications include *Introduction to Financial Models for Management and Planning* with J. Daley (CRC Press, 2009); "Life and Death of Businesses: A Review of Research on Firm Mortality," *Journal of Business Valuation and Economic Analysis* (2009); "Firm Mortality and Business Valuation," *Valuation Strategies* (September–October 2009); "The Iterative Process Using CAPM to Calculate the Cost of Equity Component of the Weighted Average Cost of Capital When Capital Structure is Changing," Appendix 7.2 in Pratt and Grabowski, *Cost of Capital: Applications and Examples*, 3rd ed. (Hoboken, NJ: John Wiley & Sons, 2008); "Growth in the Constant Growth Model," *Business Valuation Review* (Winter 2006); "Understanding the Minefield of Weighted Average Cost of Capital," *Business Valuation Review* (Fall 2005); and "Reconciling the Equity and Invested Capital Methods of Valuation When the Capital Structure is Changing," *Business Valuation Review* (March 2004). In addition, his research articles have been published in the *Journal of Finance, Journal of Financial & Quantitative Analysis, Journal of Applied Psychology, Academy of Management Journal*, and *Management Science*, among others. In addition to teaching, he provides valuation services to the business community.

Dr. Morris contributed Chapter 6 of the *Cost of Capital: Applications and Examples*, 4th ed. *Workbook and Technical Supplement* and the companion Excel worksheets that appear on the John Wiley & Sons web site.

David M. Ptashne, CFA, is an Associate Director with Ceteris, a global economic consulting firm that provides transfer pricing and business valuation services. Mr. Ptashne has performed numerous valuation studies of businesses, interests in businesses, and intangible assets across various industries, including advertising and communications, consumer products, technology, financial services, integrated oil and gas, retail, and health care. He received a Bachelor of Science degree in Finance with High Honors from the University of Illinois at Urbana-Champaign.

Mr. Ptashne contributed Chapters 2 and 4 of the *Cost of Capital: Applications and Examples*, 4th ed. *Workbook and Technical Supplement*.

Mark Shirley, CPA/ABV/CFE, has earned advanced accreditations: Certified Valuation Analyst and Certified Forensic Financial Analyst. After leaving the Internal Revenue Service in 1984, Mr. Shirley's consulting practice has concentrated on the disciplines of business valuation, forensic/investigative accounting, and financial analysis/modeling. Professional engagements have included business valuation, valuation of options/warrants, projections and forecasts, statistical sampling, commercial damage modeling, personal injury loss assessment, and the evaluation of proffered expert testimony under *Daubert* and the Federal Rules of Evidence.

Since 1988, his technical contributions have been published by Wiley Law Publications, Aspen Legal Press, and in professional periodicals, including *Valuation Examiner*, *BewertungsPraktiker* Nr. (a German-language business valuation journal), *Practical Accountant*, *CPA Litigation Services Counselor*, *Gatekeeper Quarterly*, *Journal of Forensic Accounting*, and local legal society publications. Since 1997, Mr. Shirley has authored courses for NACVA's *Fundamentals, Techniques & Theory; Forensic Institute*, and *Consultant's Training Institute*. He also has developed several advanced courses for the NACVA in applied statistics and financial modeling.

A charter member of the LA Society of CPA's Litigation Services Committee, Mr. Shirley has remained active since the committee's formation. He has been an adjunct faculty member at the National Judicial College, University of Nevada, Reno, since 1998. Mr. Shirley also serves on the Advisory Panel for *Mdex Online; The Daubert Tracker*, an online *Daubert* research database; and the Ethics Oversight Board for the NACVA.

Since 1985, Mr. Shirley has provided expert witness testimony before the U.S. Tax Court, Federal District Court, Louisiana district courts, Tunica-Biloxi Indian Tribal Court, and local specialty courts. Court appointments have been received in various matters adjudicated before the Louisiana Nineteenth Judicial District Court.

The NACVA has recognized Mr. Shirley's contributions to professional education by awarding him the Circle of Light in 2002, Instructor of the Year in 2000–2001, and multiple recognitions as Outstanding Member and Award of Excellence.

Mr. Shirley contributed Chapter 3 of the *Cost of Capital: Applications and Examples*, 4th ed. *Workbook and Technical Supplement* and Appendix III of the *Workbook and Technical Supplement* which appears on the John Wiley & Sons web site.

Acknowledgments

This book has benefited immensely from review by many people with a high level of knowledge and experience in cost of capital and valuation. These people reviewed the manuscript, and the book reflects their invaluable efforts and legions of constructive suggestions:

Bruce Bingham
Capstone Advisory Group LLC
New York, NY

Stephen J. Bravo
Apogee Business Valuation
Framingham, MA

James Budyak
Valuation Research Corp.
Milwaukee, WI

David Clarke
The Griffing Group
Oak Park, IL

Stan Deakin
Mosaic Capital LLC
Los Angeles, CA

Donald A. Erickson
Erickson Partners, LLC
Dallas, TX

Aaron A. Gilcreast
PricewaterhouseCoopers LLC
Atlanta, GA

Professor Joao Gomes
The Wharton School of the
University of Pennsylvania
Philadelphia, PA

Mark Lee
Eisner LLP
New York, NY

Dan McConaughy
Grobstein, Horwath LLP
Sherman Oaks, CA

George Pushner
Duff & Phelps LLC
New York, NY

Raymond Rath
PricewaterhouseCoopers LLC
Los Angeles, CA

Jeffrey Tarbell
Houlihan Lokey
San Francisco, CA

Terence Tchen
Houlihan Lokey
Los Angeles, CA

Marianna Todorova
Duff & Phelps LLC
New York, NY

Richard M. Wise
Wise, Blackman, LLP
Montreal (Quebec), Canada

In addition, we thank:

- Dustin Snyder and Elizabeth Anderson for assistance with editing and research, including updating of the bibliography; updating and shepherding the manuscript among reviewers, contributors, authors, and publisher; typing; obtaining permissions; and other invaluable help.

- David Fein of ValuSource for contributing Appendix II of the *Workbook and Technical Supplement* on ValuSource Pro.
- Noah Gordon of Shannon Pratt Valuations, Inc., for general editorial assistance.

We thank all of the people singled out for their assistance. Of course, any errors are our responsibility.[1]

Shannon Pratt
Roger Grabowski

Notation System and Abbreviations Used in This Book

A source of confusion for those trying to understand financial theory and methods is that financial writers have not adopted a standard system of notation. The notation system used in this volume is adapted from the fifth edition of *Valuing a Business: The Analysis and Appraisal of Closely Held Companies*, by Shannon P. Pratt (New York: McGraw-Hill, 2008).

VALUE AT A POINT IN TIME

P_n	= Stock price in period n
P_0	= Stock price at valuation period
P_i	= Price per share for company i (seen elsewhere as PV)
PV	= Present value
PV_b	= Present value of net cash flows due to business operations before cost of financing
PV_{keu}	= Present value of net cash flows using unlevered cost of equity capital, k_{eu}, as the discount rate
PV_{ts}	= Present value of tax shield due to interest expense on debt capital
PV_{dc}	= Present value of net distress-related costs
PV_{TSn}	= Present value of the tax shield as of time $= n$
PV_f	= Present value of invested capital
TV_n	= Terminal value at time n
M_e	= Market value of equity capital (stock)
M_d	= Market value of debt capital
M_p	= Market value of preferred equity
$MVIC$	= Market value of invested capital
	= Enterprise value
	$= M_e + M_d + M_p$
BV	= Book value of net assets
BV_n	= Book value of equity at time $= n$
BV_i	= Measure of book value (typically book value to market value) of stock of company i
F_d	= Fair value of debt
FV_{RU}	= Fair value of reporting unit
FV_{NWCRU}	= Fair value of net working capital of the reporting unit
FV_{ICRU}	= Fair value of invested capital of the reporting unit
FV_{FARU}	= Fair value of fixed assets of the reporting unit

FV_{IARU} = Fair value on intangible assets, identified and individually valued, of the reporting unit

FV_{UIVRU} = Fair value of unidentified intangibles value (i.e., goodwill) of the reporting unit

FV_{dRU} = Fair value of debt capital of the reporting unit

FV_{eRU} = Fair value of equity capital of the reporting unit

FMV_{BE} = Fair market value of the business enterprise

FMV_{NWC} = Fair market value of net working capital

FMV_{FA} = Fair market value of fixed assets

FMV_{IA} = Fair market value on intangible assets

FMV_{UIV} = Fair market value of unidentified intangibles value (i.e., goodwill)

FMV_{e} = Fair market value of equity capital

$FMV_{e,n,up}$ = Fair market value of equity at time $= n$ assuming "up" scenario (value of BE increases)

$FMV_{BE,n,down}$ = Fair market value of business enterprise at time $= n$ assuming "down" scenario (value of BE decreases)

$FMV_{e,n,down}$ = Fair market value of equity at time $= n$ assuming "down" scenario (value of BE decreases)

COST OF CAPITAL AND RATE OF RETURN VARIABLES

k = Discount rate (generalized)

k_c = Country cost of equity

k_e = Discount rate for common equity capital (cost of common equity capital). Unless otherwise stated, it generally is assumed that this discount rate is applicable to net cash flow available to common equity.

$k_{e,local}$ = Discount rate for equity capital in local country for discounting expected cash flows in local currency

$k_{e,u.s.}$ = Discount rate for equity capital in the United States

k_{BV} = Rate of return on book value, retained portion of net income, usually estimated as $= NI_{n+1}/BV_n$

k_{eu} = Cost of equity capital, unlevered (cost of equity capital assuming firm financed with all equity)

k_{local} = Cost of equity capital in local country

k_i = Discount rate for company i

k_{ni} = Discount rate for equity capital when net income rather than net cash flow is the measure of economic income being discounted

$k_{(pt)}$ = Discount rate applicable to pretax cash flows

k_p = Discount rate for preferred equity capital

k_d = Discount rate for debt (net of tax effect, if any) (Note: For complex capital structures, there could be more than one class of capital in any of the preceding categories, requiring expanded subscripts.)
  $= k_{d(pt)} \times (1 - \text{tax rate})$

$k_{d(pt)}$ = Cost of debt prior to tax effect

k_A = Discount rate for the firm's assets

k_{TS} = Rate of return used to present value tax savings due to deducting interest expense on debt capital financing

k_{eRU} = After tax rate of return on equity capital of reporting unit

$k_{NWC(pt)}$	= Rate of return for net working capital financed with debt capital (measured before interest tax shield) and equity capital
$k_{FA(pt)}$	= Rate of return for fixed assets financed with debt capital (measured before interest tax shield) and equity capital
k_{dRU}	= Rate of return on debt capital of the reporting unit net of tax effect
	= $k_{d(pt)RU} \times (1 - \text{tax } rate)$
k_{NWCRU}	= Rate of return for net working capital of the reporting unit financed with debt capital (return measured net of the tax effect on debt financing, if any) and equity capital
k_{FARU}	= Rate of return for fixed assets financed with debt capital (return measured net of the tax effect on debt financing, if any) and equity capital
k_{IARU}	= Rate of return for identified and individually valued intangible assets financed with debt capital (return measured net of the tax effect on debt financing, if any) and equity capital
k_{UIVRU}	= Rate of return for unidentified intangibles value of the reporting unit financed with debt capital (return measured net of the tax effect on debt financing, if any) and equity capital
$k_{IA+UIV(pt)}$	= Pretax rate of return on all intangible assets, identified and individually valued, plus the unidentified intangible value financed with debt capital (measured before interest tax shield) and equity capital
c	= Capitalization rate
$c_{(pt)}$	= Capitalization rate on pretax cash flows (Note: For complex capital structures, there could be more than one class of capital in any of the preceding categories, requiring expanded subscripts.)
D/P_0	= Dividend yield on stock
DR_j	= Downside risk in the local market (U.S. dollars)
DR_w	= Downside risk in global ("world") market (U.S. dollars)
R	= Rate of return
R_i	= Return on stock i
R_d	= Rate of return on subject debt (e.g., bond) capital
$R_{m,n}$	= Return on market portfolio in current month n
R_f	= Rate of return on a risk-free security
$R_{f,n}$	= Risk-free rate in current month n
$R_{f,local}$	= Return on the local country government's (default-risk-free) paper
$R_{f,u.s.}$	= U.S. risk-free rate
$R_{local\ euro\ \$issue}$	= Current market interest rate on debt issued by the local country government denominated in U.S. dollars ("euro-dollar" debt), same maturity as debt issued by the local country government denominated in U.S. dollars
$(R_{local\ euro\ \$issue}$ $-R_{f,u.s.})$	= Yield spread between government bonds issued by the local country versus U.S. government bonds
R_n	= Return on individual security subject stock in current month
R_m	= Historical rate of return on the "market"
RP	= Risk premium
RP_m	= Risk premium for the "market" (usually used in the context of a market for equity securities, such as the NYSE or S&P 500)
RP_s	= Risk premium for "small" stocks (usually average size of lowest quintile or decile of NYSE as measured by market value of common equity) over and above RP_m
RP_{m+s}	= Risk premium for the market plus risk premium for size (Duff & Phelps *Risk Premium Report* data for use in build-up method)

RP_{s+u} = Risk premium for small size plus risk premium attributable to the specific distressed company

RP_{m+s+u} = Risk premium for the "market" plus risk premium for size plus risk attributable to the specific company

RP_u = Risk premium for company-specific or unsystematic risk attributable to the specific company

RP_w = The equity risk premium on a "world" diversified portfolio

RP_i = Risk premium for the ith security

$RP_{i,s}$ = $B_{i,s} \times S_i$ = Risk premium for size of company i

$RP_{i,BV}$ = $B_{i,BV} \times BV_i$ = Risk premium for book value of company i

$RP_{i,u}$ = $B_{i,u} \times U_i$ = Risk premium for unique or unsystematic risk of company i

RP_{local} = Equity risk premium in local country's stock market

RI_{iL} = Full-information levered beta estimate of the subject company

$E(R)$ = Expected rate of return

$E(R_m)$ = Expected rate of return on the "market" (usually used in the context of a market for equity securities, such as the New York Stock Exchange [NYSE] or Standard & Poor's [S&P] 500)

$E(R_i)$ = Expected rate of return on security i

$E(R_{div})$ = Expected rate of return on dividend

$E(R_{cap-gains})$ = Expected rate of return on capital gains

$E(R_{i,j})$ = Expected rate of return on security i for undiversified investor j

B = Beta (a coefficient, usually used to modify a rate of return variable)

B_i = Expected beta of the stock of company i

B_L = Levered beta for (equity) capital

B_U = Unlevered beta for (equity) capital

B_{LS} = Levered segment beta

B_d = Beta for debt capital

B_p = Beta of preferred capital

B_e = Beta (equity) expanded

B_{op} = Operating beta (beta with effects of fixed operating expense removed)

B_i = Beta of company i (F-F beta)

$B_{i,m}$ = Sensitivity of return of stock of company i to the market risk premium or ERP

$B_{i,s}$ = Sensitivity of return of stock of company i to a measure of size, S, of company i

$B_{i,BV}$ = Sensitivity of return of stock of company i to a measure of book value (typically measure of book-value-to-market-value) of stock of company i

$B_{i,u}$ = Sensitivity of return of stock of company i to a measure of unique or unsystematic risk of company i

B_n = Estimated market coefficient based on sensitivity to excess returns on market portfolio in current month

B_{local} = Market risk of the subject company measured with respect to the local securities market

B_w = Market or systematic risk measured with respect to a "world" portfolio of stocks

$B_{i1} \ldots B_{in}$ = Sensitivity of security i to each risk factor relative to the market average sensitivity to that factor

B_i' = True beta estimate for stock of company i based on relationship to excess returns on market portfolio of equity plus debt, $M_E + M_D$

$B_{u.s.} \times RP_{u.s.}$ = Risk premium appropriate for a U.S. company in similar industry as the subject company in local country, expressed in U.S. dollar-denominated returns

FI-Beta	= Full-information beta for industry
TB_i	= Total beta for security i
β_{cr}	= Country covariance with region
β_{cw}	= Country covariance with world
S_i	= Measure of size of company i
U_i	= Measure of unique or unsystematic risk of company i
λ	= A measure of individual stock's liquidity
$RP_1 \dots RP_n$	= Risk premium associated with risk factor 1 through n for the average asset in the market (used in conjunction with arbitrage pricing theory)
s_i	= Small-minus-big coefficient in the Fama-French regression
SMBP	= Expected small-minus-big risk premium, estimated as the difference between the historical average annual returns on the small-cap and large-cap portfolios (also shown as SMB)
h_i	= High-minus-low coefficient in the Fama-French regression
HMLP	= Expected high-minus-low risk premium, estimated as the difference between the historical average annual returns on the high book-to- market and low book-to-market portfolios (also shown as HML)
F_d	= Face value of outstanding debt
b	= 1 − Payout ratio = retention ratio
$WACC_{(pt)}$	= Weighted average cost of capital (before interest tax shield)
$WACC_{RU}$	= Overall rate of return for the reporting unit
	= Weighted average cost of capital for the reporting unit
$WACC_{(pt)RU}$	= Before interest tax shield WACC of the reporting unit
σ_i^2	= Variance of returns for security i
σ_m^2	= Variance of the returns on the market portfolio (e.g., S&P 500)
σ_e^2	= Variance of error terms
σ	= Standard deviation
σ_e	= Standard deviation of returns on firm's common equity
σ_A	= Standard deviation of returns on firm's assets
σ_B	= Standard deviation of operating cash flows of business before cost of financing
σ_{rev}	= Standard deviation of revenues
σ_{BE}	= Standard deviation of value of business enterpise
σ_{local}	= Volatility of subject (local) stock market
$\sigma_{u.s.}$	= Volatility of U.S. stock market
σ_{stock}	= Volatility of local country's stock market
σ_{bond}	= Volatility of local country's bond market
σ_i	= Standard deviation of returns for security i
σ_m	= Standard deviation of returns for the market portfolio (e.g., S&P 500)
$\sigma_{i,m}$	= Variance of returns on the security, i, and the market, m
σ_D^2	= Variance in excess returns on market of debt
σ_{ME+MD}^2	= Variance in excess returns on market portfolio of equity plus debt, $M_E + M_D$
ρ	= *Correlation coefficient* between the returns on the security, i, and the market, m
δ_r	= Regional risk not included in RP_w
CCR_{local}	= Country credit rating of local country
λ	= Company's exposure to the local country risk
t	= Tax rate (expressed as a percentage of pretax income)
h	= Holding period
$Inflation_{local}$	= Expected rate of inflation in local country
$Inflation_{u.s.}$	= Expected rate of inflation in U.S.

INCOME VARIABLES

E	= Expected economic income (in a generalized sense; i.e., could be dividends, any of several possible definitions of cash flows, net income, etc.)
F	= Fixed operating assets (without regard to costs of financing)
F_c	= Fixed operating costs of the business
NI	= Net income (after entity-level taxes)
$NCI_{e,n}$	= Net comprehensive income to common equity in period n, which includes income terms reported directly in the equity account rather than in the income statement
$NCI_{f,n}$	= Net comprehensive income to the firm in period n, which includes income terms reported directly in the equity account rather than in the income statement
CF	= Cash flow for a specific period
NCF_e	= Net cash flow (free cash flow) to equity
NCF_f	= Net cash flow (free cash flow) to the firm (to overall invested capital, or entire capital structure, including all equity and long-term debt)
NCF_{ue}	= Net cash flow to unlevered equity
D	= Dividends
$D_{e,n}$	= Distributions to common equity, net of new issues of common equity in period n
$D_{f,n}$	= Distributions to total capital, net of new issues of debt or equity capital in period n
$RI_{e,n}$	= Residual income for common equity capital
TS	= Present value of tax savings due to deducting interest expense on debt capital financing
EBT	= Earnings before taxes
$EBIT$	= Earnings before interest and taxes
$EBITDA$	= Earnings before interest, taxes, depreciation, and amortization
V	= Variable operating costs
AEG	= Abnormal earnings growth

PERIODS OR VARIABLES IN A SERIES

i	= ith period or ith variable in a series (may be extended to the jth variable, the kth variable, etc.)
n	= Number of periods or variables in a series, or the last number in a series
0	= Period 0, the base period, usually the latest year immediately preceding the valuation date
p_y	= Partial year of first year following the valuation date

WEIGHTINGS

W	= Weight
W_e	= Weight of common equity in capital structure
	= $M_e/(M_e + M_d + M_p)$
W_p	= Weight of preferred equity in capital structure

$= M_p/(M_e + M_d + M_p)$
W_d $=$ Weight of debt in capital structure
$= M_d/(M_e + M_d + M_p)$ (Note: For purposes of computing a weighted average cost of capital [WACC], it is assumed that preceding weightings are at market value.)
W_{dRU} $=$ Weight of debt capital in capital structure of reporting unit
$=$ Fair value of debt capital/FV_{RU}
W_s $=$ Weight of segment data to total business (e.g., sales, operating income)
W_{NWC} $=$ Weight of net working capital in FMV_{BE}
$= FMV_{NWC}/FMV_{BE}$
W_{NWCRU} $=$ Weight of net working capital in FV_{RU}
$= FV_{NWCRU}/FV_{RU}$
W_{FA} $=$ Weight of fixed assets in FMV_{BE}
$= FMV_{FA}/FMV_{BE}$
W_{FARU} $=$ Weight of fixed assets in FV_{RU}
$= FV_{FARU}/FV_{RU}$
W_{IARU} $=$ Weight of intangible assets in FV_{RU}
$= FV_{IARU}/FV_{RU}$
W_{UIVRU} $=$ Weight of unidentified intangibles value FV_{RU}
$= FV_{UIVRU}$ (i.e., goodwill)$/FV_{RU}$
W_{TS} $=$ Weight of TS in FMV_{BE}
$= TS/FMV_{BE}$

GROWTH

g $=$ Rate of growth in a variable (e.g., net cash flow)
g_i $=$ Dividend growth rate for company i
g_{ni} $=$ Rate of growth in net income

MATHEMATICAL FUNCTIONS

Σ $=$ Sum of (add all the variables that follow)
$\cap$ $=$ Product of (multiply together all the variables that follow)
$\bar{X}$ $=$ Mean average (the sum of the values of the variables divided by the number of variables)
G $=$ Geometric mean (product of the values of the variables taken to the root of the number of variables)
α $=$ Regression constant
ε $=$ Regression error term
ε_i $=$ Error term, difference between predicted return and realized return, R_i
∞ $=$ Infinity
$N(*)$ $=$ Cumulative normal density function (the area under the normal probability distribution)
Δ $=$ Change in . . . (whatever follows)

NOTATION FOR REAL PROPERTY VALUATION (CHAPTER 9 OF *WORKBOOK AND TECHNICAL SUPPLEMENT*)

$DSCR$	= Debt service coverage ratio
$EGIM$	= Effective gross income multiplier
NOI, I_p	= Net operating income
OER	= Operating expense rates
PV_p	= Overall value or present value of the property
k_e	= Equity discount or yield rate (dividend plus appreciation)
k_m	= Mortgage interest rate
k_p	= Property yield discount rate
c_p	= Overall property capitalization rate
c_e	= Dividend to equity capitalization rate
c_m	= Mortgage capitalization rate or constant
c_n	= Terminal or residual or going-out capitalization rate
c_B	= Building capitalization rate
c_L	= Land capitalization rate
c_{LF}	= Leased fee capitalization rate
c_{LH}	= Leasehold capitalization rate
A	= Change in income and value (adjustment factor)
P	= Principal paid off over the holding period
$1/S_n$	= Sinking fund factor at the equity discount or yield rate (k_e)
Δ_p	= Change in value over the holding period
$SC\%$	= Cost of sale
PGI	= Potential gross income
$PGIM$	= Potential gross income multiplier
EGI	= Effective gross income
NIM	= Net income multiplier
F_d/PV_p	= Face value of debt (loan amount outstanding) to value ratio
$[1-(F_d/PV_p)]$	= Equity to value ratio
M_B	= Building value
M_m	= Mortgage value
M_L	= Land value
M_{LF}	= Leased fee value
M_{LH}	= Leasehold value
I_p	= Overall income to the property
I_L	= Residual income to the land
I_B	= Residual income to the building
I_e	= Equity income
I_m	= Mortgage income
I_{LF}	= Income to the leased fee
I_{LH}	= Income to the leasehold

ABBREVIATIONS

ERP	= Equity risk premium (usually the general equity risk premium for which the benchmark for equities is either the S&P 500 stocks or the NYSE stocks)
WACC	= Weighted average cost of capital
WARA	= Weighted average return on assets

T-Bill	= U.S. government bill (usually 30-day, but can be up to one year)
STRIPS	= Separate trading of registered interest and principal of securities
CRSP	= Center for Research in Security Prices, at the University of Chicago Booth School of Business
PIPE	= Private investment in public equity
SBBI	= *Stocks, Bonds, Bills, and Inflation,* published annually by Morningstar (previously Ibbotson Associates) in both a "Classic edition" and a "Valuation edition"
CAPM	= Capital asset pricing model
DCF	= Discounted cash flow
DDM	= Discounted dividend model
TIPS	= Treasury inflation-protected security
NCF	= Net cash flow (also sometimes interchangeably referred to as FCF, free cash flow)
BE	= Business enterprise or reporting unit
NWC	= Net working capital
FA	= Fixed assets
IA	= Intangible assets
UIV	= Unidentified intangible value (i.e., goodwill)
NOPAT	= Net operating profit after taxes
PAT	= Profit after tax
	= Net Income
$RI_{e,n}$	= Residual income to equity
$RI_{f,n}$	= Residual income for total capital
EVA	= Economic value added
DY	= Dividend yield
ROCE	= Return on common equity
RNOA	= Return on net operating assets
RPF	= Risk premium factor
FLEV	= Net financial obligations/(Net operating assets − net financial obligations) (i.e., financial leverage)
SPREAD	= *RNOA* − Net borrowing costs [(financial expense − financial income, after tax)/(financial obligations − financial assets)]
SSP	= Small stock premium
io	= Implicit interest charges on operating liabilities (other than deferred taxes)
OI	= Operating income
OA	= Operating assets
OL	= Operating liabilities
OI	= Operating income
NOA	= Net operating assets
RU	= Reporting unit
NWC_{RU}	= Net working capital of the reporting unit
FA_{RU}	= Fixed assets of the reporting unit
IA_{RU}	= Intangible assets of the reporting unit
UIV_{RU}	= Unidentified intangible value (i.e., goodwill) of the reporting unit
MP Synergies	= Market participant synergies resulting from the expectation of cash flow enhancements achievable only through the combination with a market participant
E	= Exit multiple
NICE	= Nonmarketable investment company evaluation
REIT	= Real estate investment trusts
VDM	= Value driver model

MV CAPM	= Mean-variance capital asset pricing model
MS CAPM	= Mean-semivariance capital asset pricing model
VaR	= Value at risk
CVaR	= Conditional value at risk
CRP	= $[(R_{local\ euro\ \$issue} - R_{f,\ u.s.}) \times (\sigma_{stock}/\sigma_{bond})]$
CV	= Coefficient of variation

Cost of Capital Fourth Edition Workbook and Technical Supplement

Technical Supplement— Supplements to Chapters of *Cost of Capital*: *Applications and Examples*, 4th ed.

CHAPTER 1

Alternative Net Cash Flow Definitions—Supplement to Chapter 3

Introduction
Equity Cash Flow Method
Invested Capital Method
Capital Cash Flow Method
Adjusted Present Value Method
Residual Income Method

INTRODUCTION

As we discussed in Chapter 3 of *Cost of Capital: Applications and Examples,* 4th ed., we are estimating net cash flows. In that chapter we began by presenting formulations of net cash flow, which we revisit here. In later chapters we further presented other net cash flow definitions. We thought it would be useful to summarize them here.

EQUITY CASH FLOW METHOD

In the equity cash flow method, the value of equity equals present value net cash to equity. The net cash flow to equity (NCF_e) is defined as (repeating Formula 3.1 of *Cost of Capital: Applications and Examples, 4th ed.*):

(Formula 1.1)

   Net income to common equity (after income taxes)

   Plus: Noncash charges (e.g., depreciation, amortization, deferred revenues, and deferred income taxes)

   Minus: Capital expenditures (amount necessary to support projected revenues and expenses)

   Minus: Additions to net working capital (amount necessary to support projected revenues)

   Minus: Dividends on preferred equity capital

Plus: Cash from increases in the preferred equity or debt components of the capital structure (amount necessary to support projected revenues)

Minus: Repayments of any debt components or retirement of any preferred components of the capital structure

Equals: Net cash flow to common equity capital

In the cash flow to equity method, earnings (after interest expense and after income taxes) are adjusted for various items to produce net cash flow, including:

- Noncash expenses that are subtracted from revenues but do not affect cash flow, including depreciation, amortization, depletion allowance, and in some cases changes in deferred taxes.
- Amounts necessary to augment net working capital as levels of production increase. Net working capital does not include the current portion of long-term debt, any other permanent invested capital financing of a short-term nature, or increases in cash above the level necessary to sustain the business.
- Amounts invested in plant, property, and equipment to establish or maintain productive capacity in line with increases or decreases in revenues.
- Reflection of amounts to cover scheduled repayments of debt principal or additions to debt principal.
- Because we are only including amounts of investment in net working capital and capital expenditures needed for the projected revenues and expenses included in the projected net cash flows to be discounted, we can term these sustainable net cash flows.
- Net cash flow to equity is also called *free cash flow to equity* (FCF_e).

INVESTED CAPITAL METHOD

In valuing the entire *invested capital* of a business or project by discounting or capitalizing expected cash flows, *net cash flow to invested capital* or *net cash flow to the firm* (NCF_f in our notation system) is defined as (repeating Formula 3.2 of *Cost of Capital: Applications and Examples, 4th ed.*):

(Formula 1.2)

Net income to common equity (after income taxes)

Plus: Noncash charges (e.g., depreciation, amortization, deferred revenues, and deferred income taxes)

Minus: Capital expenditures (amount necessary to support projected revenues and expenses)

Minus: Additions to net working capital (amount necessary to support projected revenues)

Plus: Interest expense (net of the tax deduction resulting from interest as a tax-deductable expense)

Plus: Dividends on preferred equity capital

Equals: Net cash flow to invested capital

The amounts of capital expenditures and additions to net working capital are consistent with the projections of revenues and expenses and the amounts defined earlier (in the net cash flow to common equity capital).

In other words, NCF_f adds back interest (tax-affected because interest is a tax-deductible expense) because invested capital includes the debt on which the interest is paid. Interest is the payment to the debt component of the invested capital. It also adds back dividends on preferred stock for the same reason (i.e., invested capital includes the preferred capital on which the dividends are paid).

Net cash flow to invested capital is also called free cash flow to the firm (FCF_f).

An alternative formula for net cash flow to invested capital is:

(Formula 1.3)

Earnings before interest and income taxes

Minus: Incomes taxes on EBIT at effective income tax rate (equals earnings before interest, after-tax)

Plus: Noncash charges (e.g., depreciation, amortization, deferred revenues, and deferred income taxes)

Minus: Capital expenditures (amount necessary to support projected revenues and expenses)

Minus: Additions to net working capital (amount necessary to support projected revenues)

Equals: Net cash flow to overall invested capital

The earnings (before interest expense and after income tax) are adjusted for various items to produce net cash flow, including:

- Noncash expenses that are subtracted from revenues but do not affect cash flow, including depreciation, amortization, depletion allowance, and in some cases changes in deferred taxes.
- Amounts necessary to augment net working capital as levels of production increase. Net working capital does not include current portion of long-term debt, any other permanent invested capital financing of a short-term nature, or increases in cash above the level necessary to sustain the business.
- Amounts invested in plant, property, and equipment to establish or maintain productive capacity in line with increases or decreases in revenues.

Debt is not subtracted or added in the invested capital model because it is deducted at the conclusion of the process to derive the value of equity.

CAPITAL CASH FLOW METHOD

An alternative definition of *net cash flow to invested capital* is *capital cash flow.* In this formulation the net cash flows include the income tax benefits of the interest expense on debt capital. The literature and practitioners refer to the formulation of the weighted average cost of capital (WACC) in Formula 18.3 of *Cost of Capital: Applications and Examples*, 4th ed. as an after-tax WACC and the formulation in Formula 18.10 as the pretax WACC. For clarity we will use the term pre-interest-tax-shield WACC. The basic formula for computing the pre-interest-tax-shield WACC for an entity with three capital structure components (repeating Formula 18.10 of *Cost of Capital: Applications and Examples, 4th ed.*) is:

(Formula 1.4)

$$WACC_{(pt)} = (k_e \times W_e) + (k_p \times W_p) + (k_{d(pt)} \times W_d)$$

where: $WACC_{(pt)}$ = Weighted average cost of capital, pre-interest-tax-shield
k_e = Cost of common equity capital
W_e = Percentage of common equity in the capital structure, at market value
k_p = Cost of preferred equity
W_p = Percentage of preferred equity in the capital structure, at market value
$k_{d(pt)}$ = Cost of debt without adjusting for the interest tax shield
W_d = Percentage of debt in the capital structure, at market value

The pre-interest-tax-shield WACC capital is applied to *capital cash flows* (NCF_c), which include the tax savings from interest tax deductions on debt capital in the cash flows (repeating Formula 18.11):

(Formula 1.5)

Net income to common equity (after income taxes)

Plus: Noncash charges (e.g., depreciation, amortization, deferred revenues, and deferred income taxes)

Minus: Capital expenditures (amount necessary to support projected revenues and expenses)

Minus: Additions to net working capital (amount necessary to support projected revenues)

Plus: Interest expense

Plus: Dividends on preferred equity capital

Equals: Net capital cash flow

or

(Formula 1.6)

(repeating Formula 18.12)
Net cash flow to invested capital
+ Tax deductions resulting from interest as a tax deductible expense
= Net capital cash flows

In using the NCF_c methodology, the proper formulas for unlevering and relevering are the Practitioners' Method formulas. The formula for unlevering beta is

Formula 11.7 of *Cost of Capital*: *Applications and Examples,* 4th ed. and the proper formula for levering beta is Formula 11.8.

ADJUSTED PRESENT VALUE METHOD

In the adjusted present value method, the value of equity equals the present value of equity cash flows, as if the business were financed solely with equity capital plus the present value of the expected benefits to equity from financing part of the business capital with debt (the present value of the tax shield). The net cash flow to unlevered equity (NCF_{ue}) is defined as:

(Formula 1.7)

Earnings before interest and income taxes

Minus: Incomes taxes on earnings before interest and tax (EBIT) at effective income tax rate (equals earnings before interest, after-tax)

Plus: Noncash charges (e.g., depreciation, amortization, deferred revenues, and deferred income taxes)

Minus: Capital expenditures (amount necessary to support projected revenues and expenses)

Minus: Additions to net working capital (amount necessary to support projected revenues)

Minus: Preferred dividends, if any

Equals: Net cash flow to unlevered business enterprise

As in the cash flow to equity method, earnings (before interest expense, after income tax) are adjusted for various items to produce net cash flow, including:

- Noncash expenses that are subtracted from revenues but do not affect cash flow, including depreciation, amortization, depletion allowance, and in some cases changes in deferred taxes.
- Amounts necessary to augment net working capital as levels of production increase. Net working capital does not include current portion of long-term debt, any other permanent invested capital financing of a short-term nature, or increases in cash above the level necessary to sustain the business.
- Amounts invested in plant, property, and equipment to establish or maintain productive capacity in line with increases or decreases in revenues.

Debt is not subtracted or added in the adjusted present value method because the present value of the net benefits and costs of debt are added to the present value of the cash flows to unlevered business enterprise (i.e., the value to equity assuming there is no debt). The net cash flows of the unlevered business enterprise are discounted at the unlevered cost of equity capital, k_{eu}, which is calculated using Formula 1.8 (assuming we are basing our discount rate with capital asset pricing model [CAPM]) (repeating Formula 18.14 of *Cost of Capital: Applications and Examples, 4th ed.*):

(Formula 1.8)

$$k_{eu} = R_f + B_U(RP_m) + RP_s \pm RP_u$$

where: k_{eu} = Cost of unlevered equity capital
   R_f = Rate of return available on a risk-free security as of the valuation date
   B_U = Unlevered beta (i.e., financial risk removed)
   RP_m = General equity risk premium for the market
   RP_s = Risk premium for small size with effect of financial risk, if any, removed
   RP_u = Risk premium attributable to the specific company risk factors (u stands for unique or unsystematic risk) without regards to financial risk of debt financing

Although the various measures of economic income differ in format, they all are composed of similar elements and require comparable estimates of their future components: sales, operating expenses, noncash charges, investments in fixed assets (capital expenditures), and investments in net working capital.

RESIDUAL INCOME METHOD

Residual income is the return on common equity (expressed in dollars) in excess of the cost of equity capital, as is shown in (repeating Formula 3.4 of *Cost of Capital: Applications and Examples, 4th ed.*):

(Formula 1.9)

$$RI_{e,n} = NCI_{e,n} - [BV_{n-1} \times k_e]$$

where: $RI_{e,n}$ = Residual income for common equity capital
   $NCI_{e,n}$ = Net comprehensive income to common equity; if there are preferred dividends, they would have to be subtracted
   BV_{n-1} = Book value of net assets
   k_e = Cost of equity capital

Residual income to total capital is based on *clean-surplus* accounting statement (repeating Formula 3.5):

(Formula 1.10)

$$NOA_n = NOA_{n-1} + NCI_{f,n} - D_{f,n}$$

where: NOA = Net operating assets = Total capital of the business
   $NCI_{f,n}$ = Net comprehensive income to the firm, which includes income terms reported directly in the equity account rather than in the income statement
   $D_{f,n}$ = Distributions to total capital, net of new issues of debt or equity capital = $NCI_{f,n} - [NOA_n - NOA_{n-1}]$

Residual income is the return on total capital (expressed in dollars) in excess of the overall cost of capital (WACC) as is shown in (repeating Formula 3.6):

(Formula 1.11)

$$RI_{f,n} = NCI_{f,n} - [NOA_{n-1} \times WACC]$$

where: $RI_{f,n}$ = Residual income for total capital
        $NCI_{f,n}$ = Net comprehensive income to total capital
        NOA = Net operating assets
        $WACC$ = Overall cost of capital

Formula 1.11 is the formula typically used for the Economic Value Added (EVA) method.

Examples of Computing OLS Beta, Sum Beta, and Full Information Beta Estimates—Supplement to Chapter 10

David Ptashne

INTRODUCTION

This chapter is a supplement to Chapter 10 of *Cost of Capital: Applications and Examples,* 4th ed. Two commonly used methods of calculating beta estimates for a subject public company involve regressing returns for the subject public company against the returns of a benchmark market index over the same periods (also known as ordinary least squares regression or OLS estimate of beta) or lagged returns (sum beta estimate of beta). These public company beta estimates can also be used as proxy beta estimates for a particular division, reporting unit, or comparable closely held company.

An alternative method for estimating a beta for a subject company involves selecting and analyzing many guideline public companies that report segment data for businesses that are comparable to all or part of the business operations of the subject company. This "full-information" methodology takes into account the influence on beta of each of the business segments. This technique may be of particular interest in cases in which the valuation subject has many different types of operations and/or the most directly comparable, observable operations to the subject operations are contained within discrete business segments of larger, more diversified public companies.

We wish to thank William Susott and Brendan Achariyakosol for their assistance in preparing these examples.

COMPUTING OLS AND SUM BETA ESTIMATES—AN EXAMPLE

Estimating OLS beta and sum beta for a public company (subject company) as of a specific date (subject date) can be performed in the general steps shown using Microsoft *Excel* and common market data that can be obtained from a variety of industry data sources, such as Bloomberg or Standard & Poor's (S&P) *Compustat* or *Capital IQ*. For purposes of these examples only, the beta estimates are based on a 12-month look-back period and are computed using 13 observations of historical monthly data for OLS beta and 14 observations of historical monthly data for sum beta. Note that a 12-month look-back period was chosen for purposes of this example for simplicity. Ordinarily, we recommend computing OLS and sum beta estimates using a longer look-back period, such as 60 months, which would require 62 months of historical data to compute both estimates accurately.

Computing Realized Return Data

Exhibit 2.1 presents the basic return data that must be calculated for the subject company and market index prior to computing the OLS and sum beta estimates. Theorists prefer to estimate beta by comparing the excess returns on an individual security relative to the excess returns on the market index. By *excess return*, we mean the total return (which includes both dividends and capital gains and losses) over and above the return available on a risk-free investment (e.g., U.S. government securities). Practitioners and some financial data services calculate betas using total returns for the subject security and for the market returns instead of excess returns, which is what we have done in this example for illustrative purposes.

In this example, the subject company is Ultimate Software Group, Inc. (Ultimate Software), a public company traded on the NASDAQ, and the subject market benchmark is the S&P 500 Index. This is the same company used in Exhibit 10.6 in Chapter 10 of *Cost of Capital: Applications and Examples,* 4th ed. For simplicity, this example assumes that each beta estimate is to be computed based on a 12-month look-back period.

The steps to obtain the required realized total return data for the subject company and benchmark index for use in the computation of historical OLS and sum beta are:[1]

1. *Column A.* Obtain historic month-end closing prices (adjusted for splits, dividends, etc.) for your subject company for N + 2 months, where N is the number of months in your look-back period. In this example, because our look-back period (N) is 12 months, we have obtained N + 2, or 14 months, of historical data. In this example, the closing prices obtained from *Capital IQ* have been adjusted for dividends. If you are unsure whether your price data has been adjusted for dividends, check with your data provider.

---

[1] These steps assume the use of Microsoft *Excel*. Note that specific formulas entered into *Excel* to re-create this example might be slightly different, depending on placement of historical return data on your worksheet.

EXHIBIT 2.1 Example of Return Data for Ultimate Software and S&P 500

		Subject Company Return Data		Benchmark Index Return Data		
		A Adjusted Closing Price	B Total Return, %	C Adjusted Benchmark Index Value	D Total Return, %	E Lagged Total Return, %
1	Dec 09	$14.60	−4.64	1,453.00	1.06	−7.18
2	Nov 09	$15.31	14.85	1,437.70	−7.18	−16.79
3	Oct 09	$13.33	−50.63	1,548.80	−16.79	−8.91
4	Sep 09	$27.00	−3.71	1,861.40	−8.91	1.45
5	Aug 09	$28.04	6.90	2,043.50	1.45	−0.84
6	Jul 09	$26.23	−26.38	2,014.40	−0.84	−8.43
7	Jun 09	$35.63	−5.82	2,031.50	−8.43	1.30
8	May 09	$37.83	15.37	2,218.50	1.30	4.87
9	Apr 09	$32.79	9.08	2,190.10	4.87	−0.43
10	Mar 09	$30.06	10.27	2,088.40	−0.43	−3.25
11	Feb 09	$27.26	0.78	2,097.50	−3.25	−6.00
12	Jan 09	$27.05	−14.05	2,167.90	−6.00	−0.69
13	Dec 08	$31.47	−3.67	2,306.20	−0.69	
14	Nov 08	$32.67		2,322.30		

Note: Total return for Ultimate Software computed as ([current month's adjusted closing price]/[prior month's adjusted closing price] − 1) based on data obtained from Standard and Poor's *Capital IQ*. Total return for the selected benchmark index was computed in a similar manner, substituting the adjusted benchmark index value for the adjusted closing price of the subject company, based on data obtained from Standard and Poor's *Capital IQ*.

2. *Column B.* Compute total monthly return for your subject company, which is defined as (current month's adjusted closing price)/(previous month's adjusted closing price) less 1.

3. *Column C.* Obtain historic month-end closing values for your selected benchmark index for N + 2 months. In this example, the closing index values obtained from *Capital IQ* have been adjusted for dividends. If you are unsure whether your index data has been adjusted for dividends, check with your data provider.

4. *Column D.* Compute total monthly returns for your benchmark index, which is defined as (current month's adjusted benchmark index value)/(previous month's adjusted benchmark index value) less 1.

5. *Column E.* Compute the lagged return of the selected benchmark index. The lagged return is defined as (previous month's adjusted benchmark index value)/(adjusted benchmark index value from 2 months ago). Compare columns D and E. Note that the lagged return E for the current month is simply the index return D from the previous month. This computation of lagged return will be used in the calculation of sum beta.

Computing OLS Beta Estimate

OLS beta can be computed in *Excel* in a single cell using this formula:

$$\text{OLS Beta} = \text{Covar}(\text{Company}, \text{Market})/\text{Varp}(\text{Market})$$

where: Covar = Covariance function in *Excel*, which returns the covariance (the average of the products of deviations for each data point pair) of two arrays.

Company = Array of the subject company's total returns for months 1 to 12 for a 12-month look-back period. In *Excel*, it would be the range of cells that includes (B1:B12).

Market = Array of benchmark index total returns for months 1 to 12 for a 12-month look-back period. In *Excel*, it would be the range of cells that includes (D1:D12).

Varp = Variance function in *Excel*, which returns the variance of a user-defined population.

If you were to follow the example exactly, the resulting OLS beta estimate would equal 2.030 for the 12-month look-back period. By following the same procedures, an OLS beta estimate for Ultimate Software as of the subject date using the recommended 60-month look-back period was computed to be 1.69 (Exhibit 10.6).

Computing Sum Beta Estimate

Sum beta can be computed in *Excel* in three steps.

Step 1. Compute the market coefficient in *Excel* in a separate cell using this formula:

$$
\begin{aligned}
\text{Market coefficient} = &+(\text{Varp}(\text{Lagged}) * \text{Covar}(\text{Market}, \text{Company}) \\
&- \text{Covar}(\text{Market}, \text{Lagged}) * \text{Covar}(\text{Company}, \text{Lagged})) \\
&/(\text{Varp}(\text{Market}) * \text{Varp}(\text{Lagged}) \\
&- \text{Covar}(\text{Market}, \text{Lagged})^2)
\end{aligned}
$$

where: Varp = Variance function in *Excel*, which returns the variance of a user-defined population.

Lagged = Array of lagged total returns for months 1 to 12 for a 12-month look-back period. In Excel, it would be the range of cells that includes (E1:E12).

Covar = Covariance function in *Excel*, which returns the covariance (the average of the products of deviations for each data point pair) of two arrays.

Market = Array of benchmark index total returns for months 1 to 12 for a 12-month look-back period. In *Excel*, it would be the range of cells that includes (D1:D12).

Company = Array of subject company total returns for months 1 to 12 for a 12-month look-back period. In *Excel*, it would be the range of cells that includes (B1:B12).

The following tables show the computed variances and covariances that are required for the computation of the market coefficient in this example:

Variances	Company	Market	Lagged
	0.03356	0.00337	0.00326

Covariances	Company	Market	Lagged
Company		0.00685	0.00252
Market	0.00685		0.00094
Lagged	0.00252	0.00094	

In this example, the market coefficient is computed as:

$$\text{Market Coefficient} = (.00326 * .00685 - .00094 * .00252)$$
$$/(.00337 * .00326 - .00094\hat{}2)$$

or

$$\text{Market Coefficient} = 1.973$$

By following the same procedures, the market coefficient for Ultimate Software as of the subject date using the recommended 60-month look-back period was computed to be 1.548.

Step 2. Compute the market lagged coefficient in *Excel* in a separate cell using this formula:

$$\text{Market lagged coefficient} =$$
$$+(\text{Varp(Market)} * \text{Covar(Company, Lagged)}$$
$$- \text{Covar(Market, Lagged)} * \text{Covar(Company, Market)})$$
$$/(\text{Varp(Market)} * \text{Varp(Lagged)} - \text{Covar(Market, Lagged)}\hat{}2)$$

where: Varp = Variance function in *Excel*, which returns the variance of a user-defined population.

Market = Array of benchmark index total returns for months 1 to 12 for a 12-month look-back period. In *Excel*, it would be the range of cells that includes (D1:D12).

Covar = Covariance function in *Excel*, which returns the covariance (the average of the products of deviations for each data point pair) of two arrays.

Company = Array of subject company total returns for months 1 to 12 for a 12-month look-back period. In *Excel*, it would be the range of cells that includes (B1:B12).

Lagged = Array of lagged total returns for months 1 to 12 for a 12-month look-back period. In *Excel*, it would be the range of cells that includes (E1:E12).

The following table repeats the computed variances and covariances that are required for the computation of the market lagged coefficient in this example:

Variances	Company	Market	Lagged
	0.03356	0.00337	0.00326

Covariances	Company	Market	Lagged
Company		0.00685	0.00252
Market	0.00685		0.00094
Lagged	0.00252	0.00094	

In this example, the market lagged coefficient is computed as:

$$\text{Market Lagged Coefficient} = (.00337 * .00252 - .00094 * .00685)$$
$$/(.00337 * .00326 - .00094^2)$$

or

$$\text{Market Lagged Coefficient} = .205$$

By following the same procedures, the market lagged coefficient for Ultimate Software as of the subject date using the recommended 60-month look-back period was computed to be .369.

Step 3. Add the value computed in Step 1 to the value computed in Step 2. This is the sum beta estimate.

If you were to follow the example exactly, the resulting sum beta estimate would equal (1.973 + .205) = 2.178 for the 12-month look-back period. By following the same procedures, a sum beta estimate for Ultimate Software Group as of the subject date using the recommended 60-month look-back period was computed to be (1.548 + .369) = 1.917 (Exhibit 10.6).

COMPUTING FULL-INFORMATION BETA ESTIMATE—AN EXAMPLE

A full-information beta estimate as of a specific date can be calculated in the general steps described using *Excel* and market data of guideline public companies obtained from industry data sources, such as Standard & Poor's *Compustat* or *Capital IQ* or from the public filings of the selected guideline companies.

For purposes of this example, we are estimating a full-information beta for Exxon Mobil Corp. (Exxon), which operates in the oil and gas industry. We further distinguished the businesses of Exxon for this example as upstream operations such as exploration (Upstream), downstream operations such as refining (Downstream), Chemicals, and Other. The Other segment was used as a reservoir for all sales and operating income that were not attributable to the Upstream, Downstream, or Chemical segments, such as corporate headquarters, pipelines, and finance; a well-selected group of guideline public yet non pure play companies should represent businesses accounting for the bulk of the business of the subject company.

We have gathered selected segment-level data for 19 guideline companies, including sales and operating income information for fiscal year (FY) 2006. Our guideline companies were selected because each report segment-level results for a segment of its operations that is comparable to one or more of the main business segments of Exxon excluding Other (i.e., Upstream, Downstream, or Chemicals). Note that in our example, the Other segment only accounted for 5.5% of sales and 6.16% of operating income for the group and 0.01% of sales and 1.1% of operating income for Exxon. Our list of guideline companies is not intended to be an exhaustive list of guideline companies for Exxon but rather was selected for demonstrative purposes. We are using data for the 19 guideline companies to estimate the beta for Exxon. We will then compare the full-information beta estimate with the OLS beta estimate for Exxon.

In order to estimate a full-information beta, you must first aggregate the reported segment data for the subject company into the four identified segments. This is accomplished by the analyst with the assistance of the Standard Industrial Classification (SIC) codes assigned to each of the companies' segments as provided by *Compustat*. An example of this raw data for Exxon is shown in Exhibit 2.2.

Note that this information provides segment data for sales, operating income, depreciation, capital expenditures, and assets. For purposes of calculating this example's full-information beta estimate, we will compare the estimate using sales and operating income as the weighting factors. That is, we will weight the influence of differences in segment sales and segment operating income in the betas of the 19 guideline public companies.

The SIC codes and corresponding segments that were applicable in our example were identified to be:

SIC Code (starting with):	Segment
131 & 132	Upstream Operations
291	Downstream Operations
282	Chemicals

Notice in Exhibit 2.2 that two SIC codes are provided for some of the segments and none is provided for other segments. *Compustat* often assigns two SIC codes to a single segment; therefore, in some instances it is necessary to determine which SIC code, and, thus, which segment label best defines the sales and operating income for that segment. For instances in which two SIC codes fell into the same segment label—for example, U.S. Upstream—because both 131 and 132 correspond with upstream operations, that segment is clearly labeled as an Upstream segment. However, in some segments, such as U.S. Chemicals, the two SIC codes listed are 291 and 282, which correspond to Downstream Operations and Chemicals, respectively. In these instances, it is necessary to determine a single segment in which to classify the revenue and operating income. Based on the segment name, this is clearly more closely aligned to the Chemicals segment, and so we assigned it to Chemicals. Finally, notice that the business segment named Corporate & Financing has no SIC code assigned to it; in this instance, we determined that this should be categorized into the Other segment.

EXHIBIT 2.2 Business Segment Data for Exxon

EXXON MOBIL CORP
TICKER: XOM
SIC: 2911
GICS: 10102010

Fiscal Year Ended: December 2006

Business Segments	Segment SIC Codes		Segment Sales	% of Total	Segment Oper Inc	% of Total	Segment Depr	% of Total	Segment Car Exp	% of Total	Segment Assets	% of Total
U.S. Upstream	1,311	1,321	6,054	1.66	5,168	13.08	1,263	11.06	1,942	12.56	21,119	9.64
Non-U.S. Upstream	1,311	1,321	26,821	7.34	21,062	53.32	6,482	56.78	9,735	62.96	75,090	34.29
U.S. Downstream	2,911	NA	93,437	25.57	4,250	10.76	632	5.54	718	4.64	16,740	7.64
Non-U.S. Downstream	2,911	NA	205,020	56.10	4,204	10.64	1,605	14.06	1,757	11.36	47,694	21.78
U.S. Chemicals	2,911	2,824	13,273	3.63	1,360	3.44	427	3.74	257	1.66	7,652	3.49
Non-U.S. Chemicals	2,911	2,824		5.70	3,022	7.65	473	4.14	384	2.48	11,885	5.43
Corporate & Financing	NA	NA	37	0.01	434	1.10	534	4.68	669	4.33	38,835	17.73

Source: Compiled from Standard & Poor's *Compustat* data. Calculations by Duff & Phelps LLC. Used with permission. All rights reserved.

17

EXHIBIT 2.3   Segment Operating Income

	Segment Operating Income				Total
	Upstream	Downstream	Chemicals	Other	Segments
EXXON MOBIL CORP	26,230	8,454	4,382	434	4
ANADARKO PETROLEUM CORP	5,370	—	—	(483)	1
CANADIAN NATURAL RESOURCES	2,745	—	—	35	2
CHESAPEAKE ENERGY CORP	3,192	—	—	147	2
CHEVRON CORP	13,142	3,973	539	—	3
CONOCOPHILLIPS	10,324	4,481	—	745	3
DEVON ENERGY CORP	4,496	—	—	—	1
DOW CHEMICAL	—	—	4,893	510	2
DU PONT (E I) DE NEMOURS	—	—	2,296	1,987	2
DUKE ENERGY CORP	569	—	—	3,360	2
EL PASO CORP	640	—	—	1,110	2
HESS CORP	1,763	390	—	(237)	2
IMPERIAL OIL LTD	2,661	784	188	(114)	3
MARATHON OIL CORP	2,019	2,795	—	—	2
MURPHY OIL CORP	616	105	—	(83)	2
OCCIDENTAL PETROLEUM CORP	7,239	—	901	(239)	2
ROHM AND HAAS CO	—	—	649	106	2
SUNCOR ENERGY INC	3,114	328	—	—	2
TESORO CORP	—	1,476	—	(159)	1
WILLIAMS COS INC	530	—	—	840	2

Source: Compiled from Standard & Poor's *Compustat* data. Calculations by Duff & Phelps LLC. Used with permission. All rights reserved.

Once all of the companies' business segments were appropriately assigned into our four segment categories, we organized these data into a chart as shown in Exhibit 2.3. (Although this analysis was completed separately with sales and operating income data, for brevity we show only operating income results in the exhibit.)

Using these amounts, we then created a segment weighting for each company. The segment weighting and the OLS beta estimates for each guideline public company (using a look-back period of 60 months) are displayed in Exhibit 2.4. Although we are estimating the beta for Exxon using the other 19 guideline public companies, we display Exxon's beta estimate in this exhibit for comparison purposes.

The data in Exhibit 2.4 are then used to run the regression necessary to estimate the full-information beta for the subject company (i.e., Exxon) with operating income weights.

In order to run the regression in *Excel*, we utilized the Regression function found under Tools → Data Analysis. The Y Variable Range is the column of OLS beta estimates for the 19 guideline public companies, and the X Variable Range is

EXHIBIT 2.4 Segment Operating Income Weights and OLS Beta Estimates

	OLS Beta	Segment Operating Income Weights			
		Upstream	Downstream, %	Chemicals, %	Other, %
EXXON MOBIL CORP	0.763	66.4	21.4	11.1	1.1
ANADARKO PETROLEUM CORP	0.623	109.9	0.0	0.0	−9.9
CANADIAN NATURAL RESOURCES	0.316	98.7	0.0	0.0	1.3
CHESAPEAKE ENERGY CORP	0.596	95.6	0.0	0.0	4.4
CHEVRON CORP	0.743	74.4	22.5	3.1	0.0
CONOCOPH1LLIPS	0.642	66.4	28.8	0.0	4.8
DEVON ENERGY CORP	0.562	100.0	0.0	0.0	0.0
DOW CHEMICAL	1.066	0.0	0.0	90.6	9.4
DU PONT (E I) DE NEMOURS	1.072	0.0	0.0	53.6	46.4
DUKE ENERGY CORP	1.185	14.5	0.0	0.0	85.5
EL PASO CORP	2.219	36.6	0.0	0.0	63.4
HESS CORP	0.458	92.0	20.4	0.0	−12.4
IMPERIAL OIL LTD	0.291	75.6	22.3	5.3	−3.2
MARATHON OIL CORP	0.560	41.9	58.1	0.0	0.0
MURPHY OIL CORP	0.418	96.5	16.5	0.0	−13.0
OCCIDENTAL PETROLEUM CORP	0.498	91.6	0.0	11.4	−3.0
ROHM AND HAAS CO	0.992	0.0	0.0	86.0	14.0
SUNCOR ENERGY INC	0.371	90.5	9.5	0.0	0.0
TESORO CORP	1.723	0.0	112.1	0.0	−12.1
WILLIAMS COS INC	2.726	38.7	0.0	0.0	61.3

Source: Compiled from Standard & Poor's *Compustat* data. Calculations by Duff & Phelps LLC. Used with permission. All rights reserved.

the four columns of segment weights. In the regression tool, we then select "Labels" (to show the labels in the output), "Constant is Zero" (to force the intercept of the regression line through the origin), and a 95% confidence level. The regression output for operating income weights is shown in Exhibit 2.5.

EXHIBIT 2.5   Full-Information Regression Results Using Operating Income Weights

Summary Output

Regression Statistics

Multiple R	0.927
R Square	0.860
Adjusted R Square	0.765
Standard Error	0.466
Observations	19

Anova

	df	SS	MS	F	Significance F
Regression	4	20.030	5.008	23.047	0.000
Residual	15	3.259	0.217		
Total	19	23.290			

	Coefficients	Standard Error	t Stat	P-Value	Lower 95%	Upper 95%
Intercept	0					
Upstream	0.491	0.158	3.106	0.007	0.154	0.827
Downstream	1.446	0.360	4.016	0.001	0.678	2.213
Chemicals	0.707	0.352	2.007	0.063	−0.044	1.459
Other	2.359	0.360	6.551	0.000	1.591	3.126

Source: Compiled from Standard & Poor's *Compustat* data. Calculations by Duff & Phelps LLC. Used with permission. All rights reserved.

According to these results, the divisional beta for the segment Upstream, for example, is 0.491 with a 95% confidence interval of 0.154 to 0.827. These results also show that the R-square value of the regression is 0.860.

Using Formula 2.1, the formula for full-information beta:

(Formula 2.1)

$$RI_{iL} = \sum_{1}^{n} (W_s \times B_{Ls})$$

where: RI_{iL} = Full-information levered beta estimate of the subject company
W_s = Weight of each segment of the subject company
B_{Ls} = Levered beta estimate of each segment from the regression
n = Number of segments

We then calculate the full-information beta estimate for Exxon to be:

$$B_{Exxon} = (0.491 \times 0.664) + (1.446 \times 0.214) + (0.707 \times 0.111) + (2.359 \times 0.011)$$
$$= 0.740$$

This full-information beta estimate of 0.740 closely approximates the OLS beta estimate for Exxon as a whole of 0.763 (difference of 3.1%).

EXHIBIT 2.6 Full-Information Regression Results Using Sales Weights

Summary Output

Regression Statistics

Multiple R	0.941
R Square	0.885
Adjusted R Square	0.795
Standard Error	0.422
Observations	19

Anova

	df	SS	MS	F	Significance F
Regression	4	20.614	5.153	28.890	0.000
Residual	15	2.676	0.178		
Total	19	23.290			

	Coefficients	Standard Error	t Stat	P-Value	Lower 95%	Upper 95%
Intercept	0					
Upstream	0.384	0.205	1.874	0.081	−0.053	0.821
Downstream	0.739	0.195	3.794	0.002	0.324	1.154
Chemicals	0.625	0.348	1.796	0.093	−0.177	1.367
Other	2.087	0.249	8.378	0.000	1.556	2.618

Source: Compiled from Standard & Poor's *Compustat* data. Calculations by Duff & Phelps LLC. Used with permission. All rights reserved.

Similarly, we calculated the full-information beta estimate using sales weights. The regression results are displayed in Exhibit 2.6.

We then calculate the full-information beta estimate for Exxon to be:

$$B_{Exxon} = (0.384 \times 0.090) + (0.739 \times 0.817) + (0.625 \times 0.093) + (2.087 \times 0.000)$$
$$= 0.696$$

This yields a full-information beta estimate of 0.696. This estimate compares with the OLS beta estimate for Exxon of 0.763 (difference of 8.8%).

Why is the full-information beta estimate using operating income weights more accurate than using sales weights? Stock returns are driven by profits, not revenues. In the case of Exxon, the segment operating margin (operating income/sales) differed across segments. The Upstream segment represented 9% of the sales but 66.4% of the operating income (operating margin of 79.8%), whereas the Downstream segment represented 81.7% of the sales but only 21.4% of the operating income (operating margin of 2.8%).

CHAPTER 3

Estimating Beta: Interpreting Regression Statistics—Supplement to Chapter 10

Mark W. Shirley

INTRODUCTION

As discussed in Chapter 10 of *Cost of Capital: Applications and Examples,* 4th ed. for a publicly traded stock, beta is often estimated by regression analysis (ordinary least squares [OLS] regression). In applying regression analysis to beta estimation, excess returns on the individual security $R_i - R_f$ are regressed against the excess returns on the market $R_m - R_f$ during a look-back period. The look-back period is the historic period of sufficient time series to include data reflective of changes in macroeconomic conditions. The resulting slope of the best-fit line is the beta estimate. Formula 10.1 of *Cost of Capital: Applications and Examples,* 4th ed. repeated here as Formula 3.1 illustrates the regression formula.

(Formula 3.1)

$$\left(R_i - R_f\right) = \alpha + B \times \left(R_m - R_f\right) + \varepsilon$$

where: $R_i =$ Historical return for publicly traded stock, i
        $R_f =$ Risk-free rate
        $\alpha =$ Regression constant
        $B =$ Estimated beta based on historical data over the look-back period

$R_m =$ Historical return on market portfolio, m
$\varepsilon =$ Regression error term

The Greek letters β and α are explained in Appendix III and in the discussions of hypothetical testing and types of error. These symbols have different meanings when used in the context of regression analysis. However, error measurement (residuals) is a fundamental and critical analysis in determining the reliability of a regression line.

Comparisons of beta estimates based on excess returns or total returns, as a practical matter, yield little difference in the aggregate. But based on the fundamental formula for value (value = dividends + appreciation), if one includes only the changes in price and ignores dividends one will not obtain a meaningful beta estimate when a stock's return is predominantly comprised of dividends, such as with private companies which are closely held conduit (pass-through) entities.

Closely held conduit entities include partnerships, S corporations, and limited liability entities. These entities do not pay an entity level income tax but "pass-through" their net income to the respective equity owners, who report their allocated portion for income tax purposes. Consequently, conduit entities commonly distribute current earnings to the equity owners as reimbursement for the increased incremental income taxes on the pass-through income. Closely held conduit entities often adopt equity owner compensation plans, formal or informal, combining wage compensation, and distributions of current earnings. This creates difficulties in applying fundamental value relationships derived from samples of guideline public companies to closely held conduit entities.

Formula 3.2 illustrates the OLS regression using total return:

(Formula 3.2)

$$R_i = \alpha + B \times R_m + \varepsilon$$

where the variables are defined as they were earlier.

In theory, beta is calculated by applying the ANOVA formula illustrated in Formula 12.4 which we repeat here as Formula 3.3:

(Formula 3.3)

$$B_i = \frac{Cov(R_i, R_m)}{Var(R_m)}$$

where: $B_i =$ Expected Beta of the stock of company i
$Cov(R_i, R_m) =$ Expected covariance between the excess return $(R_i - R_f)$ on security i and the excess market return $(R_m - R_f)$
$Var(R_m) =$ Expected variance of excess return of the stock market in aggregate

Covariance measures the degree to which the return on a particular security and the overall market's return move in relationship to each other. Covariance is not a measure of volatility. Covariance measures the changes in the variances of the data sets in relationship to each other. Understanding beta estimation requires an examination of the nature of beta and what it is intended to measure.

Formula 12.5, in *Cost of Capital: Applications and Examples,* 4th ed. is repeated below as Formula 3.4, and Formula 12.6 is repeated here as Formula 3.5. They illustrate the relationship between the population correlation coefficient and beta:

(Formula 3.4)

$$\rho = \sigma_{i,m}/[\sigma_i * \sigma_m]$$

where: ρ = correlation coefficient between the returns on the security i and the market m, then
    $\sigma_{i,m}$ = standard deviation of returns on the security i and the market m
    σ_i = standard deviation of returns on the security i
    σ_m = standard deviation of returns on the market m

(Formula 3.5)

$$B_i = \rho * [\sigma_i/\sigma_m]$$

The correlation coefficient that matches beta is the expected correlation coefficient, ρ, and the expected standard deviation of returns on the security of company i and the expected standard deviation of returns on the market m. Any estimate of the correlation coefficient calculated by regressing realized returns R is only an estimate of the expected correlation ρ. Similarly, the standard deviations of realized returns on the company security i and the market m, over a look-back period, are only estimates of the expected standard deviations of returns.

There are two general ways for estimating betas: top-down and bottom-up. The top-down beta estimate for a public company is calculated from a regression of excess returns of the company's stock to the excess returns of a market portfolio.

Alternatively, a bottom-up beta can be estimated as follows:

- Identify the businesses in which the subject business operates
- Identifying guideline public companies and estimate their respective levered betas
- Unlevering the guideline public company beta yields estimates of unlevered (asset) betas
- Calculate a weighted average of the unlevered betas. The respective weights are based on the relative values (or operating income) of the businesses in which the subject business operates
- Re-lever beta using an appropriate debt-to-equity ratio for the subject business.

A bottom-up or *proxy* beta is required when the subject business is a division, reporting unit, or closely held business.

The most commonly used technique for estimating beta uses a sample of historic time series data or look-back period. This approach assumes that future period returns will not diverge materially from the historic time series returns, and an extrapolation of betas calculated using historical data will provide a reasonable estimate. To minimize the uncertainty inherent in using historic data as a proxy for future periods may require the use of historic time series spanning a complete macroeconomic cycle. For example, the U.S. economy cycles at intervals of approximately 18 years, as discussed later.

An alternative method for estimating beta requires identifying and measuring a fundamental relationship between the subject company and an industry or market index. This type of beta estimation is often referred to as fundamental beta or accounting beta estimates. Although stock return data is unavailable for closely held companies, accounting earnings are available. Changes in accounting earnings can be regressed against changes in earnings for an equity index to estimate a fundamental beta:

$$\Delta \text{Earnings (closely held firm)} = a + b \times \Delta \text{Earnings index}$$

The slope of the regression b is the fundamental beta for the closely held company. Analysis based on operating earnings yields an unlevered beta estimate whereas analysis based on net income yields a levered or equity beta estimate.

EVALUATING BETA ESTIMATION OUTPUT

The Review of Statistical Analyses in Appendix III provides a condensed primer to fundamental statistical theory. The disciplines of finance and economics incorporate advanced statistical theory, incorporating applied and stochastic calculus. Traditional academic financial accounting curriculums seldom provide a comprehensive understanding of the application of these theories. The ability to replicate the calculations is not essential, but understanding what attribute or economic phenomenon is being quantified and the level of confidence is all-important. The advanced theoretical models applied in estimating risk premiums, including binomial and risk neutral modeling, are beyond the scope of this material. However, the fundamentals discussed here can assist the analyst in structuring a logical framework from which to interpret statistical tests, such as beta, and provide a foundation for reasonable conclusions.

Chapter 10 of *Cost of Capital: Applications and Examples,* 4th ed. includes several examples of beta estimation based on regressions analysis. Chapter 10 identified two methods of estimating beta using historical returns over a look-back period: OLS and sum beta. Each of these approaches are designed to the same phenomena.

The initial analysis of the data requires the preparation of pictorial statistics, a scatter plot. A picture provides a visual rendering of the distribution of data points, which is not possible with data organized in columnar or tabular formats.

For each sample, the fundamental assumption regarding beta is that individual company returns will move in relation to the regression line of the market. Theoretically, over time, specific company betas will converge on the mean. This is a function of the inclusion of the specific company data in the population comprising the market data and efficient market theory. The scatter plot assists in visually identifying data points that may be outliers as well as the general shape of the distribution.

We can think of the specific company beta in terms of a statistical z score of a frequency distribution $\left[z = {}^{(x-\mu)}/_{\sigma}\right]$, we are concerned with the distance from the mean value.

Outlier values are easily identified by a scatter plot and their cause must be investigated. A determination must be made about their inclusion, omission, or adjustment. Outlier values assert pressure on the regression line and pull the direction of the line. The effect on the regression line is negatively correlated to the sample size and positively correlated to the magnitude of the outlier values (measured by the variance).

By observing the scatter plot for the Chapter 10 examples, one can observe the outlier values. Statistical tests quantify those values. These data points partially explain the differences in the calculated beta estimates. The added variables, which are fixed in time in the sum beta calculation, yields a beta estimate that deviates from the OLS beta estimate.

Interpreting the ANOVA output is not difficult but requires a fundamental understanding of the terms and what they measure.

The statistical analysis of historic time series data and development of prospective values (point estimator) has numerous inherent error tendencies, especially when rudimentary statistical modeling is applied. The analyst must acknowledge and address the following when constructing an opinion or conclusion:

- Data collection errors exist, particularly for short time series.
- Simple statistical models will not include all independent and dependent variable combinations.
- Errors do occur due to the incorrect application of statistical models.
- Errors occur do to random chance.
- The comparison of the mean returns of a single company or group to mean market returns is not a causal relationship defined by an independent variable and a dependent variable.
- Future economic events (particularly traded market activity) are uncertain and often volatile.
- Future economic conditions will depart from historic means, particularly in the short term.
- The number of trailing decimal places does not enhance the precision of an estimate. The analysis must adopt a consistent definition of significant digits (rounding).
- The statistical exercise develops an estimate, not an absolute value. It is a best guess based on the validity of the assumption about future economic conditions, company financial performance, limitations due to number of variables employed and volatility.

EVALUATING REGRESSION OUTPUT

All statistical analysis software and applications (Microsoft *Excel* add-ins) generate tables of regression output values. These output values are segregated into three common tables.

The regression output tables have three components:

- Regression statistics table.
- ANOVA table.
- Regression coefficient table.

Regression Statistics Table

Multiple R	$R = \sqrt{R^2}$
R Square	R^2 measures the % of variation of y around $\bar{y}$ explained by regression x_2 and x_3
Adjusted *R* squared	Adjusted R^2 used if more than one x variable

| Standard Error | A standard estimate of standard deviation of the error μ. Standard error of regression $\left({}^{SSE}/_{n-k} \right)$ |
| Observations | Number of observations used in regression (n) |

ANOVA Table

The ANOVA table disects the sum of squares (SS) into its components. The statistics presented include the elements (F-statistic) necessary for hypothesis testing of the β and α error.

$$SS_T = SS_{\text{Regression}} + SS_{\text{Residual}}$$

$$
\begin{aligned}
SS_T &= \text{Sum-of-squares total} \\
SS_{\text{Regression}} &= \text{Sum-of-squares explained by the regression} \\
SS_{\text{Residual}} &= \text{Unexplained sum-of-squares}
\end{aligned}
$$

$$R^2 = 1 - SS_{\text{Residual}}/SS_T$$

F Column (hypothesis testing)

Overall F-test of H_0: $\beta_2 = 0$ and $\beta_3 = 0$ versus H_a: at least one of β_2 and $\beta_3 \neq 0$

Significance F Column

The p-value associated with F-statistic

If $> .05$, do not reject H_0 at significance level 0.05

Regression Coefficient Table

Coefficient Column

Least squares estimate of population coefficient of jth regressor β_j

df Column

Degrees of freedom

Regression $df = 1 - $ number of groups

Residual $= n - $ number of groups

Total $= n - 1$

SS Column

Sum of Squares

MS Column

Mean Square

$MSG = SSG/DFG$

$MSE = SSE/DFE$

F Column

$F = MSG/MSE$

Standard Error Column

Standard error of least squares estimates; b_j and β_j

f-Stat Column

Computed f statistic for H_0; $\beta_j = 0$ against $H_a \neq 0$.

p-value Column

p-value for test of $H_0 = 0$ against $\beta_j \neq 0$. For one sided test $p/2$

F(number of groups $- 1, n - 1$)

Lower 95% and Upper 95% Column

Defines 95% confidence interval for β_j

Beta Estimation—TIBX Example

The regression output tables shown in Exhibit 3.1 are summarized in Exhibit 10.2 in Chapter 10 of *Cost of Capital: Applications and Examples*, 4th ed. The discussion addresses interpretation of the OLS data elements in the context of beta estimation.

The monthly returns for TIBX are annualized as follows:

$$\text{Annualized return} = [(1 + \text{monthly return})^{12}] - 1$$
$$0.02451 = [(1 + 0.00202)^{12}] - 1$$

The standard deviation of monthly returns for the market is annualized as follows:

$$\text{Annualized standard deviation} = \text{monthly standard deviation} \times (12)^{.5}$$
$$.12752 = .03681 \times (12)^{.5}$$

Let us begin with an initial assessment regarding the sufficiency of the data and the appropriate statistical measures to be applied. The sample size for both TIBX and the market index is 60 months (that is, the look-back period is 60 months).

Research has shown that the U.S. economy (micro and macro) cycle through approximately 18 year cycles.[1] The plot of historic market indices (e.g., Dow Jones Industrial Average, S&P 500) from 1925 through 2004 illustrates the repeated pattern and interval between peaks and valleys (booms and busts), corresponding to the real-estate market cycle as postulated by Foldvary. This pattern has been repeated during the interval 2004 through 2010, except with a much steeper decline slope. A negatively skewed distribution indicates, as discussed in Appendix III, a gradual sloping curve and a steeper curve after traversing the apex. The analyst needs to recognize from what part of the economic/business cycle the data was sampled. Longer time series provide an indication of how the subject company reacts to changing macroeconomic phenomena compare to the mean market indices. Precision is directly related to the size of a properly constructed sampling process and increases by the square root of the sample size, $\sqrt{n}$. In this instance bigger is definitely better and more precise.

It is essential to realize that the regression line is constructed based on the mean (average) market returns, as reported by a market index. The market statistics, mean, variance, and standard deviation, will indicate the symmetry of the frequency distribution of market returns. Further, as discussed in Appendix III, statistics can locate the subject company within the distribution of market returns based on the z-score. Locating the subject company, in terms of standard deviations from the mean, allows the use of the probability divisions of the normal curve.

$$z = {}^{(x-\mu)}/\sigma$$

---

[1] Fred E. Foldvary "The Business Cycle: A Georgist-Austrian Synthesis." *American Journal of Economics and Sociology* 56(4) (October 1997): 521–41; *The Depression of 2008*, 2nd ed. (Berkeley, CA: Gutenberg Press, 2007).

EXHIBIT 3.1 ANOVA Tables for TIBX

SUMMARY OUTPUT

Regression Statistics	
Multiple R	0.57281
R Square	0.32812
Adj. R Square	0.31653
Standard Error	0.09456
Observations	60

ANOVA

	df	SS	MS	F	Significance F
Regression	1	0.25325	0.25325	28.32442	0
Residual	58	0.51859	0.00894		
Total	59	0.77184			

	Coefficients	Standard Error	t Stat	P-value	Lower 95%	Upper 95%	Lower 95%	Upper 95%
Intercept	0.00401	0.01221	0.3282	0.74395	−0.02044	0.02846	−0.02044	0.02846
X Variable 1	1.76482	0.3316	5.32207	0	1.10104	2.4286	1.10104	2.4286

OLS Beta	1.76482

Summary Statistics			Annualized		
	TIBX	Market		TIBX	Market
Average Return	0.202%	−0.113%	Average Return	**2.451%**	**−1.343%**
Standard deviation (statistic)	11.438%	3.712%	Standard deviation (statistic)	39.621%	12.860%
Standard deviation (parameter)	11.342%	3.681%	Standard deviation (parameter)	39.290%	12.752%
Correlation Matrix					
	TIBX	Market			
Company	1.000				
Market Index	0.573	1.000			

Substituting the mean TIBX annualized return (2.451%) for the mean TIBX return and the mean market annualized return (−1.343%) for the variable μ and the market standard deviation (12.752%) yields a z-score of .2975. Based on binomial probability tables the z table provides the probability of a sample mean between μ and $(\mu + z)$. Based on a two-tailed test the calculated probability is 61.41%.

Often the analyst will apply the incorrect formula in calculating the measures. In Appendix III we discussed the different formulas for statistics (sample) and parameter (population). Because we are sampling the population of returns for both the market and TIBX, the proper formulas are for the sample (statistic).

A calculation that is not often performed is the coefficient of variation, $CV = \frac{\sigma}{\mu}$. As discussed in Appendix III, the coefficient of variation (CV) is a normalized measure of dispersion of a distribution. This measure is also referred to as unitized risk or variation coefficient. The ratio measures the dispersion of a distribution in relationship to the mean, the kurtosis of the distribution. The smaller the CV, the narrower the distribution (i.e., less volatile).

For the market index and TIBX the CV was −9.495 and 16.03, respectively. Because the market mean is negative and, therefore, the CV is also negative, the measure is undefined. The CV for TIBX indicates significantly high variance (dispersion). The negative market mean indicates that one may want to consider a longer sample period (time series), which would be more representative of longer-term market returns.

As previously discussed, the statistics R and R^2 are not the definitive determination of the usefulness of the regression analysis. The TIBX regression coefficients are $R = .57281$ and $R^2 = .32812$, indicating that only 32.812% of the change in the dependent variable y (TIBX) can be explained by changes in the independent variable x (market index).

The hypothesis test for determining if a positive relationship exists between the market and TIBX when $\alpha = .025$ (95% confidence level, two tail) is phrased as follows:

$$H_0 : \beta_1 \leq 0$$
$$H_a : \beta_1 > 0$$

The test statistic is the t-stat column for the x variable 1: 5.32207. The critical values for t for $df = n - 2$ and $\alpha = .025$ are found by referencing the area under the curve table for t values, 2.0. Because the t stat (5.32207) is greater than 2.0, the hypothetical is rejected and the conclusion supported that a linear relationship exists between TIBX and the market index.

Similarly, because the P-value (0) is less than $.025(\alpha)$ a positive relationship exists between TIBX and the market index. However, is the market a good predictor for TIBX? The expected value of y is a better predictor than the mean y. The confidence interval for beta ($\alpha = .025$) is 1.10104 to 2.4286.

The statistics for the intercept are significantly less than the x variable, indicating a low causal relationship between the variables. This is also indicated by the disparities in the CV indicating that the distribution of value for the two variables are significantly different. The conclusion is that additional data points should likely be tested (i.e., a longer look-back period) because the number of data points is likely insufficient for a very reliable beta estimate.

CHAPTER 4

Example of Computing Downside Beta Estimates—Supplement to Chapter 12

David Ptashne

Introduction
Computing Downside Beta Estimates

INTRODUCTION

This chapter is a supplement to Chapter 12 of *Cost of Capital: Applications and Examples,* 4th ed. and is a continuation of Chapter 2 of this *Workbook and Technical Supplement.* Here we present an example of how to compute downside beta for a guideline public company. Similar to OLS beta and sum beta, this guideline public company downside beta estimate can be used as a proxy beta estimate for a division, reporting unit, or closely held company.

COMPUTING DOWNSIDE BETA ESTIMATES

Estimating downside beta for a public company (subject company) as of a specific date (subject date) can be performed in the general steps shown using Microsoft *Excel*[1] and common market data that can be obtained from industry data providers, such as Standard and Poor's (S&P) *Compustat* or *Capital IQ.* For purposes of this example, we have assumed that the downside beta estimate will be based on 12 months of observed returns, which are computed using 13 observations of historic monthly data (as discussed in Chapter 2). Note that a 12-month look-back period was chosen for purposes of this example only. Ordinarily, we recommend computing this risk measure using a longer period, such as a 60-month look-back period, which would require 61 months of historical data.

We wish to thank William Susott for his assistance in preparing these examples.

[1]Although the example provided within this chapter was prepared using Microsoft *Excel 2007*, the functions discussed are also available in previous releases of *Excel*.

In this example, the subject company is Ultimate Software Group, Inc. (Ultimate Software), a public company traded on the NASDAQ, and the subject market benchmark is the S&P 500 Index.

Exhibit 4.1 presents realized returns for our subject company over the look-back period. For more detail regarding the computation of realized returns, see Exhibit 2.2.

We next present the computation of the downside beta with respect to the average total return over the look-back period. This downside beta can be computed as shown:[2]

Step 1. Compute the average return for the subject company over the look-back period. In this case, the formula is = Average(B1:B12). Let us call the cell that contains the subject company's average return value XX for purposes of this example, which has a computed value of −4.00%.

Step 2. Compute the average return for the benchmark index over the same look-back period. In this case, the formula is = Average(D1:D12). Let us call the cell that contains the benchmark index's average return value YY for purposes of this example, which has a computed value of −3.60%.

Step 3. In a separate cell in *Excel*, input = Linest(If(B1:B12<XX, B1:B12-XX,0),If(D1:D12<YY,D1:D12-YY,0), False)

where Linest is the function in *Excel* that calculates the statistics for a line by using the least squares method to calculate a straight line that best fits the data and then returns an array that describes the line. Because this function returns an array of values, it must be entered as an array formula.

Important: After entering the preceding formula, you must press Ctrl + Shift + Enter simultaneously. This is an array formula in *Excel*, and pressing Ctrl + Shift + Enter simultaneously is required to make these formulas work properly. Note, also, that *false* at the end of this formula tells *Excel* to estimate the slope of a regression without a constant.

If you wanted to compute the downside beta with respect to another reference value (e.g., zero or the risk-free rate), simply substitute the average return in cell YY with zero, the risk-free rate, or any other reference value.

If you followed the example exactly, the resulting downside beta estimate with respect to the average total return of the subject company equals 2.653. We also computed a downside beta estimate for Ultimate Software with respect to the average total return as of the subject date using the recommended 60-month look-back period to be 2.138 by following the same procedures discussed.

---

[2] These steps assume the use of Microsoft *Excel*. Also note that specific formulas entered into *Excel* to recreate this example might be slightly different depending on where on your worksheet you place historical return data.

EXHIBIT 4.1 Example of Return Data for Ultimate Software and S&P 500

		Subject Company Return Data		Benchmark Index Return Data		
		A	B	C	D	E
		Adjusted Closing Price	% Total Return	Adjusted Benchmark Index Value	% Total Return	% Lagged Total Return
1	Dec-09	$14.60	–4.64	1,453.00	1.06	–7.18
2	Nov-09	$15.31	14.85	1,437.70	–7.18	–16.79
3	Oct-09	$13.33	–50.63	1,548.80	–16.79	–8.91
4	Sep-09	$27.00	–3.71	1,861.40	–8.91	1.45
5	Aug-09	$28.04	6.90	2,043.50	1.45	–0.84
6	Jul-09	$26.23	–26.38	2,014.40	–0.84	–8.43
7	Jun-09	$35.63	–5.82	2,031.50	–8.43	1.30
8	May-09	$37.83	15.37	2,218.50	1.30	4.87
9	Apr-09	$32.79	9.08	2,190.10	4.87	–0.43
10	Mar-09	$30.06	10.27	2,088.40	–0.43	–3.25
11	Feb-09	$27.26	0.78	2,097.50	–3.25	–6.00
12	Jan-09	$27.05	–14.05	2,167.90	–6.00	–0.69
13	Dec-08	$31.47	–3.67	2,306.20	–0.69	
14	Nov-08	$32.67		2,322.30		

Note: Total return for Ultimate Software computed as ([current month's adjusted closing price]/[previous month's adjusted closing price] – 1) based on data obtained from Standard and Poor's *Capital IQ.* Total return for the selected benchmark index was computed in a similar manner, substituting the adjusted benchmark index value for the adjusted closing price of the subject company, based on data obtained from Standard and Poor's *Capital IQ.*

Iterative Process Using CAPM to Calculate the Cost of Equity Component of the Weighted Average Cost of Capital When Capital Structure Is Constant—Supplement to Chapter 18

Harold G. Martin, Jr.

I wish to thank James R. Hitchner of Financial Valuation Advisors, Inc., in Ventnor City, New Jersey, for sparking my initial interest in the invested capital model; and Mark L. Zyla of Acuitas, Inc., in Atlanta, Georgia, and Michael J. Mattson of The Financial Valuation Group in Chicago, Illinois, for their suggestions and critique of the model. Finally, I wish to acknowledge two of my associates at Keiter Stephens, Peter N. Thacker and Asif H. Charania, who assisted me in researching and updating the materials for this new edition. Any errors relating to the the application of the model are solely my own.

INTRODUCTION

This chapter is a supplement to *Cost of Capital: Applications and Examples,* 4th ed. In Chapter 18 of *Cost of Capital* the authors present an iterative process for computing the weighted average cost of capital (WACC) for a closely held company. In determining the WACC, the market values of the capital structure components— debt and equity—are required to determine the relative weights of each component. However, this sets up a circularity issue:

- Our objective is to determine the market value of equity for the closely held company based on some unknown WACC.
- To determine the WACC, we must solve for an unknown market value of equity.

Chapter 18 of *Cost of Capital* presents an estimation technique, an iterative process, which provides a method for circumventing this circularity problem. This chapter expands on the technique and considers the additional complexities introduced to the iterative process when the Capital Asset Pricing Model (CAPM) is used to calculate the equity component of WACC when the WACC is assumed to remain constant over time. Further, it illustrates how to implement the iterative process using a financial spreadsheet model.

CAPITAL ASSET PRICING MODEL AND BETA

Chapter 8 of *Cost of Capital: Applications and Examples,* 4th ed. presents an overview of CAPM. Formula 8.6 for the expanded CAPM we repeat here as:

(Formula 5.1)
$$E(R_i) = R_f + B_L(RP_m) + RP_s \pm RP_u$$

where: $E(R_i)$ = Expected rate of return on security i

$\quad R_f$ = Rate of return available on a risk-free security as of the valuation date

$\quad B_L$ = Beta levered

$\quad RP_m$ = General equity risk premium for the market (ERP)

$\quad RP_s$ = Risk premium for small size

$\quad RP_u$ = Risk premium attributable to the specific company (u stands for unique or unsystematic risk)

As explained in Chapter 10 of *Cost of Capital: Applications and Examples,* 4th ed., proxy beta estimates for the subject closely held company are often derived from guideline public company beta estimates. However, as noted in Chapter 10, the public company betas are levered betas.

To unlever the guideline public company beta estimate, we will use Formula 5.2. We use this formula for illustrative purposes as a simplification. The formula is the same as the Fernandez formula (Formula 11.9), assuming that the beta on debt capital equals zero ($B_d = 0$), or the Hamada formula (Formula 11.1) presented in Chapter 11 of *Cost of Capital: Applications and Examples,* 4th ed.:

(Formula 5.2)

$$B_U = \frac{B_L}{1 + (1 - t)\,W_d/W_e}$$

where: B_U = Beta unlevered
B_L = Beta levered
t = Income tax rate for the company
W_d = Percent debt at market value in the capital structure
W_e = Percent equity at market value in the capital structure

Once the public company beta estimate is unlevered, then the beta estimate may be relevered for the subject company using, for illustrative purposes, the simplified Formula 11.10 with $B_d = 0$ or Formula 11.2 presented in Chapter 11 of *Cost of Capital: Applications and Examples*, 4th ed.:

(Formula 5.3)

$$B_L = B_U(1 + [1 - t]\,W_d/W_e)$$

where the definitions of the variables are the same as in Formula 5.2.

In relevering the unlevered beta, we have introduced a third unknown: We need to know the market value of the subject company's equity in order to determine the relative weights to be assigned to the subject company's debt and equity for the purpose of relevering the beta.

SOLUTION: THE ITERATIVE PROCESS

Each of the next three calculations depends on a single unknown value—the market value of the subject company's equity:

1. Subject company's relevered beta.
2. WACC.
3. Market value of equity.

We can solve each of these calculations by using the iterative process to estimate the market value of equity. The next example illustrates this methodology. For purposes of illustration, we have used a capital structure consisting of solely common equity and debt. Further, in applying the income approach, we have used the capitalization of economic income method instead of the discounted economic income method to simplify the calculations. Our example is based on seven assumptions:

1. Book value of long-term interest-bearing debt: $400,000.
2. Book value of common equity: $600,000.
3. Interest rate for debt: 10% (assumed to be the market rate).
4. Income tax rate (combined federal and effective state rate): 40%.
5. Projected net cash flow to invested capital for year following the valuation date: $250,000.

6. Estimated annual compounded long-term growth rate for net cash flow to invested capital: 5%.
7. Cost of capital variables

$$R_f = 4.5\%$$
$$RP_m = 6.0\%$$
$$RP_s = 5.81\%$$
$$RP_u = 2.0\%$$
$$k_{d(pt)} = 10\%$$
$$B_{Ui} = 1.23$$
$$g = 5\%$$
$$t = 40\%$$

Step 1. Inputs for Debt and Equity

For this iteration, the book values of the subject company's debt and equity will be used as proxies for the market values for purposes of calculating the weighting of the capital components of the WACC:

Capital Component	Estimated Market Value	Percent of Capital*
Debt	$400,000	0.40
Equity	$600,000	0.60
Total	$1,000,000	1.00

*Percentages expressed as decimal equivalents.

Step 2. Calculation of Relevered Beta for the Subject Company

The next step in the iterative process is to estimate the beta for the subject company. This involves relevering the unlevered industry beta. To calculate the relevered beta for the subject company, we substitute the unlevered industry beta, the subject company tax rate, and the initial book values for debt and equity into Formula 5.3 to get Formula 5.4:

(Formula 5.4)

$$B_L = B_{Ui}(1 + [1 - t]W_d/W_e)$$
$$= 1.23(1 + [1 - .4]0.4/0.6)$$
$$= 1.7220$$

Step 3. Estimation of Cost of Equity Using the Capital Asset Pricing Model

Next we calculate an estimate of cost of equity using CAPM. We substitute the known values for the CAPM variables as well as the relevered beta just derived into Formula 5.1 to get Formula 5.5:

(Formula 5.5)
$$E(R_i) = R_f + B_L(RP_m) + RP_s + RP_u$$
$$= 0.45 + 1.7220(0.06) + 0.0581 + 0.02$$
$$= 0.2264$$

Step 4. Estimation of Weighted Average Cost of Capital

After calculating the initial estimate of the cost of equity, we next estimate the WACC. Using the same book values of the subject company's debt and equity as the weights and the cost of equity calculated using CAPM, we calculate the WACC as:

(Formula 5.6)
$$WACC = (k_e \times W_e) + (k_d[1 - t] \times W_d)$$
$$= (0.2264 \times 0.6) + (0.1[1 - 0.4] \times 0.4)$$
$$= 0.1598$$

As the WACC represents a discount rate for invested capital, we subtract the long-term growth rate of 5% to derive the capitalization rate of 10.98%.

Step 5. Capitalized Economic Income Method (Invested Capital Model)

Finally, we use Formula 5.7 (repeating Formula 4.4 in *Cost of Capital: Applications and Examples,* 4th ed.) to estimate the market value of invested capital and subtract the value of the debt to derive the estimated value of equity:

(Formula 5.7)
$$PV = \frac{NCF_1}{c}$$

where: PV = Present value
NCF_1 = Net cash flow expected in the first period immediately following the valuation date
c = Capitalization rate (WACC − g)

$$2,276,867 = 250,000/0.1098$$

The market value of invested capital, $2,276,867, minus the value of debt, $400,000, equals the estimated market value of equity, $1,876,867. However, this estimate of the market value of equity is materially different from the book value of $600,000 we used initially as a proxy and consequently results in very different market weights of debt and equity, as indicated in the next chart.

Capital Component	Estimated Market Value	Percent of Capital*
Debt	$400,000	0.1757
Equity	$1,876,867	0.8243
Total	$2,276,867	1.0000

*Percentages expressed as decimal equivalents.

Therefore, we must repeat the preceding calculations, substituting the book value of equity used in step 1, $600,000, with the calculated value of equity, $1,876,867. We continue to recalculate the value of equity until the value of the equity input in step 1 (the value used to estimate the market weights in steps 2 and 4) equals the calculated equity in step 5.

ITERATIVE PROCESS USING A FINANCIAL SPREADSHEET MODEL

Although we could repeat each of these calculations manually, the iterative process can be implemented more easily using a financial spreadsheet application and linking the cells containing the unknown weight of the equity value we are seeking to determine. The next illustration of a spreadsheet model is based on the previous example. This model is built in Microsoft *Excel*, and all formulas are presented using *Excel* definitions. Note that the version of the model presented requires a user to manually input the estimated market value of equity for each iteration. This presentation is useful in illustrating how the iterative process is performed. However, advanced users of *Excel* may wish to consider using either the *Excel* "goal seek" function or Solver, an *Excel* add-on tool, to calculate the value automatically. One can find the worksheets on the companion John Wiley & Sons web site.

Iteration 1

Worksheet 1.1 Inputs: Estimates of Debt and Equity   As previously discussed, the estimated market values of debt (C7) and equity (C8) for Iteration 1 are based on book values and serve as our initial inputs to the model. The relative weights of debt (D7) and equity (D8) are calculated.

A	B	C	D
3		Estimated	Percent
4		Market	of
5		Value	Capital
6			W
7	Long-term interest-bearing debt	400,000	0.4000
8	Equity	600,000	0.6000
9	Total capital	1,000,000	1.0000

A	B	C	D
3		Estimated	Percent
4		Market	of
5		Value	Capital
6			W
7	Long-term interest-bearing debt	400,000	= ROUND(C7/C9,4)
8	Equity	600,000	= ROUND(C8/C9,4)
9	Total capital	= SUM(C7:C8)	= SUM(D7:D8)

Worksheet 1.2 Calculation of Relevered Beta for Subject Company   Worksheet 1.2 presents the calculation of the relevered beta. The estimated market weights of debt (C17) and equity (C18) are linked to the values in Worksheet 1.1 (D7 and D8, respectively). The tax rate (D17) and beta (E19) are manual inputs to the model. The relevered beta (F19) is calculated using Formula 5.4.

A	B	C	D	E	F
13		Percent		Industry	Subject
14		of		(or Guideline Co.)	Company
15		Capital	Tax Rate	Unlevered Beta	Levered Beta
16		W	t	B_{Ui}	B_L
17	Debt	0.4000	0.40		
18	Equity	0.6000	N/A		
19	Total	1.0000		1.23	1.7220

A	B	C	D	E	F
13		Percent		Industry	Subject
14		of		(or Guideline Co.)	Company
15		Capital	Tax Rate	Unlevered Beta	Levered Beta
16		W	T	B_{Ui}	B_L
17	Debt	= D7	0.4		
18	Equity	= D8	N/A		
19	Total	= SUM(C17:C18)		1.23	= ROUND((E19* (1 + ((1-D17)* C17)/C18)),4)

Worksheet 1.3 Estimation of Cost of Equity Using CAPM   Worksheet 1.3 presents the CAPM based on Formula 5.5. All CAPM variables are manual inputs, except for beta (C26), which is linked to Worksheet 1.2 (F19). The cost of equity is calculated (D30).

A	B	C	D
23	Risk-free rate (R_f)		0.0450
24	Systematic risk		
25	Equity risk premium (RP_m)	0.0600	
26	× Beta (B)	1.7220	
27	Systematic risk		0.1033
28	Risk premium for size (RP_s)		0.0581
29	Specific (unsystematic) risk (RP_u)		0.0200
30	Cost of equity (k_e)		0.2264

A	B	C	D
23	Risk-free rate (R_f)		0.0450
24	Systematic risk		
25	Equity risk premium (RP_m)	0.06	
26	× Beta (B)	= F19	
27	Systematic risk		= ROUND((C25*C26),4)
28	Risk premium for size (RP_s)		0.0581
29	Specific (unsystematic) risk (RP_u)		0.0200
30	Cost of equity (k_e)		= SUM(D23:D29)

Worksheet 1.4 Estimation of WACC   Worksheet 1.4 calculates the WACC based on Formula 5.6. As with Worksheet 1.2, the cells containing the estimated market weights of debt (C39) and equity (C40) are linked to the values in Worksheet 1.1 (D7 and D8, respectively). The cost of debt (D39) and tax rate (E39) are manual inputs and the tax-affected rate is calculated (F39). The cost of equity (D40) is linked to Worksheet 1.3 (D30). The weighted average cost of debt (G39) and equity (G40) are calculated and summed to derive the WACC (G41). The long-term growth rate (G45), a manual input, is deducted from the WACC (G44) to derive the capitalization rate (G46).

A	B	C	D	E	F	G
				Cost of Capital		
34		Percent				Weighted
35		of		Tax	After-Tax	Average
36		Capital	Rate	Rate	Rate	Cost
37		W	k	t	k [1 − t]	WACC
38	**Calculation of WACC**					
39	Debt	0.4000	0.10	0.40	0.0600	0.0240
40	Equity	0.6000	0.2264	N/A	0.2264	0.1358
41	Total	1.0000				0.1598
42						
43	**Calculation of Capitalization rate**					
44	Discount rate for net cash flow					0.1598
45	Less long-term average growth rate					0.0500
46	Capitalization rate for net cash flow					0.1098

A	B	C	D	E	F	G
				Cost of Capital		
34		Percent				Weighted
35		of		Tax	After-Tax	Average
36		Capital	Rate	Rate	Rate	Cost
37		W	k	T	$k\,[1-t]$	WACC
38	**Calculation of WACC**					
39	Debt	= D7	0.10	0.40	= ROUND ((D39*(1 – E39)),4)	+ROUND ((C39*F39),4)
40	Equity	= D8	= D30	N/A	= + D40	+ ROUND ((C40*F40),4)
41	Total	= SUM (C39:C40)				+ ROUND (SUM(G39: G40),4)
42						
43	**Calculation of Capitalization Rate**					
44	Discount rate for net cash flow					+ ROUND (G41,4)
45	Less long-term average growth rate					0.05
46	Capitalization rate for net cash flow					+ (G44-G45)

Worksheet 1.5 Capitalized Economic Income Method (Invested Capital Model) Worksheet 1.5 presents the calculation of the value of invested capital using the capitalized economic income method based on Formula 4.1, and it also presents a calculation of the value of the equity. The net cash flow to invested capital (C50), a manual input, is multiplied by the capitalization rate (C51) linked to Worksheet 1.4 (G46) to derive the market value of invested capital (C52). From this amount, the market value of debt (C53), linked to Worksheet 1.1 (C7), is subtracted to derive the estimated market value of equity (C54).

A	B	C
50	Adjusted net cash flow to invested capital	250,000
51	Capitalization rate	0.1098
52	Indicated value of 100% of the Business Enterprise	2,276,867
53	Less interest-bearing debt	400,000
54	**Indicated value of a 100% marketable equity interest**	1,876,867

A	B	C
50	Adjusted net cash flow to invested capital	250000
51	Capitalization rate	= G46
52	Indicated value of 100% of the Business Enterprise	= ROUND(C50/C51,0)
53	Less interest-bearing debt	= C7
54	**Indicated value of a 100% marketable equity interest**	= C52−C53

As the value of the calculated equity (C54), $1,876,867, is not equal to the initial estimate of equity input in Worksheet 1.1 (C8), $600,000 (the value used to estimate the market weights in Worksheets 1.2 and 1.4), the market value of equity must be estimated again and the calculations repeated.

Iteration 2

Worksheet 2.1 Inputs: Estimates of Debt and Equity   In the second iteration, the value of equity in Worksheet 2.1 (C8) is set equal to the value derived in Iteration 1, Worksheet 1.5 (C54). The relative weights of debt (D7) and equity (D8) are then recalculated. The model then automatically performs the calculations in Worksheets 2.2, 2.3, 2.4, and 2.5.

A	B	C	D
3		Estimated	Percent
4		Market	of
5		Value	Capital
6			W
7	Long-term interest-bearing debt	400,000	0.1757
8	Equity	1,876,867	0.8243
9	Total capital	2,276,867	1.0000

Worksheet 2.2 Calculation of Relevered Beta for Subject Company

A	B	C	D	E	F
13		Percent		Industry	Subject
14		of	Tax	(or Guideline Co.)	Company
15		Capital	Rate	Unlevered Beta	Levered Beta
16		W	T	B_{Ui}	B_L
17	Debt	0.1757	0.40		
18	Equity	0.8243	N/A		
19	Total	1.0000		1.23	1.3873

Worksheet 2.3 Estimation of Cost of Equity Using CAPM

A	B	C	D
23	Risk-free rate (R_f)		0.0450
24	Systematic risk		
25	Equity risk premium (RP_m)	0.0600	
26	× Beta (B)	1.3873	
27	Systematic risk		0.0832
28	Risk premium for size (RP_s)		0.0581
29	Specific (unsystematic) risk (RP_u)		0.0200
30	Cost of equity (k_e)		0.2063

Worksheet 2.4 Estimation of WACC

A	B	C	D	E	F	G
				Cost of Capital		
34		Percent				Weighted
35		of		Tax	After-Tax	Average
36		Capital	Rate	Rate	Rate	Cost
37		W	K	t	$k\,[1-t]$	$WACC$
38	**Calculation of WACC**					
39	Debt	0.1757	0.10	0.40	0.0600	0.0105
40	Equity	0.8243	0.2063	N/A	0.2063	0.1701
41	Total	1.0000				0.1806
42						
43	**Calculation of Capitalization rate**					
44	Discount rate for net cash flow					0.1806
45	Less long-term average growth rate					0.0500
46	Capitalization rate for net cash flow					0.1306

Worksheet 2.5 Capitalized Economic Income Method (Invested Capital Model)

A	B	C
50	Adjusted net cash flow to invested capital	250,000
51	Capitalization rate	0.1306
52	Indicated value of 100% of the Business Enterprise	1,914,242
53	Less interest-bearing debt	400,000
54	**Indicated value of a 100% marketable equity interest**	1,514,242

As the value of the calculated equity (C54), $1,514,242, is not equal to the estimate of equity input in Worksheet 2.1 (C8), $1,876,867, the market value of equity must be estimated again and the calculations repeated.

Iteration 3

Worksheet 3.1 Inputs: Estimates of Debt and Equity In Iteration 3, the value of equity in Worksheet 3.1 (C8) is set equal to the value derived in Iteration 2, Worksheet 2.5 (C54). The relative weights of debt (D7) and equity (D8) are then recalculated. The model then automatically performs the calculations in Worksheets 3.2, 3.3, 3.4, and 3.5.

A	B		C	D
3			Estimated	Percent
4			Market	of
5			Value	Capital
6				W
7		Long-term interest-bearing debt	400,000	0.2090
8		Equity	1,514,242	0.7910
9		Total capital	1,914,242	1.0000

Worksheet 3.2 Calculation of Relevered Beta for Subject Company

A	B	C	D	E	F
13		Percent		Industry	Subject
14		of	Tax	(or Guideline Co.)	Company
15		Capital	Rate	Unlevered Beta	Levered Beta
16		W	T	B_{Ui}	B_L
17	Debt	0.2090	0.40		
18	Equity	0.7910	N/A		
19	Total	1.0000		1.23	1.4250

Worksheet 3.3 Estimation of Cost of Equity Using CAPM

A	B	C	D
23	Risk-free rate (R_f)		0.0450
24	Systematic risk		
25	Equity risk premium (RP_m)	0.0600	
26	× Beta (B)	1.4250	
27	Systematic risk		0.0855
28	Risk premium for size (RP_s)		0.0581
29	Specific (unsystematic) risk (RP_u)		0.0200
30	Cost of equity (k_e)		0.2086

Worksheet 3.4 Estimation of WACC

A	B	C	D	E	F	G
		Cost of Capital				
34		Percent				Weighted
35		of		Tax	After-Tax	Average
36		Capital	Rate	Rate	Rate	Cost
37		W	k	t	k [1 − t]	WACC
38	**Calculation of WACC**					

39	Debt	0.2090	0.10	0.40	0.0600	0.0125
40	Equity	0.7910	0.2086	N/A	0.2086	0.1650
41	Total	1.0000				0.1775
42						
43	**Calculation of Capitalization Rate**					
44	Discount rate for net cash flow					0.1775
45	Less long-term average growth rate					0.0500
46	Capitalization rate for net cash flow					0.1275

Worksheet 3.5 Capitalized Economic Income Method (Invested Capital Model)

A	B	C
50	Adjusted net cash flow to invested capital	250,000
51	Capitalization rate	0.1275
52	Indicated value of 100% of the Business Enterprise	1,960,784
53	Less interest-bearing debt	400,000
54	**Indicated value of a 100% marketable equity interest**	1,560,784

As the value of the calculated equity (C54), $1,560,784, is not equal to the estimate of equity input in Worksheet 3.1 (C8), $1,514,242, the market value of equity must be estimated again and the calculations repeated.

Iteration 4

Worksheet 4.1 Inputs: Estimates of Debt and Equity   In the fourth iteration, the value of equity (C8) is set equal to the value derived in Iteration 3, Worksheet 3.5 (C54). The relative weights of debt (D7) and equity (D8) are then recalculated. The model then automatically performs the calculations in Worksheets 4.2, 4.3, 4.4, and 4.5.

A	B	C	D
3		Estimated	Percent
4		Market	of
5		Value	Capital
6			W
7	Long-term interest-bearing debt	400,000	0.2040
8	Equity	1,560,784	0.7960
9	Total capital	1,960,784	1.0000

Worksheet 4.2 Calculation of Relevered Beta for Subject Company

A	B	C	D	E	F
13		Percent		Industry	Subject
14		of	Tax	(or Guideline Co.)	Company
15		Capital	Rate	Unlevered Beta	Levered Beta
16		W	T	B_{Ui}	B_L
17	Debt	0.2040	0.40		
18	Equity	0.7960	N/A		
19	Total	1.0000		1.23	1.4191

Worksheet 4.3 Estimation of Cost of Equity Using CAPM

A	B	C	D
23	Risk-free rate (R_f)		0.0450
24	Systematic risk		
25	Equity risk premium (RP_m)	0.0600	
26	× Beta (B)	1.4191	
27	Systematic risk		0.0851
28	Risk premium for size (RP_s)		0.0581
29	Specific (unsystematic) risk (RP_u)		0.0200
30	Cost of equity (k_e)		0.2082

Worksheet 4.4 Estimation of WACC

A	B	C	D	E	F	G
				Cost of Capital		
34		Percent				Weighted
35		of		Tax	After-Tax	Average
36		Capital	Rate	Rate	Rate	Cost
37		W	k	t	$k\,[1-t]$	*WACC*
38	**Calculation of WACC**					
39	Debt	0.2040	0.10	0.40	0.0600	0.0122
40	Equity	0.7960	0.2082	N/A	0.2082	0.1657
41	Total	1.0000				0.1779
42						
43	**Calculation of Capitalization rate**					
44	Discount rate for net cash flow					0.1779
45	Less long-term average growth rate					0.0500
46	Capitalization rate for net cash flow					0.1279

Worksheet 4.5 Capitalized Economic Income Method (Invested Capital Model)

A	B	C
50	Adjusted net cash flow to invested capital	250,000
51	Capitalization rate	0.1279
52	Indicated value of 100% of the Business Enterprise	1,954,652
53	Less interest-bearing debt	400,000
54	Indicated value of a 100% marketable equity interest	1,554,652

As the value of the calculated equity (C54), $1,554,652, is approximately equal to the estimate of equity input in Worksheet 4.1 (C8), $1,560,784, we conclude that the market value of equity is approximately $1,555,000 in round numbers. We could continue the iterations until the two equity values equaled one another, but for purposes of illustration, the calculated value is considered reasonable.

SUMMARY

This supplement has expanded on the iterative process presented in Chapter 18 of *Cost of Capital: Applications and Examples,* 4th ed. to consider the additional complexities when the CAPM is used to calculate the equity component of WACC, assuming the WACC is constant over time. Further, it has provided an example illustrating the use of a financial spreadsheet model to perform the calculations required for the iterative process. The *Excel* worksheet for this example are reproduced in the companion John Wiley & Sons web site.

ADDITIONAL READING

Abrams, Jay B. *Quantitative Business Valuation: A Mathematical Approach for Today's Professionals*, 2nd ed. New York: McGraw-Hill, 2010.

Bishop, David M., and Frank C. Evans."Avoiding a Common Error in Calculating the Weighted Average Cost of Capital." *CPA Expert* (Fall 1997).

Evans, Frank C., and Kelly L. Strimbu. "Debt and Equity Weightings in WACC." *CPA Expert* (Fall 1998).

Hitchner, James R., ed. *Financial Valuation: Applications and Models*, 3rd ed. Hoboken NJ: John Wiley & Sons, 2010.

Martin, Harold G., Jr. "Cost of Capital." Joint presentation made with Ronald L. Seigneur at the American Institute of Certified Public Accountants National Business Valuation Conference, Las Vegas, Nevada, December 4, 2001.

Pratt, Shannon P., with Alina Niculita. *Valuing a Business: The Analysis and Appraisal of Closely Held Companies*, 5th ed. New York: McGraw-Hill, 2008.

Iterative Process Using CAPM to Calculate the Cost of Equity Component of the Weighted Average Cost of Capital When Capital Structure Is Changing—Supplement to Chapter 18

James R. Morris

INTRODUCTION

This chapter is a supplement to *Cost of Capital: Applications and Examples,* 4th ed. In the preceding chapter of this workbook, Harold Martin explained how to use the iterative process to calculate the cost of capital and the value of the firm. The iterative process is necessary because the valuation problem is circular. That is, to calculate the cost of capital and the value of the firm, we need to know the value of the firm and value of its components—the debt and equity—which, in turn, are the things we are trying to determine. We use the iterative process to converge on value estimates where the values we use as input agree with the values we get as output. The purpose of this appendix is to build on the iterative process of Chapter 5 to show how to calculate the value of the firm and equity when the capital structure is changing over time.

ASSUMPTIONS INHERENT IN WEIGHTED AVERAGE COST OF CAPITAL

The standard weighted average cost of capital (WACC) calculation is based on the assumption that the capital structure will remain unchanged over the time period of the valuation. For example, the valuation developed in Chapter 5 was based implicitly on these assumptions:

- The proportional mix of debt and equity in the capital structure, in terms of market values, would remain constant over the investment horizon.
- With a constant proportional mix of debt and equity, the costs of capital (cost of debt, cost of equity, and WACC) would remain unchanged over the investment horizon.
- The cash flow to invested capital will grow at a constant rate over an indefinitely long investment horizon.

But how do we handle it if the mix of debt and equity are expected to change over the investment horizon? The answer is that we still use the iterative technique, but the task is made slightly more complicated by the changing capital structure.

SOLUTION: ITERATIVE PROCESS WITH CHANGING CAPITAL STRUCTURE

Basically, the iteration method is the same, except that we have to perform an iteration for each period in which the capital mix has changed. The way we do this is to start at a future date when we expect the capital structure to reach long-run stability and calculate value at each date from the future, working backward in time to the present.

For example, assume that by the end of period 4 in the future, the firm is expected to reach a point where its proportional capital structure will be stable for many years into the future. In the interim, with a given amount of debt currently outstanding, the firm is expected to repay part of the debt over the next three periods to reach that stable capital structure. To handle the changing capital structure with an iterative process, we start by calculating the value at time 4, when the firm is expected to reach its stable capital structure. Then we step back to time 3 and calculate the value at time 3, based on the capital structure and cost of capital prevailing at time 3. Next we calculate value at time 2 based on capital structure and cost of capital at time 2. We continue stepping backward in time until we reach the present and calculate the value based on the present capital structure. Essentially, when we use this process, we use a sequence of one-period valuation models, starting at the end and working backward, period by period, until we reach the present valuation date.

We start the process by calculating the value of the firm at the horizon date when the firm is expected to reach a stable capital structure and stable future growth in future cash flows. In this case, assume that the value at the horizon date (terminal value) is based on the constant growth model:[1]

(Formula 6.1)

$$PV_4 = NCF_5 \left[\frac{1}{(WACC_4 - g)} \right]$$

where: $WACC_4$ = WACC with capital structure proportions that prevail at time 4
NCF_5 = cash flow to invested capital for period 5

It is assumed that from time 5 forward, cash flows will grow at a constant rate g for the indefinite future.

Having calculated terminal value for time 4 based on the capital structure at time 4, we step back to time 3 and use a one-period valuation model to calculate time 3 value:

(Formula 6.2)

$$PV_3 = NCF_4 \left[\frac{1}{1 + WACC_3} \right] + PV_4 \left[\frac{1}{1 + WACC_3} \right]$$

where: $WACC_3$ = WACC with capital structure proportions prevailing at time 3

Then we continue stepping back, using a single-period valuation model to calculate value at each date based on the cost of capital and capital structure prevailing at that date. Our process stops when we reach the present, time 0.

To calculate value, we not only have to step backward in time from the horizon to the present, but at each stage we have to use an iterative process so that the capital structure weights are based on market values instead of book values. At each stage, we start the iteration using the book values of debt and equity to calculate the weights in the WACC and the costs of equity, and perhaps debt to the extent that it depends on the capital weights. Using the book values as the starting point, we calculate the values, at that stage, of invested capital, equity, and debt. These first iteration values are used as input to calculate new capital proportions for the second iteration for that stage. The iterations continue until the calculated values equal the assumed values. That gives us the value for that stage. Then we step back to the previous stage and start the iterative value calculation over again. An example will help show this process.

---

[1] The terminal value does not have to be based on constant growth. Constant growth is used here because it is a common method. The multistage iterative process explained here would work just as well if the terminal value was based on some other valuation method. It is just that we do need to have a terminal value with which to start working backward from the terminal date to the present. And, to generate consistent values, the terminal value of invested capital must be consistent with the terminal value of equity.

ITERATIVE PROCESS USING FINANCIAL SPREADSHEET MODEL

Our example will build on the valuation presented in Chapter 5. The example is the Martin Corporation whose current and pro forma income statement and balance sheet are shown in Exhibit 6.1. Over the first four periods of the investment horizon, Martin's sales are assumed to be stable and constant. Then, after period 4, sales are assumed to grow at a constant annual rate of 5% forever. Operating costs, earnings before interest, taxes, depreciation, and amortization (EBITDA), and earnings before interest and taxes (EBIT) are proportional to sales, and stable for periods 1 to 4, and then grow with sales in subsequent periods. Similarly, total assets, and

EXHIBIT 6.1   Current and Pro Forma Financial Statements

	A	B	C	D	E	F	G
1				Martin Corporation			
2							
3	Income Statement			Forecast			
4		0	1	2	3	4	5
5							
6	Sales	1,717,033	1,717,033	1,717,033	1,717,033	1,717,033	1,802,885
7	EBITDA	590,659	590,659	590,659	590,659	590,659	620,192
8	Depreciation	114,469	114,469	114,469	114,469	114,469	120,192
9	EBIT	476,190	476,190	476,190	476,190	476,190	500,000
10	Interest	60,000	60,000	53,000	46,000	40,000	40,000
11	Earnings Before Tax	416,190	416,190	423,190	430,190	436,190	460,000
12	Income Tax	166,476	166,476	169,276	172,076	174,476	184,000
13	Net Income	249,714	249,714	253,914	258,114	261,714	276,000
14							
15	Dividends	179,714	179,714	183,914	198,114	214,095	247,304
16	Retained Earnings	70,000	70,000	70,000	60,000	47,619	28,696
17							
18				Martin Corporation			
19	Balance Sheet						
20				Forecast			
21		0	1	2	3	4	5
22							
23	Current Assets	331,960	331,960	331,960	331,960	348,558	365,986
24	Net Fixed Assets	858,516	858,516	858,516	858,516	901,442	946,514
25	Total Assets	1,190,476	1,190,476	1,190,476	1,190,476	1,250,000	1,312,500
26							
27	Current Liabilities	238,095	238,095	238,095	238,095	250,000	262,500
28	Long-term Debt	600,000	530,000	460,000	400,000	400,000	420,000
29	Equity	352,381	422,381	492,381	552,381,	600,000	630,000
30	Liabilities & Equity	1,190,476	1,190,476	1,190,476	1,190,476	1,250,000	1,312,500

current liabilities are proportional to sales, so they do not grow for the first four periods, but then must grow the same 5% rate as sales after time 4.

At the start of the investment horizon (time 0), Martin's capital structure includes $600,000 of long-term debt at an interest rate of 10%. The borrowing rate is expected to remain at 10% for the indefinite future, and the market value of debt is equal to book value at each date. The company is expected to pay off some of its debt over the next three years until it has reduced its debt to $400,000 by time 3. If the firm did not grow, its debt would remain at $400,000. However, as the firm grows after time 4, debt will be issued to finance part of the growth, with the amount of borrowing being just sufficient to maintain the book value debt-to-equity ratio at 0.667 in each future period.

With the current (time 0) book value of equity at $352,381, the debt-to-equity ratio is currently $600,000/$352,381 = 1.7, and repayment of debt will reduce it to 0.667 by time 4. Thus, we have a situation in which the capital structure is going to change over the next four years and remain stable after that. Our task is to estimate the value of the firm and the equity so as to properly take account of the changing capital structure.

Valuation

Before calculating value, we need to specify some of the cost of capital parameters.

Assume that market conditions and cost of capital parameters are the same as were used in the example in Chapter 5. These parameters are:

$$R_f = 4.5\%$$
$$RP_m = 6.0\%$$
$$RP_s = 5.81\%$$
$$RP_u = 2.0\%$$
$$k_{d(pt)} = 10\%$$
$$B_{Ui} = 1.23$$
$$g = 5\%$$
$$t = 40\%$$

With these parameters, if the firm had no debt, its cost of equity capital would be:

(Formula 6.3)
$$k_e = R_f + RP_m \times B_{Ui} + RP_s \pm RP_u$$
$$= 4.5\% + 6.0\% \times 1.23 + 5.81\% + 2.0\%$$
$$= 19.69\%$$

However, the firm has debt in its structure, so the cost of equity will be greater to reflect the financial leverage. To lever the beta, we will use Formula 5.3. We use this formula for illustrative purposes as a simplification. The formula is the same as the Fernandez formula (Formula 11.10), assuming that the beta on debt capital equals zero ($B_d = 0$) or the Hamada formula (Formula 11.2) as presented in *Cost of Capital: Applications and Examples*, 4th ed. Using book values of debt and equity as a *first approximation*, the beta for the leveraged equity at time 4 would be:

(Formula 6.4)

$$B_L = B_{Ui}\left[1 + \left(\frac{Debt_4}{Equity_4}\right)(1 - t)\right]$$

$$= 1.23\left[1 + \left(\frac{400}{600}\right)(1 - 0.40)\right]$$

$$= 1.722$$

and the cost of leveraged equity would be:

(Formula 6.5)

$$k_e = 4.5\% + (6\% \times 1.722) + 5.81\% + 2.0\%$$

$$= 22.642\%$$

With the time-4 capital structure, using book values, the weighted average cost of capital would be:

(Formula 6.6)

$$WACC_4 = W_d \times k_{d(pt)}(1 - t) + W_e \times k_e$$

$$= 0.4 \times 0.10(1 - 0.40) + 0.60 \times 0.22.64$$

$$= 15.985\%$$

It must be emphasized that these cost-of-capital estimates are only a first approximation because the capital structure weights used to calculate beta and the weights in WACC should be based on the market values of debt and equity. We do not yet know the market value of equity because that is one of the things we are trying to determine. We know the market value of debt because it is assumed to be equal to book value. Our next step is to calculate the value of invested capital and equity at each date.

Because the capital structure is changing until time 4, we will calculate value in stages, starting from the horizon date at time 4 and working backward to time 0. In addition, because the cost of capital at each stage depends on the market values of debt and equity, we need to use an iterative process at each stage. We start at the horizon date using the constant growth model shown as Formula 6.1. But first, we need to calculate the cash flows as input to our calculations. Exhibit 6.2 shows the calculation of cash flow to invested capital along with the cash flow to equity.

Stage 4

This is the same firm that was discussed in Chapter 5, so the time-4 terminal value is calculated the same way as in that example. At time 4, when the firm has reached a stable capital structure and long-run future growth is expected to stabilize at 5%, the first-iteration value of invested capital is based on book value capital weights. Using Formula 6.1, iteration 1 value of invested capital at time 4 is:

(Formula 6.7)

$$PV_4 = NCF_5\left[\frac{1}{(WACC_4 - g)}\right]$$

$$= 250,000\left[\frac{1}{0.15985 - 0.05}\right]$$

$$= \$2,275,789$$

EXHIBIT 6.2   Cash Flows to Invested Capital and Equity

	A	B	C	D	E	F	G
34				Martin Corporation			
35	**Cash Flow to Invested Capital**						
36			1	2	3	4	5
37							
38	EBITDA		590,659	590,659	590,659	590,659	620,192
39	Depreciation		114,469	114,469	114,469	114,469	120,192
40	EBIT		476,190	476,190	476,190	476,190	500,000
41	Tax (Notional: T * EBIT)		190,476	190,476	190,476	190,476	200,000
42	Operating CF (AT)		400,183	400,183	400,183	400,183	420,192
43	NWC investment		0	0	0	4,693	4,928
44	Capital investment		114,469	114,469	114,469	157,395	165,264
45	Net cash flow to invested capital		285,714	285,714	285,714	238,095	250,000
46							
47				Martin Corporation			
48	**Equity Cash Flow**						
49			1	2	3	4	5
50							
51	Net income		249,714	253,914	258,114	261,714	276,000
52	Depreciation		114,469	114,469	114,469	114,469	120,192
53	Cash flow from earnings		364,183	368,383	372,583	376,183	396,192
54	NWC investment		0	0	0	4,693	4,928
55	Capital investment		114,469	114,469	114,469	157,395	165,264
56	Debt issued		−70,000	−70,000	−60,000	0	20,000
57	Equity cash flow		179.714	183,914	198,114	214,095	246,000

where the NCF_5 of $250,000 is from the last column of line 45 of Exhibit 6.2. Subtracting the time-4 debt of $400,000 from the value of invested capital yields our iteration-1 estimate of the value of equity as:

(Formula 6.8)
$$M_e = \left(M_{e,4} + M_{d,4}\right) - M_d$$
$$= \$2,275,789 - \$400,000$$
$$= \$1,875,789$$

where M_e denotes the market value of invested equity capital, and M_d denotes the market value of invested debt capital, which in this case we assume is the same as the book value.

Note that if this were the market value of equity, the debt-to-equity ratio would be 400,000/1,875,789 = 0.2132, instead of the 0.667, based on book values that were used to start our initial calculation of the leveraged beta. Similarly, the debt to total capital ratio (W_d in the WACC formula) would be 400,000/2,275,789 = .1758

EXHIBIT 6.3   Stage 4 Iterations to Converge on Values of Invested Capital and Equity

	Iteration	1	2	3	4	5
Row						
1	Assumed equity value	600,000	1,875,789	1,513,937	1,560,123	1,553,138
2	Debt/equity	66.67%	21.32%	26.42%	25.64%	25.75%
3	Beta	1.722	1.387	1.425	1.419	1.420
4	k_e	22.64%	20.63%	20.86%	20.83%	20.83%
5	k_{WACC}	15.99%	18.06%	17.75%	17.80%	17.79%
6	Value IC	2,275,789	1,913,937	1,960,123	1,953,138	1,954,170
7	Derived value equity	1,875,789	1,513,937	1,560,123	1,553,138	1,554,170

instead of .40. To improve our value estimate, we go to iteration 2, which uses the values and weights that we derived in iteration 1. The steps for iteration 2 are the same: We calculate the values of invested capital and equity using these revised capital weights and costs of capital. The iterations are continued until we reach a point at which the derived values of invested capital and equity match the assumed values. Exhibit 6.3 presents the results of five iterations, showing the final value of invested capital being $1,954,170, with an equity value of $1,554,170. A couple of more iterations would converge to the last dollar at $1,554,037. The number of iterations we take depends on the desired accuracy. The difference between the third iteration equity value and the final converged value is an error of about 0.4%.

Note that the value at time 4, except for rounding differences, is the same as was derived in Chapter 5. The idea is that the converged value represents the value of the firm when it has reached its stable position at time 4. Now we continue to work through the stages to show how to handle the changes in capital structure that occur between time 0 and time 4.

Stage 3

We use the one-period valuation model Formula 6.2 to calculate the value at time 3:

(Formula 6.9)

$$PV_3 = \$238,095 \left[\frac{1}{1 + WACC_3}\right] + \$1,954,037 \left[\frac{1}{1 + WACC_3}\right]$$

where the $238,095 is the cash flow to invested capital at time 4 from Exhibit 6.2, and $1,954,037 is the converged value of invested capital at time 4 that we just finished calculating. We will need to use the iterative process to determine the discount rate at time 3, $WACC_3$, which depends on the market value capital structure proportions at time 3. For the first iteration, we start with the book values of debt and equity at the end of period 3, which are $400,000, and $552,381, respectively, as shown in the balance sheet (Exhibit 6.1) and shown as the initial Assumed Equity Value in row 1 of Exhibit 6.4.

Starting iteration 1 with book values, we have the debt to equity, cost of equity, and WACC, as shown in the iteration 1 column. This yields derived values of

EXHIBIT 6.4   Stage 3 Iterations for Value of Invested Capital

	Iteration	1	2	3	4	5
Row						
1	Assumed equity value	552,381	1,493,033	1,461,953	1,462,470	1,462,461
2	Debt/equity	72.41%	26.79%	27.36%	27.35%	27.35%
3	Beta	1.764	1.428	1.432	1.432	1.432
4	k_e	22.90%	20.88%	20.90%	20.90%	20.90%
5	k_{WACC}	15.80%	17.73%	17.70%	17.70%	17.70%
6	Value IC	1,893,033	1,861,953	1,862,470	1,862,461	1,862,461
7	Derived value equity	1,493,033	1,461,953	1,462,470	1,462,461	1,462,461

invested capital and equity of $1,893,033 and $1,493,033 shown in the rows 6 and 7. The equity value of $1,493,033 is used as the assumed equity value for iteration 2, and calculations are repeated, to give values of $1,861,953 and $1,461,953 for invested capital and equity, respectively. The iterations are continued in this manner until, as shown for the fifth iteration, the derived value of equity that is the output agrees with assumed value of equity that is the input for calculating the capital ratios. We have concluded that the value of invested capital at the end of period 3 is $1,862,461, and equity is $1,462,461. Now we use that value as input in the next stage to calculate the values of invested capital and equity at time 2.

Stage 2

The one-period value of invested capital at time 2 is calculated as

(Formula 6.10)

$$PV_2 = \$285,714 \left[\frac{1}{1 + WACC_2} \right] + \$1,862,461 \left[\frac{1}{1 + WACC_2} \right]$$

where $285,714 is the cash flow to invested capital at time 3. From the balance sheet we know that the time-2 book values of debt and equity are $460,000 and $492,381, respectively. Once again we have to go through the iterative process, starting with book values at time 2 and converging to value estimates for time 2. The reader undoubtedly gets the idea, so the iterations will not be shown here. The converged value of invested capital and equity at time 2 are calculated to be $1,830,379 and $1,370,379, respectively.

Stage 1

We go through the same steps, using the single-period valuation model that uses the cash flow at time 2 and the value at time 2 as the input. We go through the iterations again, starting with book values at time 1 and continuing until the process converges. The converged values at time 1 are $1,808,992 and $1,278,992 for invested capital and equity.

EXHIBIT 6.5   Model for Calculating Value of Invested Capital Showing Converged Values

	A	B	C	D	E	F	G
59					Martin Corporation		
60	Firm Valuation						
61	Period	0	1	2	3	4	5
62	Weighted average cost of capital						
63	Debt	600,000	530,000	460,000	400,000	400,000	
64	Equity—Assumed value	1,196,539	1,278,992	1,370,379	1,462,461	1,554,037	
65	Debt/total capital	33.4%	29.3%	25.1%	21.5%	20.5%	
66	Equity/total capital	66.6%	70.7%	74.9%	78.5%	79.5%	
67	Debt/equity	50.1%	41.4%	33.6%	27.4%	25.7%	
68	Cost of debt	10.0%	10.0%	10.0%	10.0%	10.0%	
69	Levered beta	1.600	1.536	1.478	1.432	1.420	
70	Cost of equity	21.91%	21.52%	21.18%	20.90%	20.83%	
71	Weighted average cost of capital	16.60%	16.98%	17.36%	17.70%	17.79%	
72							
73	Cash flow to invested capital		285,714	285,714	285,714	238,095	250,000
74	$PV_t\,(CF_{t+1})$	245,045	244,249	243,446	202,289		
75	$PV_t\,(Value_{t+1})$	1,551,494	1,564,742	1,586,933	1,660,173	1,954,037	
76							
77	Value of invested capital	1,796,539	1,808,992	1,830,379	1,862,461	1,954,037	
78	less: debt	600,000	530,000	460,000	400,000	400,000	
79	Value of equity	1,196,539	1,278,992	1,370,379	1,462,461	1,554,037	

Stage 0

The last stage is the time 0 calculation of value. We use the values from stage 1, and start with book values to initiate the iterations. We end up with estimates of the value of the Martin Corporation at time 0 of $1,796,539 for invested capital and $1,196,539 for the equity. These values are shown in the Period 0 column (column B) of Exhibit 6.5, which shows the calculation of the converged values at each stage.

Handling the Iterations

Exhibit 6.5 shows the converged results for the iterations at each of the stages in the value calculation. Two ways to work through the iterations are manually and automatically. The manual approach was used to construct Exhibits 6.3 and 6.4, which were shown to demonstrate the steps in the iteration. One can find the worksheets on the companion John Wiley & Sons web site.

Manual Iterations   Using the manual approach with a spreadsheet model like Exhibit 6.5 requires that the user start at stage 4 and plug in the equity value in cell

F64. For the first iteration, this would be the book value of equity referenced by equating cell F64 to equity in the balance sheet (= F29) in Exhibit 6.1. The derived values for the first iteration would show in cells F77 and F79 in Exhibit 6.5. The equity value in F79 from the first iteration would be plugged into cell F64 to start the second iteration. This would continue until cell F79 agrees with the input cell F64. Stage 3 would use these converged results from stage 4 and go through the iterations starting with the book value of equity in cell E64, with the derived value showing in cell E79. The stage iterations stop when E79 agrees with the input cell E64. Then we go to stage 2, reach convergence, then stage 1 and stage 0. These are the manual steps used to complete the values explained in the preceding text. Now let us look at the automatic approach.

Automatic Iterations   Microsoft *Excel* will work through these iterations automatically, so you do not have to do it manually. The steps that *Excel* follows are much like the manual approach just explained, but they are performed instantly. In the *Excel* model shown in Exhibit 6.5, we can set the input equity values in row 64 equal to the derived output equity values in row 79. For example, for stage 4 we enter in cell F64 the formula = F79. This causes a circular reference that brings up a dialog box chastising you for committing such a stupid and unforgivable error. The way to solve the circular reference is:

1. On the *Excel* Menu bar, select Tools>Options. The Options dialog box (shown in Exhibit 6.6) pops up.
2. Choose the Calculation tab, click Iteration and OK.

The model is now set to do the iterations automatically. This automatic iteration method was used to generate the values shown in Exhibit 6.5, and it does the

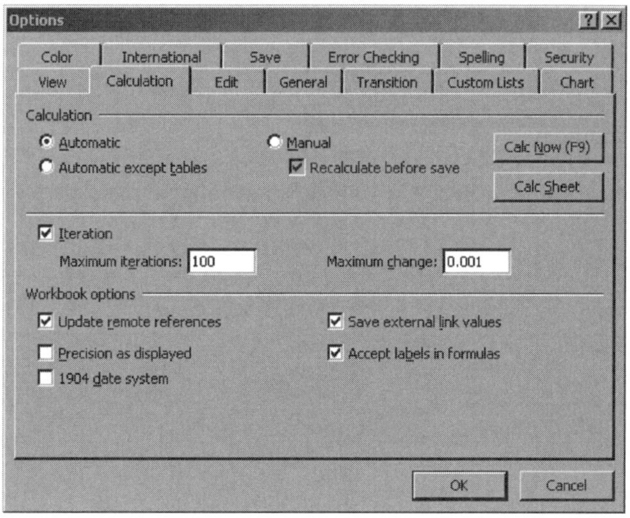

EXHIBIT 6.6   *Excel* Calculation Dialog Box

iterations down to the point where the circular references agree within the .001 shown in the Maximum Change box.[2]

EQUITY VALUE

Our discussion so far has focused on the value of invested capital, with the value of equity being a residual. Often the task is to estimate the value of equity. The analyst may want to attack the problem directly by using the equity approach, not the invested capital (WACC) approach. If we are using the equity approach with a changing capital structure, we use the same iterative approach over several stages. As with the invested capital approach, we start at the end of the investment horizon, when the firm is expected to reach a stable structure with constant growth.

We will not repeat all the steps of the iterations and stages for the equity method, having shown them for the invested capital method. We will just show the converged results in Exhibit 6.7 that are the result of using *Excel's* automatic

EXHIBIT 6.7   Model of Equity Value

	A	B	C	D	E	F	G
81					Martin Corporation		
82	**Equity Valuation**						
83	Period	0	1	2	3	4	5
84	Risk-free rate	4.50%					
85	Equity risk premium	6.00%					
86	Size premium	5.81%					
87	Company-specific premium	2.00%					
88	Unlevered beta	1.23					
89	Debt	600,000	530,000	460,000	400,000	400,000	
90	Equity	1,196,539	1,278,992	1,370,379	1,462,461	1,554,037	
91	Debt/equity	0.50	0.41	0.34	0.27	0.26	
92	Levered beta	1.600	1.536	1.478	1.432	1.420	
93	Cost of equity	21.91%	21.52%	21.18%	20.90%	20.83%	
94							
95	Equity cash flow		179,714	183,914	198,114	214,095	246,000
96	$PV_t(CF_{t+1})$	147,415	151,339	163,493	177,083		
97	$PV_t(Value_{t+1})$	1,049,124	1,127,653	1,206,887	1,285,378	1,554,037	
98							
99	Value of equity	1,196,539	1,278,992	1,370,379	1,462,461	1,554,037	
100	Plus: debt	600,000	530,000	460,000	400,000	400,000	
101	MVIC	1,796,539	1,808,992	1,830,379	1,862,461	1,954,037	

---

[2] A caution is in order. Automatic iteration works well in simple models in which there are few circular references that do not conflict. However, complex models may contain numerous inconsistent circular references, and you may not be able to converge to consistent answers for all of them. The solution is simply to do a better job of model building so as to avoid the numerous circular references.

iteration capability. All the cost of capital parameters are the same as in the invested capital example, and the equity cash flow is from line 57 of Exhibit 6.2.

Cell F99 shows the converged value at time 4 that is calculated with the constant growth model

(Formula 6.11)

$$M_{e,4} = \$246,000 \left[\frac{1}{(0.2083 - 0.05)} \right]$$
$$= \$1,554,037$$

where $246,000 is the cash flow to equity at time 5, and the long-run growth in equity cash flow is assumed to be equal to the growth of net cash flow to invested capital. Line 96 is the present value at each stage t of the cash flow at time $t + 1$, discounted at the cost of capital for period t: $NCF_{e,t+1}\left[1/(1 + k_{e,t})\right]$. Line 97 is the present value at time t of the equity value at time $t + 1$: $PV_{t+1}\left[1/(1 + k_{e,t})\right]$. Line 99 adds the present value of cash flow to the present value of the end of period value to obtain the value of equity at each date. Thus, line 99 shows all the converged values of equity. The iterations are executed automatically by equating the equity value in line 90 with the equity value in line 99 and allowing *Excel* to do the iterations. Note that the value of equity (line 99) and the value of invested capital (line 101) at each stage match the values derived using the invested capital method shown in Exhibit 6.5.

Exhibit 6.8 shows the importance of using an iterative method by showing the differences between the starting values and ending values of the costs of capital and the values of equity and invested capital. The starting costs of capital were based on the book-value weights for that period, and the converged costs of capital on the derived market-value weights. The biggest error occurs at stage 4, with a 21% difference between the starting and ending values of equity. The differences decline as we proceed from stage 4 back through time to stage 0 because by stage 0, we have already used market based capital weights in the later stages 1 through 4. Had we used book-value weights throughout, without using an iterative process, the time 0

EXHIBIT 6.8 Comparison of Costs of Capital and Value between First and Last Iterations

Period (Stage)	0	1	2	3	4
Cost of equity— first iteration	27.23%	25.25%	23.83%	22.9%	22.64%
Last iteration	21.91%	21.52%	21.18%	20.9%	20.83%
Value of equity— first iteration	$1,239,802	$1,317,541	$1,404,469	$1,493,033	$1,875,789
Last iteration	$1,196,539	$1,278,992	$1,370,379	$1,462,461	$1,554037
WACC—first iteration	13.85%	14.54%	15.22%	15.8%	15.99%
Last iteration	16.60%	16.98%	17.36%	17.7%	17.79%
MVIC—first iteration	$1,839,802	$1,847,541	$1,864,469	$1,893,033	$2,275789
Last iteration	$1,769,539	$1,808,992	$1,830,379	$1,862,461	$1,954,037

value of invested capital would have been estimated to be $2,105,080, an error of 17% over the correct converged value of 1,796,539. Furthermore, if capital weights are based on book values in each period, the values derived with the invested capital/ WACC method do not agree with the values obtained when you use the equity method, such as the method shown in Exhibit 6.7.

SUMMARY

This chapter has discussed two complications to calculating and using the cost of equity and the weighted average cost of capital. First, both are functions of the capital proportions based on market values of the sources of capital, which makes the valuation problem circular. Second, both are valid for a stable capital structure, so if the capital structure is changing over time, we need to adjust the market-value-based capital proportions to calculate costs of capital and value at each stage.

This chapter has shown how we can deal with these complications. To handle the requirement that the capital proportions are based on market values, we perform an iterative process, typically starting with book values and converging on a solution where the capital proportions are based on market-value estimates. To handle the second problem when the capital structure is changing, we work in stages, starting at a terminal value, at a point in the future when the capital structure mix will have stabilized, and working backward in time to the present, using an iterative process at each stage to reach value estimates that are based on converged market values at each stage. The *Excel* worksheets for this example are reproduced in the companion John Wiley & Sons web site.

ADDITIONAL READING

Morris, James R. "Reconciling the Equity and Invested Capital Methods of Valuation When the Capital Structure Is Changing." *Business Valuation Review* (March 2004): 36–46.
Morris, James R. "Growth in the Constant Growth Model." *Business Valuation Review* (Winter 2006): 153–162.

CHAPTER 7

Cost of Capital and the Valuation of Worthless Stock—Supplement to Chapter 16

Joanne Fong and Roger Grabowski

Any opinions presented herein are those of the authors and do not represent the official position of Duff & Phelps LLC or Ernst & Young LLP. This material is offered for educational purposes with the understanding that neither the authors, Duff & Phelps LLC or Ernst & Young LLP are engaged in rendering legal, accounting or any other professional service through presentation of this material.

The information presented in this paper has been obtained with the greatest of care from sources believed to be reliable, but is not guaranteed to be complete, accurate or timely. The authors, Duff & Phelps LLC and Ernst and Young LLP expressly disclaim any liability, including incidental or consequential damages, arising from the use of this material or any errors or omissions that may be contained in it.

We thank Brian A. Peabody of Ernst & Young LLP for his review and contribution on the tax discussion.

This chapter presents an example of the methodologies discussed in *Cost of Capital in Litigation: Applications and Examples,* Chapter 5.

INTRODUCTION

This chapter is a supplement to *Cost of Capital: Applications and Examples,* 4th ed., Chapter 16.

When is a taxpayer allowed a worthless security deduction under IRC §165(g)(3) of the Internal Revenue Code? Revenue Ruling 2003-125 (issued December 29, 2003) states the following:

> [T]he shareholder of [an] entity is allowed a worthless security deduction under §165(g)(3) if the fair market value of the assets of the entity, including intangible assets such as goodwill and going concern value, does not exceed the entity's liabilities such that on the deemed liquidation of the entity the shareholder receives no payment on its stock.

Furthermore, courts have concluded stock is worthless only when it lacks liquidating value or potential value."[1]

The concept of liquidating value applies when the owners have decided to cease operations as of the valuation date. In cases in which the aggregate fair market values of the underlying assets of the business is determined to be less than the face value of debt, no additional value is ascribed to equity.

The concept of potential future value is relevant when the owners continue operating the business as a going concern, under the existing equity structure, as of the valuation date. Even when the expected value of a business is deemed less than the face value of its debt, one frequently observes that common shares of publicly traded companies trade daily on exchanges at a positive value.

LIQUIDATING VALUE

A company has no liquidating value if there is no excess of asset value over liabilities as of a certain date. To estimate the fair market value of a business, valuation practitioners rely on three generally accepted valuation approaches: income approach, market approach, and asset approach. The income approach uses methods that convert anticipated benefits into a present single amount. The market approach uses methods that compare the subject to similar businesses that have been sold. The asset approach uses methods based on the value of the assets of that business net of liabilities.

The standard of value for U.S. federal income tax purposes is fair market value, which has been framed over the years by countless court cases. Fair market value is defined as the price that a willing buyer would pay a willing seller, both having reasonable knowledge of all of the relevant facts and neither being under compulsion to buy or to sell. See *United States v. Cartwright,* 411 U.S. 546, 551, 36 L. Ed. 2d 528,

---

[1] *Sterling Morton,* 38 B.T.A. 1278 "The ultimate value of stock, and conversely its worthlessness, will depend not only on its current liquidating value, but also on what value it may acquire in the future through the foreseeable operations of the corporation. Both factors of value must be wiped out before we can definitively fix the loss."

93 S. Ct. 1713 (1973); Treas. Reg. 20.2031-1(6). Some important implications are as follows:

- The willing buyer and the willing seller are hypothetical persons, rather than specific individuals or entities, and the peculiar characteristics of these hypothetical persons are not necessarily the same as the individual characteristics of an actual seller or an actual buyer. See *Estate of Bright v. United States*, 658 F.2d 999, 1005-1006 (5th Cir. 1981).
- The hypothetical willing buyer and willing seller are presumed to be dedicated to achieving the maximum economic advantage. See *Estate of Newhouse v. Commissioner*, supra at 218. This advantage must be achieved in the context of market and economic conditions on the valuation date.
- The hypothetical sale should not be constructed in a vacuum isolated from actual facts that affect value. See *Estate of Andrews v. Commissioner*, supra at 956.
- The fair market value of property should reflect the highest and best use to which the property could be put on the date of valuation. See *Stanley Works & Subs. v. Commissioner*, 87 T.C. 389, 400 (1986). This may or may not be the current use of the property.
- Valuation is a question of fact, and the trier of fact must weigh all relevant evidence on the date of valuation, without regard to hindsight, to draw the appropriate inferences. See *Estate of Jung v. Commissioner*, 101 T.C. 412, 423-424 (1993); *Estate of Newhouse v. Commissioner*, 94 T.C. 193, 217 (1990); *Estate of Andrews v. Commissioner*, 79 T.C. 938, 940 (1982).
- Future events foreseeable on the valuation date may be considered in deciding fair market value. See *Estate of Newhouse v. Commissioner*, supra at 218.

To determine if the stock is worthless, one must estimate the fair market value of the business and assets of the subject company as if the business and assets are being sold to a third-party buyer without regard to the existing liabilities of the subject entity. The willing seller is assumed to act to achieve the maximum proceeds, which makes it necessary to consider both the value of the underlying assets as if they are assumed to be used in the continuing business (often termed the value of the business enterprise) and their values, assuming that the willing buyer could better use the assets outside the subject business. If the sum total of the fair market value of the business and assets is less than the liabilities, the subject entity is worthless.

The principles for determining the magnitudes of the assets and liabilities differ from the generally accepted accounting principles in the United States. Both on- and off-balance sheet assets need to be considered in valuing the subject business and its underlying assets. Also, both on- and off-balance sheet contractual and contingent liabilities need to be considered in determining whether the total liabilities exceed the fair market value of the subject business and assets.

Common off-balance sheet assets are:

- Intellectual property, including know-how to produce internally developed products and know-how surrounding application of technologies.
- Key distribution and customer relationships and contracts.
- Assembled workforce.

Common off-balance sheet liabilities to be considered are:

- Pending legal judgments.
- Warranty reserves.
- Post-retirement obligations.
- Restructuring liability.

When the entity liabilities include contingent liabilities, one must include the fair market value of these liabilities in the analysis.[2] Contingent liabilities are not currently an indebtedness of the company, but may or may not become a liability dependent on the outcome of some specified future event. The fair market value of a contingent liability may be quite different from what appears on a company's financial accounting statements. Further, when a subsidiary entity ceases business operations after the IRC §165 election, the liabilities include shutdown costs such as costs for terminating leases and employees.

POTENTIAL VALUE

Although valuation practitioners routinely estimate the fair market value of a business as of a certain valuation date, the concept of potential value poses a dilemma. How does one demonstrate that stock is reasonably worthless, not only currently, but also in the foreseeable future? A stock is said to have no potential value, when the liabilities of a corporation are so greatly in excess of its assets and the nature of the assets and business is such that there is no reasonable hope and expectation that a continuation of the business will result in any profit to its stockholders.[3]

Even though the hurdle of potential value is a matter for legal interpretation, valuation practitioners can assist in the analysis by quantifying (1) the possibility the fair market value of the subject business and/or assets without regard to the existing debts (the value of the business enterprise) will exceed the face value of debt at some future point in time and (2) the probability this will occur at some future point in time.

Business cash flows (and the value of a business) in any one future given year are unknown, but they follow a probability distribution. Less risky cash flows (businesses) have a less dispersed distribution of expected cash flows, whereas more risky cash flows (businesses) have a greater dispersed distribution of expected cash flows. One generally accepted valuation approach is the income approach in which the fair market value of a business is based on the present value of the expected value of future cash flows. The expected value of cash flows is the probability weighted cash flow of the entire distribution of possible cash flows. In the case of a public company, observed market values represent the consensus estimate of the present value of expected cash flows as assessed by the marginal investor (i.e., the investor who just bought and the investor who just sold a stock). Refer to Exhibit 3.2 of *Cost of*

---

[2] See *Black & Decker Corp. v. United States*, 2004 U.S. Dist. LEXIS 22835 (D. Md. 2004); Also see *In re Tronox Incorporated, et al.*, Case No. 09-10156 (ALG) United States Bankruptcy Court, Southern District of New York.

[3] *Sterling Morton*, 38 B.T.A. 1270.

Capital: Applications and Examples, 4th ed. for examples of the riskiness of net cash flows.

In estimating (1) the value of the possibility that the business enterprise will exceed the face value of debt at some future point in time and (2) the probability that this will occur at some future point in time, one discretely considers the right "tails" of the probability distributions.

EXAMPLE

To illustrate the aforementioned concepts of 1) possibility and 2) probability, following are examples that consider the value of the equity of a nonpublic subsidiary of a large company estimated using the discounted cash flow (DCF) method and the guideline publicly traded company method. In applying these approaches, one is assuming that the assets will continue to be used in their existing use (i.e., the assets contribute to the expected cash flow of the business).

In applying the asset approach, one is typically assuming that the underlying assets will be used in alternative or additional uses. For example, a willing buyer of software maintenance contracts may be in a position of assuming and fulfilling the contracts without adding the fixed overhead of the existing business. Sometimes the value of an asset must be considered both in terms of its existing use (and its contribution to the expected cash flows of the existing business) and an alternative use. The analysis applies to both tangible assets and intangible assets. Examples include: excess land surrounding existing facilities that could be sold off without disrupting production; excess warehouse capacity that could be rented; trade names that may be used in the existing business and could potentially be used for product extensions, which, to date, have not been introduced; and so forth.

POSSIBILITY THAT VALUE OF THE BUSINESS ENTERPRISE EXCEEDS THE FACE VALUE OF DEBT— PRICING EQUITY AS A CALL OPTION

There are a number of widely used and accepted approaches to estimate the fair market value of equity in a highly leveraged capital structure.[4] Often these models are structured in terms of the aggregate value of stock of an existing overleveraged entity. Black and Scholes[5] noted that all ownership claims, such as common stock, corporate bonds, or warrants, can be viewed as combinations of simple option contracts.

---

[4] A probabilistic model is the most appropriate valuation method when the expected payoff function is non-linear, as is the case with highly-leveraged equity. Types of probabilistic models include the Black-Scholes option pricing model, probability weighted expected outcome, lattice, and Monte Carlo simulation. The selection of an appropriate valuation methodology is based on facts and circumstances.

[5] Fischer Black and Myron Scholes, "The Pricing of Options and Corporate Liabilities," *The Journal of Political Economy* (May/June 1973): 637–654.

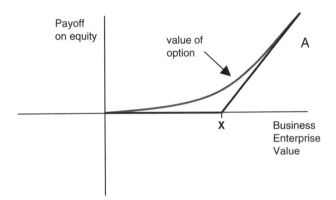

EXHIBIT 7.1   Value of a Call Option

For example, equity holders have the equivalent of an option to buy the assets of the company, given they first repay the debt holders. In other words, the value of equity can be viewed as the value of a call option on the assets, with an exercise price equal to the face value of debt. Also, the value of debt represents the "risk-free" right of debt holders to receive the return of their loaned monies and accrued interest, minus the value of default risk. In other words, the value of debt can be viewed as a risk-free bond minus the value of a put option on the assets.

The value of equity as a call option is the price a hypothetical buyer would pay for the possibility that the fair market value of the business enterprise will exceed the face value of debt (F_d or X on the graph) over a specified future horizon. This can be depicted as in Exhibit 7.1. Line A represents the intrinsic value (or payoff) from a call option at time T. When the business enterprise value, $FMV_{BE,0}$, is less than the face value of debt (i.e., $FMV_{BE,0} < Fd$), the equity holder will let the option expire worthless, that is, default on the debt. When the $FMV_{BE,0}$ is greater than the face value of debt (i.e., $FMV_{BE,0} > Fd$), the equity holder will exercise the option, that is, repay the debt holders and own the assets.

This same diagram also illustrates the value of a call option, in relation to its intrinsic value. Viewing equity as a call option is more significant when the $FMV_{BE,0}$ is approximately equal to the face value of debt. When "near the money," the value of a call option is the farthest above intrinsic value and, therefore, the value of optionality is the greatest. When deep out of the money or deep in the money, the value of a call option is closer to intrinsic value.

But in this formulation the value of equity as a call option is the price a hypothetical buyer would pay to acquire the business and/or assets without regard to the existing debts (the value of the business enterprise). The price that the hypothetical buyer would pay assumes that the buyer will finance the business and assets based upon the current debt capacity of such businesses and current market conditions.

For purposes of illustration, we present a simplified analysis based on a probability distribution of risky future cash flows (i.e., DCF method with scenarios) and a method based on business enterprise volatilities of public guideline companies (i.e., the guideline public company method). Both methods estimate the value of equity in a manner equivalent to its value in terms of a call option on the assets of the firm.

Discounted Cash Flow Method Using Scenarios and Option Pricing Model

In the standard application of the DCF method applied to invested capital, one estimates the fair market value of equity based on the present value of expected (i.e., probability-weighted) net cash flows to invested capital minus the face value of debt. This application provides an estimate of the liquidating value of equity as of the valuation date. When the fair market value of the business enterprise is less than the face value of debt, zero value is ascribed to the fair market value of equity.

Adopting the standard DCF method using scenarios, though, we can use a one-step binomial model (on the premise of no arbitrage) to value the possibility that the fair market value of the business enterprise will exceed the face value of debt (i.e., we estimate the value of equity as a call option). The fair market value of equity is determined based on a hypothetical construction of a risk-free portfolio at time 0 consisting of owning some percentage (p, expressed as a decimal; e.g., 20% = .20) of the business enterprise (BE) and shorting the equity. As the constructed portfolio is risk-free, the liquidating payoff at time n is the same in the up scenario and the down scenario. Additionally, the value of the risk-free portfolio at time 0 is equal to the present value of the liquidating payoff at time n, discounting at the risk-free rate. See Exhibit 7.2, which shows how a DCF with scenarios can be thought of in an option framework.

The DCF analysis indicates the fair market value of equity at time 0 based on a probability distribution of risky cash flows that a business can be expected to generate in the future. Our application of the DCF method is comprised of six steps:

Steps for Time n:

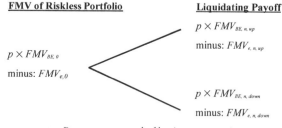

FMV of Riskless Portfolio

$p \times FMV_{BE,0}$

minus: $FMV_{e,0}$

Liquidating Payoff

$p \times FMV_{BE,n,up}$

minus: $FMV_{e,n,up}$

$p \times FMV_{BE,n,down}$

minus: $FMV_{e,n,down}$

where:

p = Percentage owned of business enterprise

$FMV_{BE,0}$ = Fair market value of business enterprise at valuation date

$FMV_{e,0}$ = Fair market value of equity at valuation date

$FMV_{BE,n,up}$ = Fair market value of business enterprise at time = n assuming up scenario (value of BE increases)

$FMV_{e,n,up}$ = Fair market value of equity at time = n assuming up scenario (value of BE increases)

$FMV_{BE,n,down}$ = Fair market value of business enterprise at time = n assuming down scenario (value of BE decreases)

$FMV_{e,n,down}$ = Fair market value of equity at time = n assuming down scenario (value of BE decreases)

EXHIBIT 7.2   Valuation Using DCF Method with Scenarios

1. Discount the expected up (down) future net cash flows to time n value at a cost of capital that considers the relative risk of achieving the cash flows and the time value of money. This cost of capital should consider the amount of debt financing that would be used by the pool of willing buyers (the WACC in our examples), not the existing debt of the over-leveraged business. This will provide indications of $FMV_{BE,n,up}$ and $FMV_{BE,n,down}$.

2. $FMV_{BE,n,up}(FMV_{BE,n,down})$ minus the face value of debt (F_d) equals $FMV_{e,n,up}$ $(FMV_{e,n,down})$.

3. Solve for p, the liquidating payoff, which is the same in the up and down scenario, under our premise of no arbitrage, $p \times FMV_{BE,n,up} - FMV_{e,n,up} = p \times FMV_{BE,n,down} - FMV_{e,n,down}$.

Steps for Time 0

4. Discount the expected future cash flows to present value at a rate of return that considers the relative risk of achieving the cash flows and the time value of money. This will provide an indication of $FMV_{BE,0}$.

5. Discount the liquidating payoff to present value at the risk-free rate. This will provide an indicated value of the riskless portfolio.

6. $p \times FMV_{BE,0}$ minus the value of the riskless portfolio equals $FMV_{e,0}$.

See Exhibit 7.3 for an example, under the discounted cash flow method, on valuing the possibility that the business enterprise will exceed the face value of debt at some future point in time. In the example, the $FMV_{BE,0}$ is directly correlated with time, and is approximately 1% of expected $FMV_{BE,0}$ assuming a two-year horizon (i.e., $n = 2$).

Guideline Public Company Method and Option Pricing Model

This illustration of the guideline public company method considers the fair market value of equity utilizing the Black-Scholes option pricing model and observed equity volatilities of public guideline (i.e., comparable) companies; the companies chosen should reflect the likely leverage that the willing buyer would use, not the debt of the subject over-leveraged business. We can estimate the fair market value of equity as a call option based on a few input assumptions. The basic Black-Scholes call option equation is as follows (repeating Formula 16.4 in *Cost of Capital: Applications and Examples*, 4th ed.):

(Formula 7.1)

$$FMV_{e,0} = FMV_{BE,0}N(d_1) - F_d^{R_f(n-i)}N(d_2)$$

where: $FMV_{BE,0}$ = Fair market value of business enterprise value at time 0

$N(^*)$ = Cumulative normal density function

$$d_1 = \frac{log\left(\frac{FMV_{BE,0}}{F_d}\right) + \left(R_f + \frac{1}{2}\sigma^2\right)(n-i)}{\sigma\sqrt{n-i}} = \frac{log\left(\frac{FMV_{BE,0}}{F_d}\right) + R_f(n-i)}{\sigma\sqrt{n-i}} + \frac{1}{2}\sigma\sqrt{n-i}$$

F_d = Face value of outstanding debt

R_f = Risk-free rate

$n - i$ = Time to maturity of debt or time to a liquidating event from period i to period n

σ_{BE} = Standard deviation of the value of the business enterprise

$d_2 = d_1 - \sigma\sqrt{n-i}$

EXHIBIT 7.3 Valuation of Worthless Stock

Value of Possibility that $FMV_{BE,n}$ Exceeds F_d
Discounted Cash Flow Method Scenario Analysis and Binomial Option Model
Dollars in Thousands

Probability			Net Cash Flows for Projection Year n					Terminal Value
			1	2	3	4	5	
20%	<20%		$86	$95	$106	$118	$132	$1,137
60%	20–80%		$62	$71	$82	$94	$108	$931
20%	>80%		$38	$47	$58	$70	$84	$725
Expected net cash flows, $\bar{X}$			$62	$71	$82	$94	$108	$931

Other assumptions	
WACC (midyear convention used in calculating PV factors)	15.0%
Long-term growth rate	3.0%
R_f	5.0%
F_d	$1,000

STANDARD DCF METHOD	Expected Net Cash Flows for Projection Year n					Terminal Value
	1	2	3	4	5	
Expected net cash flows	$62	$71	$82	$94	$108	$931
PV factor	0.9325	0.8109	0.7051	0.6131	0.5332	0.5332
Present value of net cash flows	$58	$58	$58	$58	$58	$496
Sum of present value of net cash flows	$785					
Minus: F_d	$1,000					
Indicated $FMV_{e,0}$	$0					

RESULTS OF SCENARIO ANALYSIS AND BINOMIAL OPTION MODEL

	Projection Year n				
	1	2	3	4	5
$FMV_{BE,n,up}$ (i.e., 20%)	$1,036	$1,090	$1,139	$1,184	$1,219
$FMV_{BE,n,down}$ (i.e., 80%)	$787	$835	$878	$915	$943
$FMV_{e,n,up}$ (i.e., 20%)	$36	$90	$139	$184	$219
$FMV_{e,n,down}$ (i.e., 80%)	$0	$0	$0	$0	$0
p	15%	35%	53%	68%	79%
$FMV_{BE,0}$	$785	$785	$785	$785	$785
$p \times FMV_{BE,0}$	$115	$276	$419	$538	$623

(continued)

EXHIBIT 7.3   (*Continued*)

	Projection Year n				
	1	2	3	4	5
Riskless portfolio$_0$ $(p \times FMV_{BE,0} - FMV_{e,0})$	$109	$266	$404	$513	$582
$FMV_{e,0}$	$5	$11	$16	$25	$40
% of $FMV_{BE,0}$	1%	1%	2%	3%	5%

The guideline public company method indicates the fair market value of equity at time 0 based on unlevered equity volatilities of guideline public companies, used as proxy for the subject company. (See *Cost of Capital: Applications and Examples*, 4th ed., Chapter 11 for a method to unlever equity volatilities.)

Our application of the guideline public company method is comprised of two steps:

1. Gather estimates for $FMV_{BE,0}$, n, σ_{BE}, and R_f. An estimate of σ_{BE} can be observed from guideline public companies.
2. Using the Black-Scholes option pricing model, calculate $FMV_{e,0}$.

See Exhibit 7.4 for an example of an analysis using Formula 7.1 on valuing the possibility that the business enterprise will exceed the face value of debt at some future point in time. In the example, the $FMV_{e,0}$ is directly correlated with time and is approximately 1% of $FMV_{BE,0}$ assuming a two-year horizon (i.e., $n = 2$).

EXHIBIT 7.4   Analysis Using Black-Scholes Call Option Pricing Model

Assumptions

$FMV_{BE,0}$	$785
F_d = Face Value of Debt	$1,000
σ_{BE} = Standard Deviation	10.0%
R_f = Risk – Free Rate	5.0%

RESULTS OF ANALYSIS

	Projection Year $n-i$				
	1	2	3	4	5
d_1	−1.867	−0.931	−0.443	−0.108	0.149
d_2	−1.967	−1.072	−0.616	−0.308	−0.074
$FMV_{e,0}$	$1	$10	$27	$49	$73
% of $FMV_{BE,0}$	0%	1%	3%	6%	9%

POTENTIAL FUTURE VALUE: PROBABILITY THAT VALUE OF THE BUSINESS ENTERPRISE EXCEEDS THE FACE VALUE OF DEBT

Although the FMV_{BE} may be less than the face value of debt today, there is some probability that the FMV_{BE} will exceed the face value of debt over a specified future horizon. Based on statistical theory, we present a method based on a probability distribution of risky future net cash flows (DCF method) and a method based on a probability distribution of observed volatilities of market values of stocks of guideline public companies (guideline public company method).

Discounted Cash Flow Method Using Scenarios and Option Pricing Model

The DCF method indicates the probability that the FMV_{BE} will exceed the face value of debt at some future point in time, based on a probability distribution of risky net cash flows that a business can be expected to generate in the future. Depending on expectations, the probability distribution may be represented by a normal or other standard statistical distribution. Continuing with the earlier DCF example, we assume that the risky future net cash flows follow a normal distribution, which can be described by its mean and standard deviation.

Our generalized application of the DCF method is comprised of three steps:

Step 1. Gather estimates for $FMV_{BE,0}$, $\bar{X}$, σ_{BE}, and n.

Step 2. Based on the probability distribution of the cash flows and an estimated probability, calculate $FMV_{BE,n}$.

Step 3. Repeat step 2, using a different estimated probability, until the calculated $FMV_{BE,n}$ approximately equals the face value of debt.

See Exhibit 7.5 for an example using the DCF method of estimating the probability that the FMV_{BE} will exceed the face value of debt at some future point in time. From the example, the probability is directly correlated with time and is approximately 20%, assuming a one-year horizon (i.e., $n = 1$). See Exhibit 7.6 for a table of the right-hand side of the cumulative normal density function.

Guideline Public Company Method and Option Pricing Model

The Black-Scholes option pricing model assumes that continuously compounded single-period returns are normally distributed, which implies $FMV_{BE,n}$ is lognormally distributed (see Appendix III). Formula 7.2 is the equation[6] that uses the distribution's mean and standard deviation to indicate the probability that the business enterprise is equal to a certain value:

---

[6] For a derivation and discussion of this equation, see John C. Hull, *Options, Futures and Other Derivative Securities*, 6th ed. (Englewood Cliffs, N.J.: Prentice-Hall, 2005), Chapters 10 and 11.

EXHIBIT 7.5 Valuation of Worthless Stock

Probability that FMV_{BE} exceeds F_d
Discounted Cash Flow Method Scenario Analysis and Binomial Option Model
Dollars in Thousands

Probability		Net Cash Flows for Projection Year n					Terminal Value
		1	2	3	4	5	
20%	<20%	$86	$95	$106	$118	$132	$1,137
60%	20–80%	$62	$71	$82	$94	$108	$931
20%	>80%	$38	$47	$58	$70	$84	$725
Expected net cash flows, $\bar{X}$		$62	$71	$82	$94	$108	$931

Other Assumptions

WACC (using midyear convention)	15.0%
Long-term growth rate	3.0%
R_f	5.0%
F_d	$1,000

RESULTS OF ANALYSIS

Probability	Net Cash Flows for Projection Year n					Terminal Value
	1	2	3	4	5	
5%	$109	$118	$129	$141	$155	$1,333
10%	$100	$110	$120	$133	$147	$1,259
15%	$91	$101	$111	$124	$138	$1,183
20%	$86	$95	$106	$118	$132	$1,137
25%	$81	$90	$101	$113	$128	$1,095
30%	$77	$86	$97	$109	$123	$1,058
35%	$73	$82	$93	$105	$119	$1,024
40%	$69	$78	$89	$101	$116	$992
45%	$65	$75	$85	$98	$112	$960
50%	$62	$71	$82	$94	$108	$931

Probability	FMV_{BE} for Projection Year n					
	0	1	2	3	4	5
5%	$1,168	$1,227	$1,284	$1,338	$1,388	$1,429
10%	$1,098	$1,155	$1,211	$1,264	$1,311	$1,351
15%	$1,026	$1,082	$1,136	$1,187	$1,232	$1,269
20%	$981	$1,036	$1,090	$1,139	$1,184	$1,219
25%	$942	$996	$1,048	$1,097	$1,140	$1,174
30%	$907	$960	$1,012	$1,060	$1,102	$1,135
35%	$874	$927	$978	$1,025	$1,066	$1,098
40%	$844	$896	$946	$993	$1,033	$1,064
45%	$813	$865	$915	$960	$1,000	$1,030
50%	$785	$837	$886	$931	$969	$998

☐ = FMV_{BE} exceeds F_d

Note: the scenarios in the box represent the scenarios when FMV_{BE} exceeds F_d.

EXHIBIT 7.6 Standard Normal Probability Distribution

Standard Normal Probabilities: (The table is based on the area P under the standard normal probability curve, below the respective z-statistic

where $z = \frac{(x - \mu)}{\sigma}$

Z	0.00	0.01	0.02	0.03	0.04	0.05	0.06	0.07	0.08	0.09
0.0	0.5000	0.5040	0.5080	0.5120	0.5160	0.5199	0.5239	0.5279	0.5319	0.5359
0.1	0.5398	0.5438	0.5478	0.5517	0.5557	0.5596	0.5636	0.5675	0.5714	0.5754
0.2	0.5793	0.5832	0.5871	0.5910	0.5948	0.5987	0.6026	0.6064	0.6103	0.6141
0.3	0.6179	0.6217	0.6255	0.6293	0.6331	0.6368	0.6406	0.6443	0.6480	0.6517
0.4	0.6554	0.6591	0.6628	0.6664	0.6700	0.6737	0.6772	0.6808	0.6844	0.6879
0.5	0.6915	0.6950	0.6985	0.7020	0.7054	0.7088	0.7123	0.7157	0.7191	0.7224
0.6	0.7258	0.7291	0.7324	0.7357	0.7389	0.7422	0.7454	0.7486	0.7518	0.7549
0.7	0.7580	0.7612	0.7642	0.7673	0.7704	0.7734	0.7764	0.7794	0.7823	0.7852
0.8	0.7882	0.7910	0.7939	0.7967	0.7996	0.8023	0.8051	0.8079	0.8106	0.8133
0.9	0.8159	0.8186	0.8212	0.8238	0.8264	0.8290	0.8315	0.8340	0.8365	0.8389
1.0	0.8414	0.8438	0.8461	0.8485	0.8508	0.8531	0.8554	0.8577	0.8599	0.8621
1.1	0.8643	0.8665	0.8686	0.8708	0.8729	0.8749	0.8770	0.8790	0.8810	0.8830
1.2	0.8849	0.8869	0.8888	0.8907	0.8925	0.8944	0.8962	0.8980	0.8997	0.9015
1.3	0.9032	0.9049	0.9066	0.9082	0.9099	0.9115	0.9131	0.9147	0.9162	0.9177
1.4	0.9192	0.9207	0.9222	0.9236	0.9251	0.9265	0.9279	0.9292	0.9306	0.9319
1.5	0.9332	0.9345	0.9358	0.9370	0.9382	0.9394	0.9406	0.9418	0.9430	0.9441
1.6	0.9452	0.9463	0.9474	0.9485	0.9495	0.9505	0.9515	0.9525	0.9535	0.9545
1.7	0.9554	0.9564	0.9573	0.9582	0.9591	0.9599	0.9608	0.9616	0.9625	0.9633
1.8	0.9641	0.9649	0.9656	0.9664	0.9671	0.9678	0.9686	0.9693	0.9700	0.9706
1.9	0.9713	0.9719	0.9726	0.9732	0.9738	0.9744	0.9750	0.9756	0.9762	0.9767
2.0	0.9773	0.9778	0.9783	0.9788	0.9793	0.9798	0.9803	0.9808	0.9812	0.9817

(*continued*)

EXHIBIT 7.6 (Continued)

Z	0.00	0.01	0.02	0.03	0.04	0.05	0.06	0.07	0.08	0.09
2.1	0.9821	0.9826	0.9830	0.9834	0.9838	0.9842	0.9846	0.9850	0.9854	0.9857
2.2	0.9861	0.9865	0.9868	0.9871	0.9875	0.9878	0.9881	0.9884	0.9887	0.9890
2.3	0.9893	0.9896	0.9898	0.9901	0.9904	0.9906	0.9909	0.9911	0.9913	0.9916
2.4	0.9918	0.9920	0.9922	0.9925	0.9927	0.9929	0.9931	0.9932	0.9934	0.9936
2.5	0.9938	0.9940	0.9941	0.9943	0.9945	0.9946	0.9948	0.9949	0.9951	0.9952
2.6	0.9953	0.9955	0.9956	0.9957	0.9959	0.9960	0.9961	0.9962	0.9963	0.9964
2.7	0.9965	0.9966	0.9967	0.9968	0.9969	0.9970	0.9971	0.9972	0.9973	0.9974
2.8	0.9974	0.9975	0.9976	0.9977	0.9977	0.9978	0.9979	0.9980	0.9980	0.9981
2.9	0.9981	0.9982	0.9983	0.9983	0.9984	0.9984	0.9985	0.9985	0.9986	0.9986
3.0	0.9987	0.9987	0.9987	0.9988	0.9988	0.9989	0.9989	0.9989	0.9990	0.9990
3.1	0.9990	0.9991	0.9991	0.9991	0.9992	0.9992	0.9992	0.9992	0.9993	0.9993
3.2	0.9993	0.9993	0.9994	0.9994	0.9994	0.9994	0.9994	0.9995	0.9995	0.9995
3.3	0.9995	0.9995	0.9996	0.9996	0.9996	0.9996	0.9996	0.9996	0.9996	0.9997
3.4	0.9997	0.9997	0.9997	0.9997	0.9997	0.9997	0.9997	0.9997	0.9998	0.9998
3.5	0.9998	0.9998	0.9998	0.9998	0.9998	0.9998	0.9998	0.9998	0.9998	0.9998
3.6	0.9998	0.9999	0.9999	0.9999	0.9999	0.9999	0.9999	0.9999	0.9999	0.9999
3.7	0.9999	0.9999	0.9999	0.9999	0.9999	0.9999	0.9999	0.9999	0.9999	0.9999
3.8	0.9999	0.9999	0.9999	0.9999	0.9999	0.9999	0.9999	1.0000	1.0000	1.0000
3.9	1.0000	1.0000	1.0000	1.0000	1.0000	1.0000	1.0000	1.0000	1.0000	1.0000
4.0	1.0000	1.0000	1.0000	1.0000	1.0000	1.0000	1.0000	1.0000	1.0000	1.0000

(Formula 7.2)

$$\ln FMV_{BE,0,n-i}\phi\left[\ln FMV_{BE,0} + \left(WACC - \sigma_{BE}^2/2\right)(n - i), \sigma_{BE}\sqrt{n - i}\right]$$

where: $WACC$ = Expected overall cost of capital on the business enterprise without regard to the current level of debt and other definitions are as in Formula 7.1.

σ_{BE} = standard deviation of returns on the business enterprise

$\ln$ = natural logarithm

Continuing with the guideline public company method example above, the probability that FMV_{BE} will exceed the face value of debt at some future point in time is estimated based on business enterprise volatilities of guideline public companies (leveraged based upon the financing that the hypothetical willing buyer would use in acquiring the business and/or assets but without regard to existing debt of the over-leveraged subject entity). The probability is a function of a business enterprise's expected volatility and time. This illustration of the guideline public company is comprised of three steps:

1. Gather estimates for $FMV_{BE,0}$, $WACC$, σ_{BE}, and n. An estimate of σ_{BE} can be observed from guideline companies.
2. Using the equation for a lognormal distribution and an estimated probability, calculate $FMV_{BE,n}$.
3. Repeat step 2, using a different estimated probability, until the calculated $FMV_{BE,n}$ approximately equals F_d.

See Exhibit 7.7 for an example of applying the guideline public company method to estimating the probability that the business enterprise will exceed the face value of debt at some future point in time. In the example, the probability is directly correlated with time and is approximately 15%, assuming a one-year horizon (i.e., $n = 1$).

ADDITIONAL CONSIDERATIONS

There are certain valuation-related issues that often arise for taxpayers in the context of claiming a worthless stock deduction. A subsidiary whose equity is potentially deemed worthless may also find it difficult to meet all interim principal and interest payments and continue operations. As such, the parent company may be faced with interim decisions about whether to contribute substantial additional equity capital and restructure or let the subsidiary enter bankruptcy. Although the worthless stock deduction rules do not require additional equity capital infusions, it may be economically advantageous to do so. Therefore, as part of a complete analysis, it is necessary to consider the economically motivated actions of a hypothetical investor along with the company's expected future cash flows, as they relate to compliance with debt covenants.

When there is related party debt, the Internal Revenue Service may challenge the characteristic of this intercompany debt about whether it is bona fide indebtedness

EXHIBIT 7.7   Analysis Using Lognormal Probability Distribution

Assumptions

$FMV_{BE,0}$	$785
Expected return = $WACC$	15.0%
σ_{BE} = Standard Deviation	10.0%
F_d	$1,000

RESULTS OF ANALYSIS

	FMV_{BE} for Projection Year n					
Probability	0.00	0.25	0.50	0.75	1.00	1.25
5.0%	$785	$884	$949	$1,010	$1,071	$1,132
10.0%	$785	$868	$924	$978	$1,032	$1,086
15.0%	$785	$857	$908	$957	$1,006	$1,056
20.0%	$785	$849	$896	$942	$987	$1,034
25.0%	$785	$842	$885	$928	$971	$1,015
30.0%	$785	$836	$876	$916	$956	$998
35.0%	$785	$830	$868	$906	$944	$983
40.0%	$785	$825	$859	$895	$931	$968
45.0%	$785	$820	$852	$885	$920	$955
50.0%	$785	$814	$844	$876	$908	$941

$\boxed{}$ = FMV_{BE} exceeds F_d

Note: The scenarios in the box represent the scenarios when FMV_{BE} exceeds F_d.

for federal tax purposes or may instead be viewed as an equity infusion. Therefore, it is important that companies properly execute and maintain enforceable loan agreements between the parent and the subsidiary, with a stated interest rate and due date, and otherwise document the economic relationship as one would were the monies loaned to an unrelated third party. In assessing the true substance of an intercompany advance, courts look to the rights and obligations between the parties.[7] In a liquidation analysis pursuant to IRC §165(g)(3), assets are deemed distributed first to debt, then with respect to the liquidation preference of preferred stock, and then finally to common equity.[8] The standard for determining worthlessness on the common equity is whether there is sufficient property to distribute to shareholders after satisfaction of higher priority claims.[9]

---

[7] See *Fin Hay Realty Co. v. United States*, 389 F.2d 694, 697 (3rd Cir. 1968); *Estate of Mixon v. United States*, 464 F.2d 394 (5th Cir. 1972); and *Bauer v. Commissioner*, 748 F.2d 1365 (9th Cir. 1984).

[8] Section 166 allows a deduction as an ordinary loss to the portion of intercompany loans not satisfied in liquidation. Section 331 permits a deduction as a capital loss to the portion of preferred stock not recouped in liquidation. Section 165 permits a deduction as a capital loss to worthless stock.

[9] See *H.K. Porter Co. v. Commissioner*, 87 T.C. 689 (1986); and *Commissioner v. Spaulding Bakeries*, 252 F.2d 693 (2nd Cir. 1958), aff'g, 27 T.C. 684 (1957).

Moreover, the IRS in the past has denied taxpayer claims for worthless stock deductions on the grounds that the stock became worthless in a prior year.[10] A taxpayer must prove with objective evidence that the stock in question became worthless during the taxable year in which the deduction is claimed. Whether a loss due to worthlessness is actually sustained during the taxable year is a factual determination varying according to the circumstances of each case. No definite legal test is provided by the statute for the determination of the year in which the loss is to be deducted. The general requirement losses are deducted in the year in which they are sustained calls for a practical, not a legal test.[11] The regulations refer to losses "actually sustained during the taxable year" as fixed by "identifiable events."

SUMMARY

Determining when stock is worthless is a question of both fact and law. Courts have concluded stock is worthless only when it lacks liquidating value or potential value. We have presented here a methodology to indicate (1) the value of the possibility and (2) the probability that the fair market value of the business enterprise will exceed the face value of debt at some future point in time. Viewing equity as a call option, there is always some value to the possibility of a future payoff. This is similar to a lottery ticket, where many are willing to pay some nominal amount for the chance, however remote, of hitting the jackpot. Moreover, there is always some statistical probability that a specified event outcome will materialize in the future. As such, in the context of worthless stock deductions and what is worthless, tax professionals must define the issue of de minimis value and/or probability.

---

[10] See *Morton v. Commissioner*, 38 B.T.A. 1270, 1279 (1938), aff'd, 112 F.2d 320 (7th Cir. 1940).

[11] See *Boehn v. Commissioner*, 326 U.S. 287, 293 (1945).

Technical Supplement— Specific Applications of *Cost of Capital*

CHAPTER 8

Cost of Capital of Private Investment Company Interests

William H. Frazier

INTRODUCTION

This chapter presents a fairly vigorous method of incorporating both the discount for lack of control (DLOC) and the discount for lack of marketability (DLOM) into the cost of capital (discount rate) for minority interests in private investment companies (PICs). At the end of the chapter there is an example that shows that this method produces approximately the same result as the traditional method of subtracting the DLOC and the DLOM at the end after developing an as- if publicly traded equivalent value.

The nonmarketable investment company evaluation (NICE) method is a valuation method under the income approach.[1] It is designed especially to determine the fair market value of equity interests in PICs by estimating the cost of capital that reflects the incremental risk of the subject PIC compared to the portfolio of its holdings. PIC refers to closely held investment entities (e.g., family limited partnerships (FLPs) and limited liability companies (LLCs)) that hold investment assets such as stocks, bonds, and real estate. Occasionally, these entities may own an operating business.

In the traditional market approach to valuing equity interests in PICs, the major objectives are to determine the appropriate discounts for lack of control and lack of marketability. These discounts, when applied to the net asset value (NAV) of the entity, provide estimates of fair market value. The NICE method does not use commonly applied discounts. Rather, lack of control and lack of marketability are viewed as investment risks that are embodied in the cost of capital for the subject interest. The NICE method solves for the price a typical investor would likely pay for the subject interest in the PIC in view of the investment risks and expected returns.

The NICE method is not a replacement for the more traditional PIC valuation methodologies. However, neither is it merely a corroboration or sanity check. It is a stand-alone valuation methodology.

The worksheets for the example discussed are available on the John Wiley & Sons web site.

THE PRIVATE INVESTMENT COMPANY

A primary business purpose for most PICs is asset appreciation and preservation; therefore, PICs generally will limit distributions to an amount of the equity holders' tax obligations arising from entity income, such as dividends, interest, and capital gains. This limitation on distributions may even be stated in the organizational documents. Where applicable, the NICE method can incorporate distributions in excess of income tax obligations.

In most PICs, the true economic return to the equity holders is expected to be derived from the eventual liquidation of the entity. The liquidation date can be a very distant event, often with a range of ten years from the valuation date and ending, in many cases, at a date potentially 40–50 years from the formation of the entity.

Under the NICE method, the value of an equity interest in a PIC is based upon the rates of return (ROR) required by both the buyer and the seller over the projected holding period. In the case of the buyer, the required ROR (RROR) will be the expected *ex ante* ROR from the investment. In the case of the seller, the price at which he or she is willing to sell will be influenced by the historical ROR from the investment, available reinvestment rates of return in the marketplace, and, of course, the expected ROR of the equity interest should he/she choose not to sell.

In light of lack of control and lack of required company reporting, a reasonable investor will likely require a ROR greater than otherwise could be required in a direct investment in publicly traded securities of comparable risks to those of the PIC. The degree of the ROR enhancement will vary based on the asset class. Generally

---

[1] Will Frazier, "Nonmarketable Investment Company Evaluation," *Valuation Strategies* (November/December 2006): 4–15.

speaking, the safer (less volatile) the asset class, the lower the required adjustment. Thus, the RRORs for a hypothetical buyer and seller of a PIC interest over a lengthy but uncertain holding period will be expressed by a range or spread above the entity-level RORs of the various asset classes held. Furthermore, since the holding period of the investment in a PIC is uncertain, a static ROR applicable to all possible future periods is a mathematical impossibility. Because of mean reversion of future rates of return and varying levels of illiquidity based on the expected holding period, the expected ROR will vary over time.

We will determine two paths of possible annual returns representing the minimum and maximum reasonable returns for the PIC based on the assets it holds. While the range of the holding period is uncertain, we do know that if we can determine a price that satisfies a reasonable compromise between the buyer's and seller's objectives, we have identified the fair market value of the investment.

The seller has his/her own outlook and expectations for the financial characteristics of an interest in a PIC. The buyer has his/her own unique views, too. These individual views are examples of investment value or intrinsic value—not fair market value. But the synthesis of these two viewpoints is the point at which the transaction takes place. This is fair market value. What the NICE method attempts to do is replicate the most likely investment behavior of the buyer and the seller. We assume that the pool of willing buyers and the willing seller are motivated to conclude a transaction, seeking the highest possible economic advantage, but are rational and their behavior conforms to the realities of the marketplace.

RELATIONSHIPS BETWEEN TIME TO A LIQUIDITY EVENT AND VALUE

Fair market value is the price at which a knowledgeable hypothetical buyer would buy and a hypothetical seller would sell based on (1) the expected economic returns to the interest; (2) the expected risks of realizing those expected returns; and (3) consideration of alternative investments and rates of return available in the marketplace.

The length of the expected period until a liquidity event is critical to the determination of fair market value. In all financial calculations, time is an essential element. One cannot calculate the interest cost of a loan, the present value of an annuity, or the future value of an investment without the element of time. To ignore the time element in the valuation calculus violates the primary principle of the time value of money.

The concepts of the length of time until a liquidity event occurs and liquidity, while not synonymous, are highly interrelated. Investors gravitate to investments whose economic return patterns best fit their particular needs. This phenomenon was noted and analyzed by Amihud and Mendelson:[2]

> Illiquidity can be measured by the cost of immediate execution. An investor willing to transact faces a tradeoff: He may either wait to transact at a favorable price or insist on immediate execution at the current bid or ask

[2] Yakov Amihud and Haim Mendelson, "Asset Pricing and the Bid-Ask Spread," *Journal of Financial Economics* 17 (1986): 223–250.

price. The quoted ask (offer) price includes a premium for immediate buying, and the bid price similarly reflects a concession required for immediate
sale . . . The resulting testable hypothesis is that asset returns are an increasing and concave function of the spread.

Thus, the authors show that the more illiquid an asset (or asset class) is, the
greater the RROR, although with increasing illiquidity the ROR increases at a decreasing rate. That is, the relationship of return and illiquidity is not a linear one.

Private Investment Companies Are Very Long-Term Investments

The fundamental assumption of the NICE method is that the length of time until the
PIC provides liquidity is unknown and not reasonably ascertainable. When the period is known or reasonably predictable, the NICE method is not needed. Value can
be calculated by a simple discounted cash flow analysis. Based on this author's experience in hundreds of PIC valuations, having a predictable period until the PIC will
provide cash distributions in excess of imputed income taxes is a rare exception.

The NICE method assumes a very long-term and illiquid investment. An investment horizon of less than ten years would certainly not represent an investment
entity with the foregoing characteristics.[3] The terms of the majority of FLPs we have
seen are approximately 40–50 years. Theoretically, LLCs have an infinite life; however, it is hard to imagine why there would be any practical difference in holding
periods between an FLP and LLC. For this reason, we generally use 50 years as the
practical maximum possible termination date of a PIC, unless we know otherwise.

In fact, the very long-term nature of a PIC investment may be what attracts hypothetical buyers. There are few, if any, investment products available to those investors seeking excess returns via investing in illiquid, long-lived investment
vehicles. Although the universe of potential buyers would be small for an investment
in a PIC, this type of investment could represent an attractive investment for an institutional investor with an indefinite time horizon. Most likely, this buyer would be a
foundation; endowment; family; or a charity, which allocates only small portions of
its portfolios to alternative investments.

Mean Reversion of Returns

Mean reversion is the change of the market return in the direction of a reversion
level as a reaction to a prior change in the market return. After a positive change

---

[3] In early 2009, this author's firm conducted a study of 100 family limited partnerships that
the firm had valued, prior to 1999, for estate or gift tax purposes. Of these partnerships,
68% were still in existence. The average age of these partnerships was 12 years. Of the 32
partnerships that have been terminated, the average age from filing to cancellation was eight
years. The total assets in the 100 partnerships were approximately $1.5 billion. The asset
composition of the partnerships was 60% equities, 10% municipal bonds, 10% real estate,
4% cash, and the remaining 16% was evenly divided among a number of smaller asset classes. The average NAV of each family limited partnership, then, was approximately $15 mil-
lion. (See William H. Frazier, "The Pomeroy Bill Sledgehammer," *Trusts & Estates* (May
2009).)

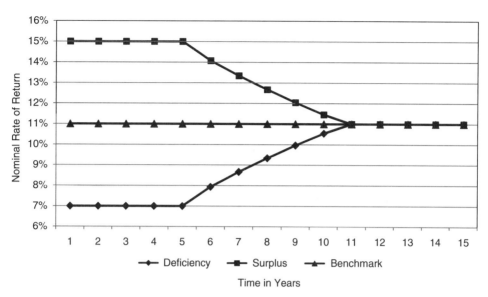

EXHIBIT 8.1 Example of Mean Reversion of Portfolio Returns

in the actual returns, mean reversion causes a negative subsequent change and vice versa.

The pricing motivation of the buyer is to extract a greater ROR from the PIC interest than that which is being earned by the underlying assets comprising the PIC's portfolio. The buyer expects to be able to outperform the PIC portfolio in a manner similar to what might happen in the marketplace if one invested with a top-ranked money manager. That money manager might charge a fee greater than average but the skill of the manager causes the investment's return to outperform the market (i.e., earn an excess return). However, as we will show, the excess return diminishes over time for almost all investment managers. Knowing this, it would be unreasonable for a buyer of a PIC interest to expect his/her investment to do anything other than mirror the realities of the marketplace. Over time, any excess returns earned will revert to the long-term mean for that asset class.

The chart in Exhibit 8.1 depicts two mean reverting paths we might expect in a typical portfolio. Here, we have assumed the mean long-term return benchmark for large-cap common stock is 11% (labeled "benchmark"). Above the mean, we see an asset initially outperforming the mean by 400 basis points. The top line (labeled "surplus") portrays a return of 15% for the first five years. After this, the excess return begins to diminish. By year eleven, the return has virtually reverted to the mean. Similarly, we portray an underperforming asset with the line below the 11% mean (labeled "deficiency"). Here, the returns are constant at 7% for five years but then begin mean reverting as well.

Empirical evidence of mean reversion can be seen in returns earned in the marketplace by mutual funds. We examined Morningstar data for investment managers in the large-cap blend asset class as of December 31, 2007. Our study included 341 equity mutual funds that had been in existence for at least 10 years. We analyzed their historical returns over time (i.e., over 1 year, 3 years, 5 years, 10 years, and 15 years); as only 141 funds reported 15-year data, the results were doubled to

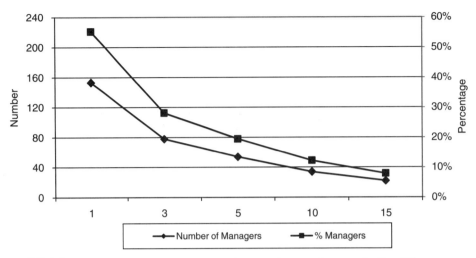

EXHIBIT 8.2   Mutual Fund Managers Outperforming Average Returns for Fund Type

compensate for the smaller sample. The number of managers and the percentage of managers that consistently outperform the average of the group declines precipitously over time (Exhibit 8.2).

If we extrapolate the lines shown in Exhibit 8.2, we can see that, after year 15, the number of managers consistently outperforming the benchmark will be essentially zero by year 20.

For this reason, if our benchmark ROR for the PIC interest incorporates a premium over the asset class benchmark 10-year returns, the premium, or excess returns, should disappear after about 10 years. Furthermore, the returns revert to the mean at a steady rate. In practice, although mean reversion occurs, its exact timing cannot be forecast.

Our research is supported by the previous research of Malkiel. In discussing this topic, he in turn cites the work of others[4]:

> Fama and French found that 25 to 40 percent of the variation in long holding period returns can be predicted in terms of a negative correlation with past returns. Similarly, Poterba and Summers found substantial mean reversion in stock market returns at longer horizons.

Furthermore, Malkiel (among many others) supports our contention that the performance of mutual fund managers lacks persistence:[5]

> A remarkably large body of evidence suggests that professional investment managers are not able to outperform index funds that simply buy and hold the broad stock market portfolio. The first study of mutual fund performance was undertaken by Jensen (1969). He found that active mutual fund

---

[4] Burton G. Malkiel, "The Efficient Market Hypothesis and Its Critics," *Journal of Economic Perspectives* 17(91) (2003): 10.
[5] Ibid: 30–31.

managers were unable to add value and, in fact, tended to underperform the market by approximately the amount of their added expenses. I repeated Jensen's study with data from a subsequent period and confirmed the earlier results (Malkiel, 1995). Moreover, I found that the degree of "survivorship bias" in the data was substantial; that is, poorly performing funds tend to be merged into other funds in the mutual fund's family complex thus burying the records of many of the underperformers . . . Survivorship bias makes the interpretation of long-run mutual fund data sets very difficult. But even using data sets with some degree of survivorship bias, one cannot sustain the argument that professional investors can beat the market.

Malkiel's study does show that professionally managed equity mutual funds underperformed the S&P 500 index by almost 200 basis points (two percentage points) over the past 10-, 15-, and 20-year periods.

LACK OF CONTROL

An investor in a typical noncontroling, minority interest in a PIC (e.g., a limited partner in a typical FLP or a minority member in a typical LLC) has no control over entity management issues such as market timing of purchases and sales of assets, the hiring and firing of managers, and paying dividends or distributions. Lastly, he/she has very limited influence on PIC governance issues such as replacing the managing general partner, amending the entity governance agreement, or the liquidation of the entity. Academic studies indicate that corporate governance significantly affects financial policy and performance and, therefore, enters into pricing considerations.

Because of lack of control and the unfamiliarity with the operation and entity management of the PIC, a reasonable investor will require an ROR greater than could otherwise be obtained in the public market for portfolios of assets with similar risk held outside the PIC.

Asymmetrical Information and Lack of Control

Asymmetrical information can be defined as information that is known to some people but not to other people. This economic concept was discussed by Akerlof.[6] The classical argument is that some sellers with inside information about the quality of an asset will be unwilling to accept the terms offered by a less informed buyer. Conversely, buyers are wary of paying for an asset about which they are not fully informed. This is also referred to as adverse selection.

The academic literature usually refers to the cost of asymmetrical information as a liquidity cost. Almost all the literature we typically cite deals with publicly traded stock, and academics describe any cost or negative characteristic that serves to

---

[6] George Akerlof, "The Market for Lemons," *The Quarterly Journal of Economics* 84(3) (August 1970): 488–500.

diminish a stock's price as a cost of liquidity.[7] This concept is helpful in understanding the return variances of the stocks in the PIC's portfolio. Here, however, we are concerned with the equity interest in the PIC.

Without question, the equity interests in closely held entities like PICs suffer from acute information asymmetry. Limited partners and minority holders of other forms of PICs receive little or no information concerning managerial activities and asset values. Many receive only an income tax return each year. Compare this to the minority owners of publicly traded investment entities such as closed-end funds or mutual funds. These shareholders can review asset values daily and receive quarterly detailed information on the funds' assets and performance. The annual report is highly detailed. In addition, these equity holders have the added assurance that the information sent to them is audited and filed with and reviewed by the SEC.

Incremental Required Rate of Return for Asymmetrical Information and Lack of Control

Because of these financial risks associated with asymmetrical information and lack of control, the willing buyer of an interest in a PIC will require a greater ROR than he/she would earn by purchasing such interest at prorata NAV. A purchase at NAV would simply earn the buyer the same ROR as the PIC earns. Assuming there is nothing special about the investment management of the PIC, the buyer could just as easily buy the same (or close to the same) assets in the marketplace at NAV and not suffer the consequences of information asymmetry or illiquidity. Accordingly, in order to induce the buyer to buy, a lower price and higher return must be offered. However, the two-sided equation of a negotiated transaction requires that we balance the buyer's requirements with the seller's. Although a rational seller will realize he/she must make a price concession to the buyer vis-à-vis the NAV, the objective is to give up as little as possible.

The governing mechanism for this hypothetical transaction is the reasonable expectation for future returns of the assets comprising the PIC's portfolio. That is, although buyers could replicate the portfolios on their own, how confident are they that, on their own, they would earn better returns than the premium offered by the sellers? Based on historical average returns by asset class, we know few investors can hope to outperform the benchmark for an asset class on a persistent basis. We also know the normal ranges of historical returns for the various asset classes. Any hypothetical transaction must be presumed to transpire within the bounds of normal and reasonable experience for the asset class(es) being considered.

For example, assume a PIC owned only a portfolio of diversified large-cap common stocks. Assume the PIC is expected to earn 8% return on the portfolio that we are assuming is the average 10-year return of the large-cap mutual funds. So, with average skill, the PIC should be able to achieve an 8% return, all things being equal. Accordingly, expecting our hypothetical PIC to earn 8% is not a leap of faith.

---

[7] Jonathan E. Clarke, C. Edward Fee, Shawn Thomas, "Corporate Diversification, Asymmetric Information, and Firm Value: Evidence from Stock Market Trading Characteristics," Working paper, March 9, 2000. Available at http://ssrn.com/abstract=204908.

Assume that the upper quartile 10-year average return for large-cap mutual funds is 11.5%. Only a minority of funds can achieve this level of return. Furthermore, because of the historical lack of persistence in fund returns, the upper quartile funds of today will probably not be in this position in the years to come. The buyer cannot have confidence in reasonably anticipating an 11.5% return by investing in any one specific overperforming fund today. However, the 11.5% return can be achieved with high confidence by a buyer if the seller discounts the selling price from NAV to a level that would provide an 11.5% return if the PIC management simply achieves the average 10-year return of 8%. In this way, the buyer can economically justify buying an interest in the PIC despite the risk of lack of control rather than investing directly in a mutual fund of similar risk. At this time we are ignoring the concept of illiquidity of the interest in the PIC itself.

It is reasonable to estimate that the upper quartile of asset return would set an upward bound of the required ROR range for lack of control for this asset class. It would be out of context with the market and therefore irrational for the buyer to demand a greater return (or a lower price). No rational willing seller would likely allow the buyer to earn a higher return.

Accordingly, to begin the process of estimating the incremental returns a hypothetical investor in the PIC would require, we examine rates of return realized by top ranked investment funds generally available in the marketplace. The better-performing funds (those whose returns exhibit the highest excess returns—90% percentile) set an upper threshold ROR for a minority investment in a closely held investment entity with a comparable portfolio. Such comparative returns are found in various sources but, perhaps, the most widely used source is Morningstar. The return information is provided by asset class (e.g., municipal bonds, government bonds, large-cap equity, small-cap equity, etc.) over various time periods with the longest comparison period generally being ten years (in some instances the longest comparison period is fifteen years). Here we are interested in the 10-year data since that is what we assume is our minimum expected period until a likely liquidity event.

Given the widespread availability of this information and Morningstar's reputation for such data, we believe their data provide a solid underpinning for any negotiation relating to pricing of an asset class which is based on long-term ROR expectations. The data would be used to frame the expectations of both parties. The buyer who wants as great an ROR as possible cannot reasonably expect a return which is greater than the top-performing group (i.e., the upper quartile of the category).

On the other hand, the seller knows he/she must offer the buyer an ROR that is significantly above the average of the overall universe. Otherwise, there is no incentive for the buyer to buy the PIC interest given the assumed risks of lack of control. The buyer could reasonably expect to achieve "average" returns on his/her own.[8]

---

[8] The buyer cannot expect to achieve excess returns by buying the specific top-ranked funds. As we have shown previously, individual mutual fund manager's ability to outperform benchmarks lacks persistence. The rates of return by which the top-ranked funds exceed are relatively stable. However, the identity of specific funds comprising the top-ranked list is unstable.

Example of Incremental Rate of Return for Lack of Control

Using mutual fund data published by Morningstar, we have tested the minimum incremental RROR for lack of control (MIN-IROC) and the maximum incremental RROR for lack of control (MAX-IROC) for a blend of growth and income stocks (large-cap equity blend) and municipal bonds for seven semi-annual periods beginning December 31, 2005, and ending December 31, 2008, and also for the period ending June 30, 2009. These data are shown below in Exhibit 8.3. We are using three years of data for this example whereas other people may use data over a longer period, say ten years.

EXHIBIT 8.3   MIN-IROC and MAX-IROC Data for Large Cap Equity and Municipal Bond Fund Returns

Large Cap Equity Blend Fund Returns								
	Dec-05	Jun-06	Dec-06	Jun-07	Dec 07	Jun-08	Dec-08	Jun-09
No. of funds	240	255	276	277	302	316	324	306
Category average	8.3%	7.6%	7.9%	7.2%	6.1%	3.6%	(0.6%)	(1.3%)
90th percentile	10.5%	9.9%	10.6%	9.8%	8.8%	6.6%	2.18%	1.3%
75th percentile	9.2%	8.5%	8.7%	7.8%	6.9%	4.4%	0.59%	0.1%
Minimum mariginal RROR	0.9%	0.9%	0.7%	0.6%	0.8%	0.9%	1.2%	1.4%
Maximum marginal RROR	2.2%	2.2%	2.6%	2.6%	2.7%	3.1%	2.8%	2.6%
Bid-ask spread	1.3%	1.4%	1.9%	2.0%	1.9%	2.2%	1.6%	1.2%
Spread as % avg	15.5%	17.8%	23.9%	27.6%	31.6%	61.0%	(257.8%)	(89.8%)

Muni National Long- and Intermediate-Term Bond Fund Returns								
	Dec-05	Jun-06	Dec-06	Jun-07	Dec-07	Jun-08	Dec-08	Jun-09
No. of funds	141	142	138	134	134	133	129	125
Category average	4.9%	5.0%	5.0%	4.7%	4.3%	4.1%	3.2%	4.0%
90th percentile	5.5%	5.7%	5.7%	5.4%	4.9%	4.6%	3.97%	4.8%
75th percentile	5.2%	5.3%	5.3%	5.0%	4.7%	4.4%	3.76%	4.4%
Minimum mariginal RROR	0.3%	0.4%	0.4%	0.3%	0.3%	0.3%	0.6%	0.4%
Maximum marginal RROR	0.7%	0.7%	0.7%	0.7%	0.6%	0.5%	0.8%	0.8%
Bid-ask spread	0.3%	0.3%	0.4%	0.4%	0.3%	0.2%	0.2%	0.0%
Spread as % avg	6.8%	6.9%	7.4%	7.8%	6.5%	4.9%	6.7%	0.0%

The incremental RROR for lack of control (IROC) as of June 30, 2009, for large-cap equity was approximately 140 basis points for the minimum (seller's) case and 260 basis points for the maximum (buyer's) case. The same analysis for municipal bonds indicated a MIN-IROC of 40 basis points and a MAX-IROC of 80 basis points. In this example, we have primarily relied on the data as of June 30, 2009 (with some consideration of historical return increments), the most recent available as of the valuation date, because the indicated statistics were very close to the averages from prior periods.

LACK OF MARKETABILITY OR ILLIQUIDITY

The financial mechanics of the NICE method with respect to illiquidity are modeled after a liquidity shock such as what we have recently witnessed in late 2008. That is, if we compare an interest in a PIC to a liquid interest in a share of stock of a company listed on the New York Stock Exchange (NYSE), we know that, in order to induce a buyer to buy, we must offer a financial incentive relative to that which could be earned from the liquid proxy (comparable publicly traded investment).

We have documented from numerous sources that the cost of illiquidity varies in direct proportion to the economic risk (volatility) of the investment. Since the PIC interest represents an indirect ownership interest in the subject PIC's portfolio, we must look at the PIC's portfolio piece by piece in order to construct the correct picture of the cost of illiquidity associated with owning the PIC interest.

Continuing with the example, we will examine the issue of illiquidity by assuming a PIC whose portfolio consists of an equal allocation of large-cap publicly traded stocks and municipal bonds. Because the PIC interest is viewed as a very long-term investment, we will look at very long-term rates of return for common stocks and municipal bonds.

According to *Ibbotson SBBI* statistics, large-cap common stocks have achieved an average ROR of about 10% to 11% and have experienced average annual volatility of about 20%.[9]

Historical financial data on municipal bonds are not nearly as complete and robust as those that exist for common stocks. However, the information that we have considered (shown in Exhibit 8.3) indicates that the long-term ROR for highly rated municipal bonds ranges from 3.2% to 5.0%. The volatility of returns for such bonds is about 10%.[10]

In highly simplified terms, the common stocks in the PIC's portfolio are approximately twice as risky as its municipal bonds. Because the cost of illiquidity varies in proportion to the risk of the investment, it is easily understood that the incremental RROR for the illiquidity of the PIC's common stock portfolio is significantly greater than that required for that portion of its municipal bond portfolio.

---

[9] See Exhibit 9.1 of *Cost of Capital: Applications and Examples,* 4th ed., Chapter 9.
[10] Ibid.

Summary of Research

Without question, establishing the exact incremental ROR components is difficult because, as far as we know, such data are not commonly measured or compiled in any easy-to-find financial database. There can be no doubt that an incremental ROR component is mandatory. The question is: "How much ROR and how do you justify it?"

The financial data we are seeking are not readily available. However, there have been a number of studies performed to attempt to answer these questions. Usually studies are performed on one particular asset class such as government bonds. We have compiled evidence from a number of these studies in order to establish a grid of the cost of illiquidity associated with various asset classes. Although we do not have such studies for many asset classes, the results of the studies we do have do confirm other studies that infer that the cost of illiquidity is proportional to the risk of the asset class. We can, by interpolation, estimate the cost of illiquidity for all asset classes for which we have reliable, historical volatility data.

The terms *liquid* and *illiquid* can be misleading. In truth, liquidity is a continuum, with the most liquid securities being represented by U.S. government securities and the least degree of liquidity (virtually none) being represented by an equity interest in a closely held entity. Some research clearly indicates that just because a security is publicly traded does not mean it is completely liquid. The degree to which a publicly traded security is illiquid will be reflected in its market price. When we estimate the illiquidity of the PIC interest, we are extrapolating what additional illiquidity cost would be associated with a publicly traded security if its liquidity went from its present state in the marketplace to a state of virtual illiquidity. Such events, when they do occur in the marketplace, are referred to as liquidity shocks. The effect of liquidity shocks on pricing has been shown to be directly related to the riskiness of the security.

Our opinion that illiquid securities must provide investors with a greater expected return is well supported in the financial literature. Favero, Pagano, and Von Thadden provide a summary of recent economic research into the effects of liquidity on asset price.[11] The authors first indicate that the work of Amihud and Mendelson[12] has been the basis of a vast empirical literature which now exists.

The bid-ask spread measure of illiquidity has spawned many subsequent studies of stock market data which have confirmed a significant cross sectional association between liquidity (as measured by the tightness of the bid-ask spread or trading volume) and asset returns, controlling for risk.[13]

---

[11] Carl Favero, Marco Pagano, and Enst-Ludwig Von Thadden, "Valuation, Liquidity and Risk in Government Bond Markets," IGIER Working Paper No. 281, January 2005. Available at http://ssrn.com/abstract=663002.

[12] Footnote 2 earlier.

[13] See for example, Michael Brennan and Avanidhar Subrahmanyam, "Market Microstructure and Asset Pricing: On the Compensation for Illiquidity in Stock Returns," *Journal of Financial Economics* 41 (July 1996): 441–464; Tarun Chordia, Richard Roll, and Avanidhar Subrahmanyam, "Market Liquidity and Trading Activity," *Journal of Finance* 56 (April 2001): 501–530; Vinay Datar, Narayan Naik, and Robert Radcliffe, "Liquidity and Stock Returns: An Alternative Test," *Journal of Financial Intermediation* 1 (1998): 203–219.

The authors also indicate that, besides the equity market, many other studies have focused on liquidity effects in fixed-income security markets. Again, the initiators were Amihud and Mendelson,[14] who showed that the yield to maturity of Treasury notes with six months or less to maturity exceeds the yield to maturity on the more liquid Treasury bills.

The liquidity risk view, developed in particular by Pastor and Stambough,[15] highlights that liquidity is priced not only because it creates trading costs, but also because it is itself a source of risk, since it changes unpredictably over time. Because investors care about returns net of trading costs, the variability of trading costs affects the risk of a security. In other words, even though a security is publicly traded, its price is affected by an unseen liquidity risk factor.

Gallmeyer, Hollifield and Seppi[16] propose a model of liquidity risk in which traders have asymmetric knowledge about future liquidity, so that less informed investors try to learn from the amount of current trading volume how much liquidity there may be in the future. Here, these authors agree with Pastor and Stambough, as they show that current liquidity is a predictor of future liquidity risk, and therefore is priced based on liquidity risk. Again, the importance of the notion of asymmetrical information is stressed.

Incremental Required Rate of Return for Lack of Marketability

In this section we will examine the appropriate range of incremental rates of return for lack of marketability (IROM) for different asset classes.

Government Bonds Empirical evidence of the cost of illiquidity of U.S. government bonds is difficult to find. However, Kempf and Uhrig-Homburg provide a study of bonds issued by the German government (BUNDs) and its state-operated funds (BAHN and POST). Their study covered the years 1992 to 1994. Generally speaking, the BUNDs are liquid and the BAHN and POST are illiquid.

All of the bonds can be viewed as default-risk free. At 10 years, the cost of illiquidity is about 100 basis points. Exhibit 8.4 illustrates the illiquidity cost of risk-free bonds over time and shows how the discount from face increases as the years to maturity increase. This study corroborates the statement by the Chief Investment Officer of Yale University, that debt issued by U.S. agencies and backed by the full faith and credit of the U.S. government often trades at a yield premium of 50 to 100 basis points to the far more liquid U.S. government bonds. These U.S. agency bonds are not as liquid as U.S. government obligations.[17]

---

[14] Footnote 2 earlier.

[15] Lubos Pastor and Robert Stambough, "Liquidity Risk and Expected Stock Returns," *Journal of Political Economy* 111 (2003): 642–685.

[16] Michael Gallmeyer, Burton Hollifield, and Duane Seppi, "Liquidity Discovery and Asset Pricing," Carnegie Mellon University Working Paper, 2004.

[17] Alexander Kempf and Marliese Uhrig-Homburg, "Liquidity and its Impact on Bond Prices," *Schmalenbach Business Review* (January 2000): 26–44; see also Hai Lin, Sheen Liu and Chunchi Wu, "Liquidity Premia in the Credit Default Swap and Corporate Bond Markets," February 2009. Available at http://ssrn.com/abstract=1361292.

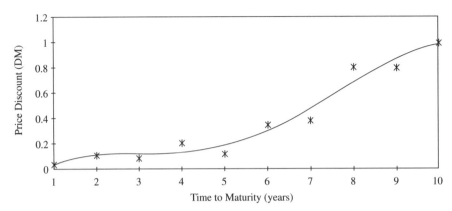

EXHIBIT 8.4   Liquidity Discount from Face Value as a Function of Years to Maturity
DM = Deutch Marks

High Yield Bonds   Kwan provides the following information regarding the illiquidity premium associated with junk bonds in 1998–a time when liquidity had virtually disappeared from this market. Between June 1998 and October 1998, the junk-bond premium increased 334 basis points. The rise was thought to not be associated with an increase in expected default risk, because no recession followed this time period. The liquidity shock of this period is one of those rare glimpses the market provides on the cost of liquidity. This situation is about as close as possible to simulating the pricing of a completely nonmarketable security such as in interest in a closely held entity. This information was helpful in our modeling of the additional required return component appropriate to a PIC holding junk bonds in the portfolio. Three hundred to 350 basis points of additional return were factored into the model for this asset class.[18]

Large-Cap Common Stocks   Archarya and Pederson describe two different facets of illiquidity: the level of liquidity and liquidity risk.[19] The level of liquidity is the degree of illiquidity in the market as a whole and how sensitive an individual stock is to it ("liquidity beta"). We have adopted the results of the Acharya study into the NICE method as the IROM for large-cap common stock.

The study covered stock prices on the NYSE and American Stock Exchange (AMEX) for the years 1963 through 1999. The maximum market-liquidity-cost stocks require a market premium of 350 basis points and the companies with the highest liquidity betas have an additional ROR requirement of 110 basis points.

The liquidity costs identified here are the covariance of:

1. Stock's illiquidity and the market's illiquidity.
2. Stock's return and the market's illiquidity.
3. Stock's illiquidity and the market's return.

---

[18] Simon H. Kwan, "Firm-Specific Information and The Correlation Between Individual Stocks and Bonds," *Journal of Financial Economic.*(January 1996): 63–80.

[19] Viral Archaya and Lesse Pedersen, "Asset Pricing with Liquidity," *Journal of Financial Economics* (August 2005): 375–410.

This study posits that the measure of the long-term average cost of illiquidity between the most liquid large-cap stocks and the least liquid is 460 basis points.[20] On average, the systematic cost of illiquidity built into the price of a share of large-cap common stock is 175 basis points. From Table 1 of the Archaya study, we conclude that the average stock also has about 50 basis points of illiquidity risk in addition to the market illiquidity cost. Thus, if our long-term average expected ROR for market equity security portion (primarily large-cap stocks) of the PIC is 11%, a small but significant portion of that return is due to illiquidity.

From the standpoint of a typical investor in a PIC, illiquidity is far more of a factor than it is for a shareholder in the least liquid stock in the Acharya study. So, if the illiquidity cost between the average stock (in terms of liquidity) and the least liquid is 235 basis points, the difference between the average large-cap stock and a (virtually) illiquid PIC interest (assuming, hypothetically, the PIC owned only large-cap common) would have to be more than 235 basis points.

The Fujimoto and Watanabe study of liquidity risk during severe liquidity shocks found that, subsequent to such shocks, illiquid portfolios have greater unconditional average returns than liquid portfolios. The return spread between the two extreme deciles is 0.48 percent per month. The study covered all NYSE and AMEX stocks between 1964 and 2004. On an annualized basis, the spread in illiquidity costs equates to an annualized return of 5.9%.[21] This is reasonably close to the 460 basis points found by Archarya and Pederson.

Small Capitalization Stocks   Our findings are consistent to those reported by Damodaran, who states that

> Ljundquist and Richardson (2003) estimate that private equity investors earn excess returns of 5 to 8 percent, relative to the public equity market, and that this generates about 24 percent in risk-adjusted additional value to a private equity investor over 10 years.[22]

These securities, for the most part, relate to the small-cap and micro-cap markets. This compares very closely to the study we performed on the same asset class and as is described in Exhibit 8.5 for investments in restricted stock of public companies.[23] The differences between the expected returns and the implied returns of the three time periods revealed a liquidity premium of about 8%.

Duration Effect of IROM   The IROM estimated above for large-cap common stocks envisions a medium-term to long-term horizon. The longer the duration of the holding period, the greater should be its return. However, academic studies proving this

---

[20] The 110 basis points associated with liquidity risk is found in smaller capitalization stocks.

[21] Akiko Watanabe and Masahiro Watanabe, "Time-Varying Liquidity Risk and the Cross Section of Stock Returns," 8th Annual Texas Finance Festival Working paper, January 9, 2007. Available at http://ssrn.com/abstract=895763.

[22] Aswath Damodaran, "Marketability and Value: Measuring the Illiquidity Discount," Working paper, July 30, 2005. Available at http://ssrn.com/abstract=841484.

[23] William Frazier, "Quantitative Analysis of the Fair Market Value of an Interest in a Family Limited Partnership," *Valuation Strategies* (January/February 2005): 6–17, 45–46.

EXHIBIT 8.5   Implied Rates of Return from Restricted Stock Investments

	Post-1997	1990–1997	Pre-1990
Assumed market price of freely traded stock	$10.00	$10.00	$10.00
Discount per time period[a]	13.0%	23.4%	32.5%
Average block size (per studies)	13.5%	14.5%	13.5%
Effective holding period (years)	2	4	6
Discounted purchase price	$8.70	$7.66	$6.75

	% Expected Rate of Return in Freely Traded Stock Price[b]	Discounted Purchase Price of Restricted Stock Investment	Holding Period	% Implied IRR of Restricted Stock Investments
Post 1997	12.7	($8.70)	2	21.6
1990–1997	12.6	($7.66)	4	28.7
Pre-1990	12.9	($6.75)	6	36.4

Notes: [a]Based on restricted-stock studies over various time periods.
[b]Microcap long-term rates of return (since 1926) from 2004, 1993, and 1984 editions of Stocks, Bonds, Bills and Inflation Yearbook, Ibbotson Associates.

point are, to date, lacking. Therefore, to avoid engaging in speculation, we believe that we are constrained by what is known. The most certain long-term differential in ROR based purely on duration may be seen in the differential between the 10-year U.S. government bonds and 30-year U.S. government bonds. According to *SBBI* data, the difference here for the previous 20 years has been about 40 basis points. This equates to an average differential of about 2 basis points per year. On the other hand, if we look at *SBBI* data back to 1926, we see virtually no difference between the average total returns on 10-year and 30-year U.S. government bonds.

The minimum IROM of 250 basis points and the maximum IROM of 300 basis points based on the studies cited earlier is taken from the public marketplace where we assume the average buyer has an investment horizon of less than 5 years.[24] In our implementation of the NICE method, IROM associated with equities grows linearly for 6 years until the minimum IROM and maximum IROM is reached. After that, growth in IROM slows to an additional IROM of 1 to 2 basis points per year. In the stated liquidation year of the Company, we have increased the total additional IROM by 50 basis points over minimum IROM and maximum IROM. We also use a 1 to 2 basis point increase for each year following the year of the inflection point in the IROM calculation for all asset classes. By *inflection point* we mean the point at which the linear rate of increase in the cost of illiquidity slows to a rate expressed by an exponential curve. A depiction of such a curve is seen in the seminal article on illiquidity and asset pricing by Amihud and Mendelson[25] as shown in Exhibit 8.6.

---

[24] The Archaya study cites a holding period for long-term equity of just twenty-nine months.
[25] Amihud and Mendelson. P. 230.

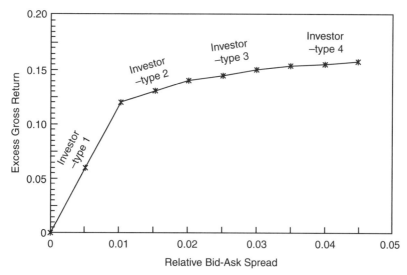

EXHIBIT 8.6 Duration Effect of IROM

Example of Incremental Rate of Return for Lack of Marketability Exhibit 8.7 provides guidance to the additional increments of return required for various asset classes held in many PICs based on research we have completed. We have direct sources of information for the data points related to risk-free government bonds, junk bonds, and small-cap common stocks. We have interpolated the estimated required return components for the other asset classes. This was done by comparing volatility and relative risk—the two key components to the cost of liquidity. In our calculation, we first determined the differences between the known components of the risk-free and small-cap asset classes and extrapolated the indicated required return based on the volatility of the asset class. However, based on our research, we know that risk is a major player in the cost of illiquidity. The price of an asset with less-than-optimal liquidity but with low risk will not be influenced by nearly the same degree as an asset with poor liquidity and significant default risk.[26]

EXAMPLE VALUATION OF PIC INTEREST

Exhibit 8.8 presents the NAV balance sheet of ABC, LLC (the "Company"). At the hypothetical valuation date of June 30, 2009, ABC had an aggregate NAV of $10 million. Assets consist of a portfolio of $5 million of large cap equity (a blend of growth and income stocks) and $5 million of AAA-rated municipal bonds.

---

[26] Maria Vassalou, Jing Chen and Lihong Zhou, "The Relation between Liquidity Risk and Default Risk in Equity Returns," EFA 2006 Zurich Meetings working paper, July 16, 2006. Available at http://ssrn.com/abstract=922622.

EXHIBIT 8.7   Estimated Incremental Illiquidity Premiums with Historical Returns and Standard Deviation by Asset Class

Asset Class	% Historical Volatility	Minimum PIC Illiquidity Premium (basis points)	Maximum PIC Illiquidity Premium (basis points)
Estimated Incremental Illiquidity Premiums with Historical Returns and Standard Deviation by Asset Class			
U.S. government bonds (10 yr.)[a]	**5.1**	50	100[e]
Municipal[d]	5.1	75	125
Corporate bonds[c]	8.7	100	150
Junk bonds[c]	**22.0**	**300**	350
U.S. large-cap[a]	20.3	200	250
International large-cap[b]	19.4	225	275
North American real estate equities[b]	20.4	275	325
U.S. small-cap[a]	**34.1**	**500**	600[f]

Boldface: sourced result; other: interpolated result.

Note: Basis points equal hundredths of a percent. For example, 50 basis points equals 0.5%.

Sources:

[a] *1997 SBBI Yearbook*

[b] Commercial Real Estate. Ibbotson. 2006. Standard deviations calculated for years 1990–2005.

[c] "Using Yield Spreads to Estimate Expected Returns on Debt and Equity," by Ian A. Cooper, Sergei A. Davydenko.

[d] Lehman Brothers Municipal Bond Index, 1995–2005.

[e] Dr Alexander Kempf and Dr Marliese Uhrig Homburg.

[f] Frazier. *Valuation Strategies*. 2005.

We allocated the NAV of the PIC interest to these asset classes on a weighted average basis.

The term of the PIC ends on December 31, 2050, and representatives of the management of the PIC indicated that there was no intent by the PIC to pursue a liquidity event for the foreseeable future. The PIC is expected to reinvest cash returns into similar asset classes as its existing asset mix. We are valuing a 10% equity interest in the PIC.

PIC Portfolio Return

The weighted average expected return of any portfolio of securities may be calculated by determining (1) the various asset classes or categories comprising the portfolio (also referred to as "asset allocation"); (2) the expected holding period or investment horizon of the portfolio ("duration"); and (3) the appropriate benchmark returns for the various asset classes corresponding to the expected holding period.

EXHIBIT 8.8 Net Asset Value Balance Sheet

ABC, LLC
Net Asset Value Balance Sheet
As of June 30, 2009

	Market Value	% of Total
Assets		
Municipal bonds	$5,000,000	50.0%
Large-capitalization, marketable equity securities	5,000,000	50.0%
Total assets	$10,000,000	100.0%
Liabilities and members' capital		
Liabilities	$0	0.0%
Members' capital (net asset value)	10,000,000	100.0%
Total liabilities and members' capital	$10,000,000	100.0%
Net asset value allocable to a 10.0% member interest	**$1,000,000**	

Sources: Market values of marketable investments as of valuation date, per Bloomberg.

The fair market value of the PIC interest must reflect a price (or investment) wherein the expected future return at any given point during the expected term of the PIC is reasonable, that is, a return that is neither too high (from the seller's standpoint) nor too low (from the buyer's standpoint). The important difference between this analysis and a simple IRR analysis is that there is no way to know (with certainty) the period where the PIC will experience a liquidity event (e.g., terminating the PIC and distributing its assets or making a distribution in excess of imputed income taxes to the investors in the PIC). Therefore, our analysis will encompass a range of potential holding periods. The reasonable range of the term of the PIC, as of the valuation date, would be from a minimum of 10 years and a maximum of 42 years (based on remaining legal term of the PIC).[27]

Summary of ROR Differential

When we add the incremental RRORs for lack of control and illiquidity for the minimum and maximum cases, we now have all the data points required to complete our analysis. Exhibit 8.9 describes the PIC's expected returns by asset class (inputs in NICE model) and for the PIC as a whole. Also shown are the individual asset class IROCs and IROMs for both the minimum (Table 1) and maximum (Table 2) cases.

The weighted average expected return from the underlying assets of the PIC is between 7.6% and 8.0%. The hypothetical willing seller of the PIC interest is asking the buyer to accept a ROR scenario (MIN RROR) with a rate of 10.1% in years 1 through 10 and 10.2% in year 42. The average weighted average MIN RROR is

---

[27] Of course, it is possible that the PIC might liquidate at any time. However, as the expectation that the PIC might be liquidated at any time period other than the very long-term is highly unlikely; we have for simplicity assumed a small but equal probability of liquidation in any one year after year 10.

EXHIBIT 8.9   Summary of Rate of Return Differential

Table 1 Minimum Rate of Return Differential

ABC, LLC

Summary of Minimum ROR Differential

I. Average Expected Returns by Asset Class

	LT Ave	10 yr	18 yr	26 yr	34 yr	42 yr
Municipal bonds	5.5%	5.5%	5.5%	5.5%	5.5%	5.5%
Large-cap stocks	10.5%	9.8%	10.5%	10.5%	10.5%	10.5%
Weighted Average ROR of Company	7.6%	8.0%	8.0%	8.0%	8.0%	

II. Minimum Marginal Required Return Component for Lack of Control

	10 yr	18 yr	26 yr	34 yr	42 yr
Municipal bonds	0.2%	0.0%			
Large-cap stocks	1.5%	0.4%			
Weighted Average Lack of Control Component	0.9%	0.2%			

III. Minimum Marginal Required Return Component for Illiquidity

	10 yr	18 yr	26 yr	34 yr	42 yr
Municipal bonds	0.8%	0.9%	1.0%	1.1%	1.3%
Large-cap stocks	2.6%	2.7%	2.8%	2.9%	3.0%
Weighted Average Illiquidity Component	1.7%	1.8%	1.9%	2.0%	2.1%

Minimum Required Return (I. + II. + III.)

	10 yr	18 yr	26 yr	34 yr	42 yr
Municipal bonds	6.5%	6.4%	6.5%	6.6%	6.8%
Large-cap stocks	13.8%	13.6%	13.3%	13.4%	13.5%
Weighted Average RROR of Interests	10.1%	10.0%	9.9%	10.0%	10.2%
Differential	2.5%	2.0%	1.9%	2.0%	2.1%

Source: Nonmarketable Investment Company Evaluation model, HFBE.

9.8% over the periods. The hypothetical willing buyer is bidding a price, which results in a ROR (MAX RROR) with 11.4% in years 1 through 10 and declining to 10.7% in year 42. The average weighted average MAX RROR is 10.6% over the periods.

Table 2 Summary of Maximum Rate of Return Differential

ABC, LLC
Summary of Maximum ROR Differential

I. Average Expected Returns by Asset Class

	LT Ave	10 yr	18 yr	26 yr	34 yr	42 yr
Municipal bonds	5.5%	5.5%	5.5%	5.5%	5.5%	5.5%
Large-cap stocks	10.5%	9.8%	10.5%	10.5%	10.5%	10.5%
Weighted Average ROR of Company	**7.6%**	**8.0%**	**8.0%**	**8.0%**	**8.0%**	

II. Maximum Marginal Required Return Component for Lack of Control

	10 yr	18 yr	26 yr	34 yr	42 yr
Municipal bonds	0.4%	0.0%			
Large-cap stocks	2.8%	0.8%			
Weighted Average Lack of Control Component	**1.6%**	**0.4%**			

III. Maximum Marginal Required Return Component for Illiquidity

	10 yr	18 yr	26 yr	34 yr	42 yr
Municipal bonds	1.3%	1.4%	1.5%	1.6%	1.8%
Large-cap stocks	3.1%	3.2%	3.3%	3.4%	3.5%
Weighted Average Illiquidity Component	**2.2%**	**2.3%**	**2.4%**	**2.5%**	**2.7%**

Maximum Required Return (I. + II. + III.)

	10 yr	18 yr	26 yr	34 yr	42 yr
Municipal bonds	7.2%	6.9%	7.0%	7.1%	7.3%
Large-cap stocks	15.6%	14.4%	13.8%	13.9%	14.0%
Weighted Average RROR of Interests	**11.4%**	**10.6%**	**10.4%**	**10.5%**	**10.7%**
Differential	3.7%	2.6%	2.4%	2.5%	2.7%

Source: Nonmarketable Investment Company Evaluation model, HFBE.

Determination of Curve of Best Fit

In order to determine the fair market value of the PIC interest using the Income Approach, we have analyzed the implied rates of return to a hypothetical willing buyer of the interest over a range of possible periods in which a liquidity event could occur from 10 years to 42 years (based on the remaining legal term of the PIC). For simplicity, we assume an equal probability of liquidation in any one year.

The indicated fair market value is the price at which the buyer expects he will never receive a return that is too low in view of the risks and the seller can expect the buyer will not be receiving a return that is too high (at the seller's expense). The model solves for the one price that best satisfies this condition. Earlier we determined the MIN RROR (based on the seller's asked price) and MAX RROR (based on the buyer's bid price) for each period in which a liquidity event might occur from 10 years to 42 years. If the period when a liquidity event were to occur were known, then we could simply assume that the fair market value of the interest was the price at which the ROR of the interest approximated the midpoint of the MIN RROR and MAX RROR (previously determined) for that specific period. However, there is a large degree of uncertainty regarding the ultimate period of the liquidity event; therefore, the buyer and seller will ultimately arrive at a price for which the ROR of the interest best satisfies the minimum RROR and maximum RROR spread for the multiple periods in which a liquidity event may occur.

For a PIC with a single period in which a liquidity could occur, the optimization process is easily understood. For example, if the MIN RROR was determined to be 10% and the MAX RROR was determined to be 14%, NICE would select a price that minimizes the total variation for a single holding period, which would result in an RROR of the interest of 12%.[28] In the case of determining the fair market value of a PIC interest with an uncertain time to a liquidity event, the NICE approach is to iteratively solve for a price, which results in an RROR of the interest that minimizes the total variation between the MIN RROR and the MAX RROR for the entire series of holding periods from 10 to 42 years.[29]

The software we developed around the NICE methodology uses a commercially available optimization engine, which iteratively minimizes the fair market value by adjusting the price of the interest until the total variation is minimized (approaches zero). This approach is calculation intensive and requires several thousand iterations; however, computer optimization models can complete this process in a relatively short time.

Graphically the curve of best fit, which shows the ROR of the interest based on the multiple possible liquidity event periods, is illustrated in Exhibit 8.10 where the interest ROR line appears between the MIN RROR (labeled "minimum expected return") and the MAX RROR (labeled "maximum expected return") lines as equally as is possible.

---

[28] In this example (with a single liquidity event period) the total variation is the difference between (i) the difference between the MIN ROR and the ROR of the interest of negative 2 percent (10 percent minus 12 percent) and (ii) the difference between the MAX ROR and the ROR of the interest of positive 2 percent (14 percent minus 12 percent), which equals zero (negative 2 percent plus 2 percent).

[29] For a PIC with multiple possible times of a liquidity event, the total variation is the difference between (i) the sum of the difference between the MIN ROR and the ROR of the interest for each holding period and (ii) the sum of the difference between the MAX ROR and the ROR of the interest for each holding period.

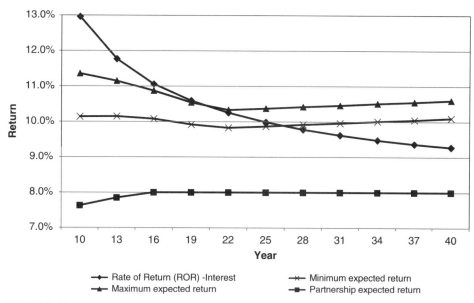

EXHIBIT 8.10 Curve of Best Fit

EXHIBIT 8.11 Fair Market Value—Income Approach ABC, LLC Determination of Fair Market Value—Income Approach (a) as of June 30, 2009

Net asset value allocable to a 10.0% member interest	$1,000,000
Less: fair market value per NICE method (rounded)	−607,000
Implied total discount from NAV	$393,000
Implied total discount from NAV as a percentage ($393,000/$1,000,000)	39.3%

As summarized in Exhibit 8.11, the NICE method results in a fair market value for a 10% interest in the PIC of $607,105. This is equivalent to a combined discount for lack of control and lack of marketability of 39.3%.

SUMMARY

The NICE method is a valuation method under the income approach. It is designed especially to determine the fair market value of equity interests in PICs.

Unlike the traditional method under the asset-based approach, the NICE method does not extrapolate discounts in its operation. The NICE method uses modern portfolio theory and financial mathematics to estimate value. What the NICE method solves for is simply the price one would pay for the interest in the PIC in view of the investment risks and expected returns.

Traditional valuations of interests in PICs involve a determination of the following:

1. PIC's NAV.
2. Discount for minority interest (or lack of control).
3. Discount for lack of marketability (or illiquidity).

The NICE method involves the determination of:

1. Expected average annual total return from the PIC's assets.
2. Additional economic return required because of lack of control.
3. Additional economic return required because of illiquidity.

The NICE method is focused on exactly the same risks as the traditional method. We express these risks in terms of income adjustments as opposed to asset value adjustments. Regardless of which method is used, the risks to be considered for any one particular partnership are the same. Therefore, the valuations from applying both methods should also be relatively close.

Because of lack of control and the unfamiliarity with the functionality of partnership management, a reasonable investor will require an ROR greater than otherwise could be obtained in the public marketplace by investing directly in similar assets to those held by the partnership. This risk is sometimes referred to as asymmetrical information. The degree of the ROR enhancement will vary based on the asset class. Generally speaking, the safer (less volatile) the asset class, the smaller the required adjustment. For most investment asset classes, data required for determining the incremental required rate of return can be found in public sources such as Morningstar. An additional consideration here is the inevitable mean reversion of the incremental required rate of return. That is, in order for the pricing construct here to be consistent with market realities, the incremental return resulting from the negotiation between the buyer and seller is temporary. Studies have proven investors cannot permanently outperform the long term average returns for a particular asset class.

The economic return for the PIC interest is highly correlated with the life-span of the PIC. Usually such investments receive little current income and look to liquidation for the economic return. As PICs are established as very long-term vehicles to provide for long-term capital appreciation, the NICE method assumes there will be no liquidation of the PIC for at least 10 years after its formation and with a practical maximum terminus of 50 years. Numerous studies give evidence to the additional rate of return requirements for illiquid assets of varying asset classes. In addition, we know that the cost of liquidity is a function of time, although not a linear one. The longer an asset is held (or economic return foregone, the higher the cost). So, unlike IROC, which declines over time, IROM, increases (at a decreasing rate) over time.

IROC and IROM are found from both the perspective of the buyer and the seller for each asset class. These increments are added to the expected returns of the PIC for the corresponding asset classes, creating a required rate of return for the seller (MIN-RROR) and a corresponding required rate of return for the buyer (MAX-RROR). Thus, minimum and maximum bounds are now established simulating the bid-ask spread of a typical market transaction. Because we do not know when the PIC might liquidate, such spreads are found for each year in which the PIC might reasonably be liquidated. Fair market value of the fractional interest in the PIC is determined by finding that one price that provides the best balance in the range of annual bid-ask spreads. Graphically, this is depicted as the curve of best fit.

CHAPTER 9

Cost of Capital of Real Property— Individual Assets

Terry V. Grissom and James R. MacCrate

INTRODUCTION

This chapter presents development of the cost of capital for individual real property investments and provides practical applications for the valuation of income-producing assets, such as apartment or office buildings, industrial properties, and development properties. In conjunction with the other chapters in this book, this chapter assists the reader in understanding the differences between the current practices applied in business valuation and those applied in real estate valuation. The income and the cost of capital associated with the ownership of real property rights are the focus of this section. This is different from the income and cost of capital that might be earned by a business enterprise operating on the property, such as a marina, hotel, fitness club, or restaurant, or a portfolio of properties, such as a real estate operating company or a real estate investment trust.

The authors thank Maureen D. McGoldrick of MDM Appraisals for her assistance.

Real estate is a unique asset class with distinguishing characteristics. Real estate is immobile, durable, or indestructible, and each parcel is different in that no two parcels can be in the same location. As a result, a body of law has evolved concerning real property rights or interests in real estate or realty. The rights inherent in the ownership of real estate are generally referred to as the bundle of rights. These include the rights of possession, control, enjoyment, and disposition. These rights are divisible and can be transferred by legal documents, such as a lease, a mortgage, or a deed. The value of real estate is the value of the real property or the rights inherent in the ownership of real estate or realty and is based on its capacity to support and house economic activities.

In essence, real property value is based on the behavioral response to a site and a facility's productive capacity. The productive capacity is a function of its physical attributes, rights inherent in the ownership of real estate or realty, and its economic location. The income generated as a function of a property's productive capacity accounts for its fundamental value, which, when compared to comparable property assets, becomes its basis of exchange or market value. Changes in behavioral responses to the factors comprising productive capacity as well as variables defining the productive capacity itself become the basis of value and income volatility over time. Recognizing and measuring the sources of volatility impact and affect the cost of capital observed for property assets over time.

Although there are three traditional approaches to value—the cost, sales comparison (or market), and income approaches—this chapter focuses on the income approach for income-producing properties. Market value is the present worth of the anticipated future benefits derived from the ownership of real estate. Market value is based on typical financing, which influences the future benefits that affect the price that investors pay for real estate. The cost of capital includes those benefits or returns to the equity and debt positions. Definitions of terms such as *net income* and *cash flow* may differ from those used previously in this text. This chapter defines these terms in the context of real estate valuation; they should not be confused with the terms as defined in financial textbooks.

TYPICAL STRUCTURE OF A REAL ESTATE TRANSACTION

Because of the special characteristics associated with real property investments, such investments can be analyzed based on their physical, legal, or financial components. The financial components include debt and equity investments. Equity investments can be in various forms, such as an individual investor, joint ventures, partnerships, syndications, or public securities. Because most real estate is acquired with debt financing, the cash flow from the real property investment must satisfy the return requirements of debt investors in order to attract debt as well as equity investors.

The mortgage or debt component may include various categories and can be obtained from commercial banks, life insurance companies, governmental agencies (e.g., Federal National Mortgage Association, Federal Home Loan Mortgage Corporation, Federal Housing Association, etc.), pension plans, real estate investment trusts (REITs), mutual funds, hedge funds, opportunity funds, credit companies, and private lenders. Commercial collateralized mortgage obligations (CMOs) had become an increasingly important vehicle for debt financing before the 2008 crisis.

These are rated by Moody's, Fitch, or Standard & Poor's. The secondary markets can have considerable influence on real estate finance.

Historically, it was recommended that real estate should be valued free and clear of all encumbrances including existing mortgage debt.[1] If the typical investor obtains debt to acquire the real property interests, then you should consider the typical financial structure that is utilized to acquire the asset. The definition of market value has evolved to assume cash to the seller or a cash-equivalent price.[2] More importantly, market participants consider debt to be crucial to the consummation of a satisfactory transaction. Many investors prefer financial leverage to improve the actual return on the investment and allow for diversification. Because market value is the most probable price that a typical investor is willing to pay, if the transaction price is influenced by financing, the cost and typical terms of financing should be considered in estimating market value. This idea supports the position that the source of capital and structure of the capital vehicle used in financing the property can have a significant affect on the value of the property that is collateralized.

The capital structure associated with an entity that utilizes the real property as part of its business operations can be different from an owner/investor who leases the property to third parties. For example, a corporation that has a high credit rating may be able to obtain unsecured debt to acquire real property assets at a substantially lower cost. There may also be additional tax benefits that accrue to owner-users that lower their after-tax effective cost of capital. When the real property is acquired as an investment, the real property is provided as collateral to obtain mortgage financing. The cost and the amount of financing are primarily driven by the capital markets.

REAL PROPERTY COMPETES WITH OTHER ASSET CLASSES

Investors have many investment alternatives available in the current environment. In order to attract equity and debt investors, the expected returns or forward-looking returns must be commensurate with the perceived investment risks as compared to alternative investments (mortgage investments, stocks, bonds, etc.) and other factors influencing the return on real estate.

Many real estate analysts use the convention of benchmarking the property rate of return to the risk-free rate using 10-year U.S. government bonds. The expected inflation rate and perceived risk over 10 years is factored into the yield on a 10-year bond. In comparison to real estate investments, 10-year U.S. government bonds are highly liquid, require no investment management, and are perceived to have assured

---

[1] William N. Kinnard Jr., *Income Property Valuation* (Lexington, Mass.: Heath-Lexington Books, 1971), 145.

[2] *Cash equivalent price* is defined as "a price expressed in terms of cash, as distinguished from a price expressed totally or partly in terms of the face amounts of notes or other securities that cannot be sold at their face amounts. Calculating the cash-equivalent price requires an appraiser to compare transactions involving atypical financing to transactions involving comparable properties financed at typical market terms." Appraisal Institute, *The Dictionary of Real Estate Appraisal*, 4th ed. (Chicago: Appraisal Institute, 2002).

income. In contrast, real estate investments in individual real property assets are highly illiquid, require intensive management, and have substantial investment risks that affect the cost of capital. Investors in real estate should be compensated for the additional investment risk over and above the risk-free rate for relative lack of liquidity, and for the additional management burden.[3]

The investment risk[4] premium should encompass such risk factors as:

- Market or business risk
- Financial risk
- Capital market risk
- Inflation risk
- Environmental risk
- Legislative risk

Market or business risk is related to factors that occur in the real estate market that may affect the operations of the real estate. This may include changes in demand and supply impacting the forecasted net operating income. Market risks can be influenced by property type, location, and position of the real estate market cycle.

By leveraging the property, the investor increases the financial risk associated with that particular investment, but the expected return (and ideally, the realized return) also is increased. Positive leverage occurs when cost of debt is less than the unleveraged return on the real property. The loan-to-value ratio is defined as the ratio of money borrowed on a property to the property's fair market value. As the loan-to-value ratio increases, the risk associated with a specific investment increases. The cost of debt also increases as the loan-to-value ratio increases. The degree of financial risk is directly related to the amount of debt and type of debt.

Capital market risk is associated with changes that might occur in the capital markets that impact mortgage rates, expected equity, and property yield rates. The value of the investment may be affected if these rates increase or decrease. Changes in mortgage interest rates, the availability of debt and equity, and the expected rates of return on alternative investments can affect investment performance. This was clearly evident during the financial crisis that occurred in the latter part of 2008.

Inflation risk is always present because real estate investments are highly illiquid. The expected cash flow from the operation of the real estate investment may lose its purchasing power. A real estate investment may not keep pace with inflation if the leases are not properly structured.

Environmental issues are always present and continuously changing from the risks associated with new contaminants at the property level as well as in the market in which the property is located. Environmental issues may include a nuclear accident, a gasoline spill, or a new product that has been used that has been reclassified as an environmental hazard. In addition, weather conditions can affect the cost of operating the property (e.g., insurance expense for properties along the Gulf Coast).

---

[3] The discount for lack of marketability is built into the discount or capitalization rate, as it is in venture capital rates in business appraisals.

[4] Appraisal Institute, *Advanced Income Capitalization* (Chicago: Appraisal Institute, 2001), 7–3; William B. Brueggeman and Jeffrey D. Fisher, *Real Estate Finance and Investment*, 13th ed. (New York: McGraw-Hill, 2006), 385–387.

Legislative risk is always present in real estate investments at the local, state, and federal level. The *1986 Tax Reform Act* had a negative impact on the demand for real estate by decreasing tax depreciation benefits to investors and, hence, real property values, especially as the 1986 act directly followed the *1981 Tax Reform Act*, which created generous benefits to corporations and real estate investments. Despite the volatility generated by these extreme regulatory shifts, additional uncertainty can arise as local municipalities control zoning, building codes, and other regulations that can impact the cost of development, the operation of the real estate, and the net proceeds from sale of the property, such as a transfer tax.

The cost of capital for real property is affected by the same risk factors that affect the cost of capital for a corporation. It is the degree of risk that varies between the macro- and microeconomic factors for each type of investment that may be different.

DIRECT CAPITALIZATION METHOD

In real property valuation, direct capitalization is defined as:

> A method used to convert an estimate of a single year's income expectancy into an indication of value in one direct step, either by dividing the income estimate by an appropriate rate or by multiplying the income estimate by an appropriate factor.
>
> A capitalization technique that employs capitalization rates and multipliers extracted from sales. Only the first year's income is considered. Yield and value change are implied, but not identified.[5]

Embedded in a market-derived overall rate are the market-oriented assumptions concerning the future income expectations or the performance of similar properties. The market-oriented assumptions result in changes in projected income and value over time. The expected annual compound rate of change in income and value can be added to the overall capitalization rate to indicate the property yield or discount rate. These same variables form the input to the years purchase (YP) method multiplier, primarily employed in the United Kingdom and Europe.

Overall Direct Capitalization

The capitalization formula for business valuation was presented in Chapter 4 of *Cost of Capital: Applications and Examples,* 4th ed. as:

(Formula 9.1)

$$PV = \frac{NCF_1}{c}$$

where: PV = Present value
NCF_1 = Net cash flow expected in first period
c = Capitalization rate

---

[5] Brueggeman and Fisher, *Real Estate Finance and Investment.*

In real property valuation, the direct capitalization formula becomes:

$$PV_p = \frac{I_p}{c_p}$$

where: PV_p = Overall value or present value of the property
I_p = Overall income to the property
c_p = Overall property capitalization rate

Using the reconstructed operating statement shown in Exhibit 9.10 in Appendix 9A, the property's net operating income is $524,052. If the market-supported capitalization rate for a project at stabilized occupancy was 10%, the indicated value is:

$$PV_p = \frac{I_p}{c_p} = \frac{\$524,052}{10\%} = \$524,052, \text{ Rounded } \$524,000$$

Note that I_p is measured before income taxes and depreciation.

This basic formula can be modified to analyze the financial, physical, or legal interests in real property if the appropriate income stream can be estimated. Multipliers are a derivative of the direct capitalization overall rate. The net income multiplier is the reciprocal of the overall rate. This is the construct of the YP method in perpetuity employed in the United Kingdom. Multipliers can be applied to the potential gross income, effective gross income, net operating income, or the equity cash flow. If income factors or multipliers are applied, the formulas generally are used to produce an indication of the property's value. It is important to adequately define the type of income being estimated in order to employ the correct techniques to estimate proper value.

Exhibit 9.1 displays the various relationships. The financial components are established by debt and equity interests; the legal components are established by contracts, such as leases creating the leasehold and leased fee interests; the physical components include land, building, furniture, fixtures, equipment, and other non-fixed property.

Some important terms are:[6]

Leased Fee Estate: An ownership interest held by a landlord with the right of use and occupancy conveyed by lease to others; usually consists of the right to receive rent and the right to repossession at the termination of the lease.

Fee Simple Estate: Absolute ownership unencumbered by any other interest or estate, subject only to the limitations imposed by the governmental powers of taxation, eminent domain, police power, and escheat.

Leasehold Estate: The interest which a tenant or lessee acquires under a lease including rights of use and occupancy for a stated term under certain conditions (e.g., the payment of a premium and/or rent).

---

[6] Appraisal Institute, *The Dictionary of Real Estate Appraisal*, 5th ed. (Chicago: Appraisal Institute, 2010).

EXHIBIT 9.1 Income Components, Rates, Factors, Symbols, and Formulas for Direct Capitalization

Value	Income Streams	Income Factors	Formula
Property value (PV_p) Property value (PV_p) Property value (PV_p)	Potential gross income (PGI) Effective gross income (EGI) Net operating income (NOI, I_p)	Potential gross income multiplier ($PGIM$) Effective gross income multiplier ($EGIM$) Net income multiplier (NIM)* *YP method	$PV_p = PGI \times PGIM$ $PV_p = EGI \times EGIM$ $PV_p = NOI$ or $I_p \times NIM$
Financial Components		Rates	
Equity value (M_e) Mortgage value (M_m)	Equity income (I_e) Mortgage income (I_m)	Equity Dividend Rate or Equity Capitalization Rate (c_e) Mortgage Capitalization Rate (c_m)	$M_e = I_e/c_e$ $M_m = I_m/c_m$
Physical Components			
Land value (M_L) Building value (M_B)	Land income (I_L) Building income (I_B)	Land capitalization rate (c_L) Building capitalization rate (c_B)	$M_L = I_L/c_L$ $M_B = I_B/c_B$
Legal Components			
Leased fee value (M_{LF}) Leasehold value (M_{LH})	Income to the leased fee (I_{LF}) Income to the leasehold (I_{LH})	Leased fee capitalization rate (c_{LF}) Leasehold capitalization rate (c_{LH})	$M_{LF} = I_{LF}/c_{LF}$ $M_{LH} = I_{LH}/c_{LH}$

Note: Different symbols may be used by different authors and organizations, such as the Appraisal Institute.

Based on the preceding information, the property value can be estimated by summing the parts of the components:

(Formula 9.2)

$$PV_p = \text{Equity Value } (M_e) + \text{Mortgage Value } (M_m)$$
$$= \text{Land Value } (M_L) + \text{Building Value } (M_B)$$
$$= \text{Leased Fee Value } (M_{LF}) + \text{Leasehold Value } (M_{LH})$$

If the financial components, the value of the equity positions and the value of the mortgages are added, the overall value of the property is indicated. The financial components may include various equity and debt positions that are entitled to receive specific cash flows from an investment in real property.

The value of the property may also be estimated by adding the physical components, the land and building values, which may be expanded to include fixtures, equipment, and other specific items commonly referred to as personal property. If personal property is included, the indication of value includes more than the real property. This would be typical for a hotel or marina.

In theory, the sum of the parts equals the whole, indicating that the value of the leased fee plus the value of the leasehold provides an indication of the overall value of the property. This is true if the values of all the parts are known, including the value associated with special benefits, such as tax benefits. This is not always the case in the valuation of the legal components of real property rights.

The property yield rate can be estimated at stabilized occupancy if the long-term growth in cash flow and value are stable:

(Formula 9.3)

$$c = k - g$$

where: $c = $ Capitalization rate
$\quad\quad k = $ Discount or yield rate
$\quad\quad g = $ Expected long-term sustainable growth rate in the cash flow available to subject investment

This is quite similar to the formula presented in real estate texts,[7] which is:

(Formula 9.4)

$$c = k - A$$

where: $c = $ Capitalization rate
$\quad\quad k = $ Discount or yield rate
$\quad\quad A = $ Expected change in income and value (adjustment factor)

A represents the relative change in value and is often expressed as Δ_a. To calculate A, a periodic adjustment factor representing the appropriate time period is

---

[7] Charles B. Akerson, *Capitalization Theory and Techniques Study Guide* (Chicago: Appraisal Institute, 1984), 59.

EXHIBIT 9.2 Derivation of Indicated Overall Capitalization Rates from Comparable Sales for Apartments

Sale Number	1	2	3	4	5
Date of sale	10/1/2008	12/14/2008	10/25/2008	1/24/2009	2/25/2009
Sale price	$3,350,000	$3,300,000	$4,100,000	$4,275,000	$3,750,000
Address	4112 Fourth Ave	555 E 21st St	19 Linden Blvd	829 E 9th St	2516 Bedford Ave
City	Johnstown	Johnstown	Johnstown	Johnstown	Johnstown
State	New York	New York	New York	New York	New York
Total units	100	58	53	54	52
Potential gross income	$596,085	$593,688	$559,044	$606,759	$579,996
Vacancy & credit loss	($46,048)	($20,779)	($21,261)	($16,314)	($20,025)
Free rent concessions	($16,806)	($5,937)	($2,689)	($2,952)	($2,800)
Additional income	$5,600	$3,500	$5,590	$4,500	$5,800
Effective gross income	$538,831	$570,472	$540,684	$591,993	$562,971
Operating expenses	($297,931)	($326,528)	($251,570)	($303,379)	($303,379)
Capital reserve	($24,247)	($20,300)	($18,550)	($18,900)	($18,900)
Net operating income	$216,653	$223,644	$270,564	$269,714	$240,692
Indicated overall rate (c_O)	6.47%	6.78%	6.60%	6.31%	6.42%

multiplied by the total change in value. Subscripts are used to indicate the applicable rates to the various components, such as equity and debt.

Exhibit 9.2 illustrates the development of overall rates from competitive property sales of comparable properties. For example, property one sold for $3,350,000. Its net operating income equaled $216,653. Its overall capitalization rate equaled 6.47% ($216,653 ÷ $3,350,000).

Multipliers often can be extracted from transactions of similar properties. If the effective gross income multiplier (EGIM) can be developed from similar properties that are comparable, the overall rate can be established as long as the operating expense ratios (OER) are similar. The OER is defined as the ratio of the total operating expenses to the effective gross income. The basic formula is:

(Formula 9.5)

$$c_p = \frac{(1.00 - OER)}{EGIM}$$

where: $OER =$ Operating expense rates
$EGIM =$ Effective gross income multiplier

Exhibit 9.3 Summarizes the development of EGIMs and the extraction of overall rates from the five comparable sales provided in Exhibit 9.2.

Band of Investment Method

The band of investment method estimates the overall rate based on the weighted average of the financial components of a capital investment. The net operating income can be used only to satisfy the debt and equity requirements. The equity

EXHIBIT 9.3 Derivation of EGIMs and Overall Property Capitalization Rates

Sale Number	1	2	3	4	5
Date of sale	10/1/2008	12/14/2008	10/25/2008	1/24/2009	2/25/2009
Sale price	$3,350,000	$3,300,000	$4,100,000	$4,275,000	$3,750,000
EGIM	6.22	5.78	7.58	7.22	6.66
OER	59.79%	60.80%	49.96%	54.44%	57.25%
Indicated overall rate (c_p)	6.47%	6.78%	6.60%	6.31%	6.42%

capitalization rate (c_e) is a single year's cash flow to the equity position divided by the equity invested. The mortgage capitalization rate (c_m) is the annual debt service (ADS or I_m) divided by the principal amount or face value of the loan (F_d). Generally, the typical loan-to-value ratio (F_d/PV_p) is known as well as the typical terms of the loan. The annual debt service can be calculated based on this information. The equity capitalization rate, also known as the equity dividend rate or cash on cash return, can be extracted from comparable sale information or obtained by interviewing or surveying market participants. The basic formula, which can be modified for various classes of equity and debt, is:

(Formula 9.6)

$$\text{Equity Component} = \lfloor 1 - (F_d/PV_p) \rfloor \times c_e$$
$$\text{Plus} : \text{Debt Component} = (F_d/PV_p) \times c_m$$
$$\text{Equals} : \text{Overall Rate} = c_p$$

where: c_e = Dividend capitalization rate
$1 - (F_d/PV_p)$ = Equity to value ratio
F_d/PV_p = Loan to value ratio
c_m = Mortgage capitalization rate or constant
c_p = Overall property capitalization rate

The band-of-investment method is a term used in real estate appraisal that is analogous to the WACC in business appraisal for the overall cost of capital for the firm (see Chapter 3 of *Cost of Capital: Applications and Examples*, 4th ed.), except that the cost of debt includes repayment of principal and the equity component includes return of—as well as on—equity investment. This approach is most appropriate when the equity dividend capitalization rate can be well supported based on extraction from comparable sales. The preceding sales are utilized to estimate the equity capitalization rate or the cash on cash return in Exhibit 9.4.

Exhibit 9.4 indicates a range in equity dividend capitalization rates between 5.00% and 5.99%. Greatest emphasis would be placed on the most comparable property, taking into consideration the quality, quantity, and the reliability of the data that was analyzed.

EXHIBIT 9.4 Derivation of Equity Dividend Capitalization Rates from Comparable Sales for Apartments

Sale Number	1	2	3	4	5
Date of sale	10/1/2008	12/14/2008	10/25/2008	1/24/2009	2/25/2009
Sale price	$3,350,000	$3,300,000	$4,100,000	$4,275,000	$3,750,000
Loan-to-value ratio	73%	75%	75%	68%	72%
Mortgage amortization term	30	30	30	30	30
Interest rate	5.68%	5.80%	5.70%	5.65%	5.70%
Annual debt service	$169,953	$174,266	$214,168	$201,363	$188,050
Cash flow to equity	$46,700	$49,378	$56,396	$68,351	$52,642
Equity invested	$904,500	$825,000	$1,025,000	$1,368,000	$1,050,000
Indicated c_e	5.16%	5.99%	5.50%	5.00%	5.01%

The indicated overall rate for the subject property can now be developed using Formula 9.6 on these assumptions:

Typical Mortgage Terms

Loan-to-value ratio	70%
Interest rate	5.70%
Amortization period	30 years
Payments	Monthly
Balloon payment	10 years

The formula is as follows:

$$\text{Equity Component} = \lfloor 1 - (F_d/PV_p) \rfloor \times c_e$$
$$\text{Plus} : \text{Debt Component} = (F_d/PV_p) \times c_m$$
$$\text{Equals} : \text{Overall Rate} = c_p$$

Inserting the sample data, we get:

$$\text{Equity Component} = 30\% \times 5.49\% = 1.65\%$$
$$\text{Plus} : \text{Debt Component} = 70\% \times 6.96\% = 4.88\%$$
$$\text{Equals} : \text{Overall Rate} = c_p = 6.53\%$$

The indicated overall rate falls within the range provided by the comparable property sales.

Ellwood Formula

Prior to the introduction of financial calculators and desktop computers, L. W. Ellwood developed a mortgage-equity capitalization formula that takes into account the equity yield rate (k_e) and the mortgage terms, including equity build-up through the amortization of the loan and the anticipated change in value over the investment holding period. Ackerson developed a formulation of Ellwood in a band of investment model as discussed earlier and illustrated below.[8] The Ellwood technique incorporates the aspects and components of periodic cash flow analysis allowing for property appreciation or loss, the effect of leveraging benefits via mortgage amortization and equity build-up and investor expectations in the traditional capitalization valuation format. It also integrates the impact of holding-period expectations, which are often less than perpetuity or mortgage-amortization periods. Despite integrating the dynamic aspects of cash flow analysis with expectations and making them explicit, by retaining its links to traditional capitalization formats, the Ellwood formula is applicable only for level income streams or income streams that change systematically.[9,10] Mathematical factors can be used to convert a systematically changing income pattern to a level annuity.[11,12]

If the required equity yield rate on the investment is known, the property discount rate can be estimated and equates to the IRR or discount rate used in the discounted cash flow model. The equity yield rate is not equal to the equity dividend rate, which represents a cash flow rate. In effect, the difference in the equity yield rate (k_e) and the equity dividend rate (c_e) produces the potential growth in the equity position over the holding period in the calculated form $(k_e - c_e = \Delta_e)$ Assuming a level income stream, the Ellwood formula is:

(Formula 9.7)

$$c_p = \left[(F_d/PV_p) \times c_m\right] + \left[(1 - F_d/PV_p) \times k_e\right] - \left[(F_d/PV_p) \times P \times 1/S_n\right] - \Delta_p 1/S_n$$

where: P = Percentage of principal paid off over the holding period
$1/S_n$ = Sinking fund factor at the equity yield rate (k_e)
Δ_p = Change in value over the holding period in Formula 9.7.

For example, based on market research, this information has been developed and applied within the Ackerson framework of the Ellwood model:

Typical Mortgage and Equity Terms

Loan-to-value ratio	70%
Interest rate	5.70%
Amortization period	30 years
Payments	monthly
Balloon payment	10 years
Typical holding period	10 years
Required equity yield rate	12%
Change in value over the holding period	20%
Type of income stream	Level

---

[8] Ibid.
[9] Terry V. Grissom and Julian Diaz, *Real Estate Valuation: Guide to Investment Strategies*, (New York: John Wiley & Sons, 1991), 284–322.
[10] Roger Gibson, "Ellwood Is Discounted Cash Flow before Taxes," *Appraisal Journal* 54(2) (July 1986): 406–415.
[11] Roger Cannaday and Peter Colwell, "A Unified Field Theory of the Income Approach to Appraisal—Parts 1, 2, and 3," *The Real Estate Appraiser and Analyst* 47(1, 2, 3) (1981), 5–10, 29–43, 25–37.
[12] Grissom & Diaz, ibid.

Applying Formula 9.7 we get:

$$
\begin{aligned}
c_p &= \left[(F_d/PV_p) \times c_m\right] + \left[(1 - F_d/PV_p) \times k_e\right] - \left[(F_d/PV_p) \times P \times 1/S_n\right) - \Delta_p 1/S_n \\
&= (0.70 \times 0.0696) + [(1 - 0.70) \times 0.12] - (0.70 \times 0.15726 \times 0.0570) \\
&\quad - (0.20 \times 0.0570) \\
&= 6.71\%
\end{aligned}
$$

As noted, the Ellwood model was developed as an accrual or stabilized discounted cash flow model prior to the advent of computers and calculators. It improved the capitalization process in the period between 1959 into the 1990s to reflect the financial and economic analysis and procedures used in industry. Technical advances in computers enabled the universal application of discounted cash flow analysis. However, as suggested by the citations noted, the Ellwood technique offers a link between the discounted cash flow analysis and direct capitalization rates developed from the market. Specifically, the generalized expression of Ellwood introduced by Gibbons of the form $(k_p - c_p = \Delta_p)$[13], can be developed using c_ps derived from market transactions with k_ps or IRRs derived from actual investments of specific properties or comparable transactions to derive market or property specific expectations of growth or change $[E(\Delta_p)]$ in value during designated economic periods.

Solvency and Gettel or Underwriter's Method The progression from traditional multiplier and direct capitalization techniques to current applications of discounted cash flow models afforded by technological advances enables the consideration of a central concern of property valuation and the analysis of capital cost calculations. The linkage of capital cost calculations with value, income productivity of assets, and the rates and yield measures produced must also address solvency or the capacity of the asset to cover its operational and capital obligations. These issues are inherent in the capitalization techniques discussed thus far. They can be made explicit in the discounted cash flow model. As with Ellwood, an intermediate procedure was offered by Gettel in 1978.[14] Gettel integrated the debt coverage ratio (DCR) solvency standard used by lenders into the capitalization process and calculation of the cost of capital.

Also called the debt service coverage ratio (DSCR) as well as the DCR, the technique is a solvency risk management measure allowing or requiring a buffer between the debt carried by an asset and the income that the asset produces. The DSCR or DCR equals the ratio of net operating income to the annual debt service. If the net operating income from the asset (NOI) per period is just enough to cover the periodic debt service (DS) of the mortgage, NOI = DS or NOI-DS = 0, then the DCR is 1. That is NOI/DCR = 1. This is a break-even solvency position for the owner of the property. From a risk management perspective, the lender/underwriter will require a DCR $\geq$ 1 (NOI/ADS $\geq$ 1, such as 1.1, 1.2, etc). A DCR of 1.1 or 1.2 infers that the income is 10% to 20% higher than the debt service payments. This protects the

---

[13] James Gibbons, "Equity Yield," *Appraisal Journal* 48(1) (January 1980): 35–44.

[14] Ronald E. Gettel, "Good grief, ANOTHER method of selecting capitalization rates?!" *Appraisal Journal* 46(1) (January 1978): 90–100.

solvency of the property's capacity to pay its debt up to a decline of 10–20% decline in the NOI of the property asset. Using this ratio as an underwriting tool for risk management, lenders establish the maximum ratio that will be permitted in order to provide sufficient cash flow to cover the debt.

For market cost of capital analysis, the focus is on establishing market level or typical DCR measures and policy levels. However, for specific investors or property owners, lenders may lower the debt coverage ratio for certain clients and under specific conditions (e.g., loan guarantees provided by the equity holder). The DSCR method can be well supported in an active mortgage market when properties are generally acquired with debt (as witnessed between 2003 and 2007). It is an appropriate model during stable periods as indicated by Lusht and Zerbst.[15]

One of the strengths of this approach is that all the factors can be derived from market participants. Mortgage terms, including the debt coverage ratio, loan-to-value ratio, amortization period, interest rate, maturity, and number of payments per year, can be obtained from lenders. Published information from the American Council of Life Insurance and other sources can provide additional support for institutional investors.

The basic formula is:

(Formula 9.8)

$$c_p = DSCR \times c_m \times \left(F_d/PV_p\right)$$

where: $DSCR$ = Debt service coverage ratio and all other variables as defined earlier.

Exhibit 9.5 illustrates the development of the overall rate using the DSCR method based on the sale information from Exhibit 9.2.

At times of low capital availability (e.g., 2008–2009 financial crisis) or inflationary periods, it may be necessary to analyze actual transactions and compare the expected return to the equity by abstraction with this method. The market transactions may indicate a higher capital cost and lower value, because the loan to value ratio is lower, requiring more equity at a higher cost.

Using this method, along with the other techniques previously considered, supports the previous overall capitalization rate estimates.

The overall rate can be abstracted from property yield rates if the assumptions concerning the anticipated changes in value can be supported. For example, by interviewing market participants and researching published data, property yield rates

EXHIBIT 9.5 Example Derivation of Overall Property Capitalization Rates from Comparable Sales for Apartments, Debt Service Coverage Ratio (DSCR) Method

Sale Number	1	2	3	4	5
DSCR	1.27	1.28	1.26	1.34	1.28
Mortgage constant	6.95%	7.04%	6.96%	6.93%	6.96%
Loan-to-value ratio	73%	75%	75%	68%	72%
Indicated overall property rate (c_p)	**6.47%**	**6.78%**	**6.60%**	**6.31%**	**6.42%**

[15] Kenneth M. Lusht and Robert H. Zerbst, "Valuing Income Property in an Inflationary Environment," *The Real Estate Appraiser and Analyst* (July–August 1980): 11–17.

were estimated to be approximately 8.25%, and the expected compound rate of change in income and value was reported to be 2.0%.

Applying Formula 9.4, we get the indicated overall property capitalization rate:

$$
\begin{aligned}
c_p &= k - A \\
&= 8.25\% - 2.0\% \\
&= 6.25\%
\end{aligned}
$$

Estimating the Capitalization Rate

Any real property interest that produces an income can be valued by direct capitalization. Several methods are available to estimate the appropriate capitalization rate for the specific real property interest being valued. The approach that is most applicable depends on the quantity, quality, and reliability of the available market information. More than one approach may be necessary to develop the appropriate capitalization rate. Methods to develop a capitalization rate include:

- Interviewing market participants.
- Reviewing published surveys.
- Abstracting from comparable sales.
- Abstracting from multipliers developed from comparable sales.
- Developing by the band of investment method.
- Mortgage-equity analysis.
- Estimating by the DSCR method.
- Abstracting from yield rates.

Potential buyers determine the assumptions that are utilized to estimate the transaction price that is paid for real property interests. Various published surveys are available that indicate the overall rates that are being applied to estimate value. Examples of these sources include:

- RERC *Real Estate Report*.
- RealtyRates.com™ *Quarterly Investor Survey*.
- *Korpacz Real Estate Investor Survey*®.
- American Council of Life Insurance *Quarterly Report* (ACLI).
- National Council of Real Estate Investment Fiduciaries (NCREIF).
- International Property Database (IPD).
- Real Capital Analytics (RCA).

Commercial real estate brokers, such as Cushman & Wakefield, CB Richard Ellis, and Colliers International, also publish surveys. These reports provide broad parameters of the appropriate rates based on the expectations and experience of market participants. They also may not reflect the type of property and associated risks that are being analyzed.

Actual transactions provide a clear indication of the market interaction between buyers and sellers. The "going-in" capitalization rate can be extracted from the sale information. The "going-in" capitalization rate is obtained by dividing a property's expected net operating income for the first year after purchase by the sale price of the property.[16] Recent comparable sales provide excellent support for market-derived capitalization rates if the information has been confirmed by the participants involved in the transaction. The comparable sales must represent a competitive investment with similar risk characteristics to the property that is being evaluated. These factors include:

- Market conditions.
- Buyer and seller motivation.
- Property type.
- Property rights.

The method that should be used to develop the overall rate is based on a number of factors, and the analyst must realize that each approach has certain strengths and weaknesses. More than one method should be employed. The methods applied to develop the overall rate must be supportable and defensible. Market value is estimated based on the actions of typically informed and knowledgeable investors. Therefore, the most appropriate method is the method that reflects the typical actions of the most probable investors. The quantity and quality of data is important to provide support for the indicated overall rate. The information collected must also be reliable.

Overall rates developed from each method can be very persuasive and easy to understand. Confirmation of the information, however, is difficult and time consuming, but it is extremely important because many services that provide this information do not have the expertise to extract the correct information. Thus, erroneous data may be provided. A number of adjustments might be required based on the information that is developed, such as:

- Property rights conveyed.
- Property type.
- Nonrealty components included.
- Near-term capital expenditures.
- Adjustment for rent concessions.
- Rent loss due to absorption.
- Present value adjustment for tenant improvement costs and leasing commissions.
- Adjustment for above- or below-market rents.
- Excess land.

The preceding list is not all-inclusive but may have an impact on the transaction or sale price. It must be remembered that the going-in capitalization rate must be consistent with market expectations and reflect the expected income pattern from the real property investment. If the net income is declining or stable, the capitalization rate will be higher than a similar asset with an increasing

---

[16] Appraisal Institute, *Dictionary of Real Estate Appraisal*, 4th ed. (Chicago: Appraisal Institute, 2002).

income stream, and vice versa. The basic formula for a capitalization rate can be modified by factors to adjust for changing income patterns, such as increasing and decreasing annuities.

Different investors treat capital outlays differently. It is important to understand the calculation that was used to develop the overall rate. Some investors deduct an annualized amount for nonrecurring capital expenditures, leasing commissions, and tenant improvement costs prior to capitalizing the income into value, while others do not. As long as the rates are developed in a similar method, it should not make a difference. The estimated market value is the same if these expenses are handled correctly.

An appraisal is a snapshot in time based on observations at a specified point in time. Any changes in market conditions that occur in the future can impact the future estimates of market value. If mortgage rates increase and the debt coverage ratio changes in the future, the estimated market value of the property can be severely impacted by negative leverage. If market participants do not factor future market expectations into the analysis correctly, any refinancing of the property can have a negative impact of the performance of the property.

Residual Methods

Today the traditional residual methods are rarely employed to develop capitalization rates. In the residual methods, it is assumed that the income is divided among the physical, financial, and legal components. The residual methods include land, building, mortgage, equity, property, leasehold, and leased fee. Current applications of residual methods are used generally for special-purpose properties, leasehold valuation, and feasibility analysis and in built-up areas with limited transactions. These methods should be employed only if the assumptions concerning the known information are supportable and defensible. An expanded version of the land residual method or a special application of a profit residual technique is employed in development valuation analysis. Development valuation is considered a distinct appraisal approach in the United Kingdom and the basis of feasibility analysis internationally. The land residual can also be employed as a useful technique in down markets when limited land sales can be identified. These specific valuation and cost of capital procedures are discussed in detail in several of the cited supportive literature.

If the information concerning one component includes its present value, its capitalization rate, the capitalization rate for the unknown component, and the net operating income for the real property, the residual income for the unknown component can be estimated and capitalized into value. The residual income is the amount that remains after the income required to support the investment in the other components has been met. The values of all the components are now known and can be combined and divided into the net operating income to provide an indication of the appropriate overall rate, which is really a weighted average of the returns required to satisfy the investments in the components.

Exhibit 9.6 summarizes the steps for each of the residual methods including the variables that must be known in order to apply a land, building, mortgage, or equity residual method.

EXHIBIT 9.6   Residual Methods

Land residual	Estimate net operating income	(NOI, I_p)
	Estimate building value	(M_B)
	Derive building capitalization rate	(c_B)
	Calculation of building income	$(c_B \times M_B = I_B)$
	Deduct income to the building	$(I_p - I_B = I_L)$
	Equals residual income to the land	(I_L)
	Derive land capitalization rate	(c_L)
	Estimate land value	$(I_L/c_L = M_L)$
	Plus: building value	$(M_L + M_B = PV_p)$
	Equals property value	(PV_p)
	Calculate overall rate	$(I_p/PV_p = c_p)$
Building residual	Estimate net operating income	(NOI, I_p)
	Estimate land value	(M_L)
	Derive land capitalization rate	(c_L)
	Calculation of land income	$(c_L \times M_L = I_L)$
	Minus: income to the land	$(I_p - I_L = I_B)$
	Equals: residual income to the building	(I_B)
	Derive building capitalization rate	(c_B)
	Estimate building value	$(I_B/c_B = M_B)$
	Plus: land value	$(M_B + M_L = PV_p)$
	Equals: property value	(PV_p)
	Calculate overall rate	$(I_p/PV_p = c_p)$
Mortgage residual	Estimate net operating income	(NOI, I_p)
	Estimate equity value	(M_e)
	Derive equity capitalization rate	(c_e)
	Calculation of equity income	$(c_e \times M_e = I_e)$
	Minus: income to the equity	$(I_p - I_e = I_m)$
	Equals: residual income to the mortgage	(I_m)
	Derive mortgage capitalization rate	(c_m)
	Estimate mortgage value	$(I_m/c_m = M_m)$
	Plus: equity value	$(M_m + M_e = PV_p)$
	Equals: property value	(PV_p)
	Calculate overall rate	$(I_p/PV_p = c_p)$
Equity residual	Estimate net operating income	(NOI, I_p)
	Estimate mortgage value	(M_m)
	Derive mortgage capitalization rate	(c_m)
	Calculation of mortgage income	$(c_m \times M_m = I_m)$
	Minus: income to the mortgage	$(I_p - I_m = I_e)$
	Equals: residual income to the equity	(I_e)
	Derive equity capitalization rate	(c_e)
	Estimate equity value	$(I_m/c_m = M_m)$
	Plus: mortgage value	$(M_e + M_m = PV_p)$
	Equals: property value	(PV_p)
	Calculate overall rate	$(I_p/PV_p = c_p)$

   The residual methods are based on the theory that the overall rate is the weighted average of the returns required to satisfy the investment in the components, in particular land and building. Mortgage-equity analysis and discounted cash flow analysis permit a sophisticated analysis of the various financial components in a transaction.

DISCOUNTED CASH FLOW METHOD

The overall value of the property is equal to the present value of the income stream plus the present value of the reversion of the property at the end of the projection period, which is shown in Formula 9.9:

(Formula 9.9)

$$PV_p = \frac{CF_1}{(1+k_p)} + \frac{CF_2}{(1+k_p)^2} + \frac{CF_3}{(1+k_p)^3} + \cdots \frac{CF_N}{(1+k_p)^n}$$
$$+ \frac{\{(NOI_{n+1}/C_n) - [(NOI_{n+1}/c_n) \times SC\%]\}}{(1+k_p)^n}$$

where:
CF = Cash flow for a specific period
k_p = Overall rate of return or discount rate for property (property yield rate)
NOI_{n+1} = Net operating income in the year following the projection term
c_n = Terminal or residual or going-out capitalization rate in final year n used to capitalize NOI_{n+1}
$SC\%$ = Cost of sale

The last term is the reversion (i.e., proceeds) from the sale of the property.

The net operating income is capitalized by the terminal capitalization rate or the so-called going-out capitalization rate. The terminal capitalization rate is usually, but not always, greater than the going-in capitalization rate. It is reasonable to assume that this rate will be greater because the improvements are older and the economic life may be reduced accordingly. In addition, there is more risk in forecasting the net operating income in the future. Ideally, the building is stabilized at that point in time. If not, adjustments may be required. The costs associated with selling the property must be deducted from the proceeds of sale at the end of the projection period.

The cash flow and the reversion from the sale of the property are developed before deduction for interest, taxes, depreciation, and amortization. These items are considered if the analyst's function is to estimate investment value, not market value.

Semiannual, quarterly, or monthly discounting and capitalization are typically not used in estimating the market value of real property. Application of different time periods can affect the analysis. These conventions were used during the late 1970s when the inflation rate and the returns on money market accounts were quite high in comparison to historical averages. The proper approach would be market oriented, in which case most real property investors expect to receive the cash flows annually. For development properties, a shorter time period often is used.

Different discount rates may be applied to the cash flows and the property reversion. If the real property is leased on a long-term basis to a creditworthy tenant, the risks associated with collecting the cash flow may be low and warrant a discount rate that might be comparable to the yield on the bonds that are available for a similar time period. The future sale price of the property may be quite speculative and will warrant a substantially higher discount rate to reflect the risk differential. The discount rate is also the weighted average of the yields associated with both components of the cash flow, from operations and the sale of the property.

ESTIMATING THE PROPERTY DISCOUNT RATE

The property (overall) rate of return or discount rate (sometimes called property yield rate) is defined as:

> the rate of return on the total capital invested, including both debt and equity. Generally, if the objective is to estimate market value, the real property is analyzed on a before-tax basis. The overall yield rate takes into consideration changes in net income over the investment period and net reversion at the end of the holding period. It is applied to cash flow before debt service.[14]

The property discount rate is forward looking and, therefore, cannot be abstracted from current comparable sales information without confirmation of the assumptions employed by the buyer to determine the price that was paid for an asset. The discount rate incorporates the investor's compensation for the apparent risks, associated with a specific investment as discussed previously.

Not only do potential investors look at the risks previously mentioned, but they will also be cognizant of the yields on alternative investments and historical returns produced by similar investments. Investors often set a "target" or "hurdle" rate representing the minimum acceptable return. Investors are well aware of the cost of debt, which is influenced by inflation expectations and fluctuations in general in the capital markets as well as the supply and demand for debt. The expected property yield rate normally should exceed the weighted average cost of debt.

In theory, the property discount rate should be the sum of its parts: the real rate of return plus the expected inflation rate plus the risk premium (known as the build-up or summation method). The risk premium adjustment includes many previously mentioned factors that are difficult to quantify. Many consider it almost impossible to build up a discount rate by measuring the risks of each component.

The property yield rate can be developed by the band of investment method provided that the assumptions used are market supported. The discount rate is the weighted average return on the financial components, equity, and debt. The basic formula is:

(Formula 9.10)

$$k_p = \left[(F_d/PV_p) \times k_m\right] + \left[(1 - (F_d/PV_p) \times k_e\right]$$

where: k_p = Property yield discount rate

k_m = Mortgage interest rate

k_e = Rate of return on equity investment and all other variables as defined in Formula 9.6.

Based on the information provided earlier, the property discount rate can be estimated by applying Formula 9.10:

Typical Mortgage Terms

Loan-to-value ratio	70%
Interest rate	5.70%
Amortization period	30 years
Payments	Monthly
Balloon payment	10 years
Equity yield rate	14%

The formula is as follows:

Equity Component $= \lfloor (1 - (F_d/PV_p) \times k_e \rfloor$ Plus : Debt Component $= (F_d/PV_p) \times k_m \rfloor$

Equals : Property Yield Discount Rate $= k_p$

Inserting the example data,

we get : Equity Component	$= 30\% \times 14.0\% = 4.20\%$
Plus : Debt Component	$= 70\% \times 5.7\% = 3.99\%$
Equals : Property Discount Rate	$= 8.19\%$

Formula 9.10 can be modified to include multiple equity investments and mortgages, such as mezzanine loans. The total weights must equal 100%. The typical real property investment includes debt, which provides support for this approach to develop the discount rate. The property discount rate provides for the required return on the mortgage and the expected return on the equity invested.

This method provides only an indication of the property discount rate during the first period. During subsequent periods, the equity component is increasing as the mortgage is amortized. The equity investor is seeking the same yield on the additional equity each year. This approach is widely used despite its shortcomings, which become obvious when interest rates are increasing or decreasing and the terms of any refinancing assumptions are changed.

The property discount rate can be estimated from overall capitalization rates if the anticipated changes in income and property value are known. Overall rates can be obtained from recent transactions. If the buyers are interviewed, the assumptions concerning the future changes in value and income can be established. If the income and value are expected to increase at a constant compound rate of growth, the formula to estimate the discount rate is derived from Formula 9.4 repeated here:

(Formula 9.11)

$$k_p = c_p + A$$

where all variables are as defined in Formula 9.4.

The comparable sales indicated a range in capitalization rates between 6.31% and 6.78%, with average of 6.50%. If it is assumed that market participants expect value and income to increase at a compound rate of growth of 2.00% per year, the indicated discount rate from applying Formula 9.11 is:

$$k_p = c_p + A$$
$$= 6.50\% + 2.0\%$$
$$= 8.50\%$$

EXHIBIT 9.7   Example Derivation of Property Discount Rates from Comparable Sales for Apartments

Sale Number	1	2	3	4	5
Date of sale	10/1/2008	12/14/2008	10/25/2008	1/24/2009	2/25/2009
Sale price	$3,350,000	$3,300,000	$4,100,000	$4,275,000	$3,750,000
Net operating income	$216,653	$223,644	$270,564	$269,714	$240,692
Growth in income per year	2.00%	1.50%	1.75%	1.75%	2.25%
Increase in value in five years	2.00%	1.50%	1.75%	1.75%	2.25%
Cash flow per year					
0 (purchase price)	−$3,350,000	−$3,300,000	−$4,100,000	−$4,275,000	−$3,750,000
1	$216,653	$223,644	$270,564	$269,714	$240,692
2	$220,986	$226,999	$275,299	$274,434	$246,108
3	$225,405	$230,404	$280,117	$279,237	$251,645
4	$229,913	$233,860	$285,019	$284,123	$257,307
5 (includes reversion)	$3,933,182	$3,792,405	$4,761,534	$4,951,481	$4,454,388
Inferred property discount rate k_p	8.47%	8.28%	8.35%	8.06%	8.67%

Formula 9.11 can be altered to accommodate level, increasing, or decreasing annuities. The property discount rates and the equity dividend capitalization rates can be extracted from comparable sales if the assumptions developed by the purchaser to prepare the expected cash flows prior to acquisition have been verified. Exhibit 9.7 summarizes the calculations for the comparables provided, based on the assumptions developed by the purchasers.

Based on the information obtained from the market, the indicated range in property discount rates is between 8.06% and 8.67%.

Discount rates can also be estimated by surveying market participants. Published surveys are available summarizing the expectations and experience of investors. For example, Exhibit 9.8 explains information obtained from *Korpacz Real Estate Investor Survey*® published by Pricewaterhouse Coopers.

This survey provides benchmarks that can be used along with other market information to support the discount rate. The discount rates reported can be compared to 10-year U.S. government bonds over time to provide an indication of the risk premium associated with a real estate investment in a central business district (CBD). Clearly, a wide range is indicated, and further research is required to support the final selection of an appropriate discount rate.

Tests of reasonableness should be performed. Yields on alternative investments can be analyzed and compared to the expected yields forecasted over time to indicate the trends that have occurred and test the expected yield. Exhibit 9.9 displays a comparison of 10-year U.S. government bonds and Moody's Baa yields to the expected yields on real estate.

The indicated trend for the expected property discount rates was downward beginning after 2001 through 2007 because the cost of debt kept declining. The real estate and credit markets froze in 2008 because the spreads narrowed and did not compensate for the risk. The spreads have widened and may continue to do so because real estate is experiencing the largest decline in

EXHIBIT 9.8 Discount Rate Survey Data

National Central Business District Office Market
Fourth Quarter 2XXX

	Current Quarter	Last Quarter	Year Ago
DISCOUNT RATE (IRR)[a]			
Range	6.00%–10.00%	6.25%–10.00%	7.00%–10.00%
Average	8.11%	8.34%	8.65%
Change (basis points)	—	−23	−54
OVERALL CAP RATE (OAR)[a]			
Range	4.50%–9.00%	4.50%–9.50%	4.50%–9.50%
Average	6.94%	7.07%	7.35%
Change (basis points)	—	−13	−41
RESIDUAL CAP RATE			
Range	6.00%–10.00%	6.75%–10.00%	7.00%–10.00%
Average	7.78%	7.98%	8.23%
Change (basis points)	—	−20	−45
MARKET RENT CHANGE RATE[b]			
Range	0.00%–7.00%	0.00%–7.00%	−3.00%–5.00%
Average	3.25%	3.04%	2.10%
Change (basis points)	—	+21	+115
EXPENSE CHANGE RATE[b]			
Range	1.50%–4.00%	1.50%–4.00%	1.50%–3.00%
Average	2.98%	2.98%	2.85%
Change (basis points)	—	0	+13

[a]Rate on unleveraged, all-cash transactions.
[b]Initial rate of change.
Note: Basis point equals hundredth of a percent.

EXHIBIT 9.9 Comparison of Bond Yields to Real Estate Discount Rates

	In Percent									
	2000	2001	2002	2003	2004	2005	2006	2007	2008	2009
Survey—real estate discount rate	11.41	11.49	11.09	10.22	9.56	8.97	8.30	8.17	8.32	10.06
Federal funds rate	6.24	3.89	1.67	1.13	1.35	3.22	4.97	5.02	1.92	0.12
Bank prime loan	9.23	6.91	4.67	4.12	4.34	6.19	7.96	8.05	5.09	3.25
Treasury constant maturities	6.03	5.02	4.61	4.01	4.27	4.29	4.8	4.63	3.66	3.43
Conventional mortgages	8.06	6.97	6.54	5.82	5.84	5.86	6.41	6.34	6.04	4.92
Moody's seasoned Baa	8.37	7.95	7.80	6.76	6.39	6.06	6.48	6.48	7.44	6.38
Real estate vs. Moody's Baa spread	3.04	3.54	3.29	3.46	3.17	2.91	1.82	1.69	0.88	3.68
Real estate vs. treasury spread	5.38	6.47	6.48	6.21	5.29	4.68	3.50	3.54	4.66	6.63

property values since the Great Depression. The spreads between Moody's Baa and the 10-year constant maturity bonds was relatively constant between 2000 and 2003, at which time the spreads began to narrow. There appears to be very little correlation with the federal funds rate and the bank prime rate. There is always a risk forecasting into the future based on the historical trends, but the basic parameters are established for supporting a discount rate or a range for the expected property discount rate. The general implication of the narrowing spread of the debt and equity asset classes is a disjointing of property and capital markets. This will alter the risk exposures impacting property investment and the associated cost of capital.

Other tests of reasonableness may include:

- In theory, the going-in capitalization rate plus the annual compound rate of change in income over the projection period should be quite comparable to the property discount rate.
- Generally, the rate of return on equity or equity yield rate should be higher than the property discount rate and the mortgage interest rate.
- The equity yield rate should be higher than the equity dividend rate if it is anticipated that income and value will increase over time. Just the opposite is being observed in some (2009) markets.

What other steps can one take in today's distressed markets with few sales? Active/potential sellers and buyers have always been the source of current market discount rates and cap rates. If anyone knows the discount rates and cap rates that match the current market conditions, it is those who are actively seeking to dispose or invest in commercial real estate. Even if some potential sales do not close, the potential sellers understand their discount rates and cap rates and potential buyers know theirs.

One procedure is to go back to the comparable market sales of one to two years prior to the valuation, contact the sellers and buyers, and get their input on how they would price the same transaction on the valuation date using the same property, the same historical performance characteristics, existing historical leases, and so forth, but taking account of the different economy, leasing, and capital markets conditions. This is a highly targeted investor survey.[17]

SUMMARY

This chapter introduced the methods and applications utilized to develop the appropriate returns on individual, income-producing, real property investments. The basic concepts are quite similar to business valuation concepts, but additional factors must be considered in the analysis of income-producing real estate and the consideration of external and explicit financial funding.

---

[17] Peter F, Korpacz, "The Illusive Cap Rate," *Valuation Briefs*, RICS Americas, (January 14, 2010).

Valuing Real Property

INTRODUCTION

This appendix focuses on the income associated with the ownership of real property rights. This is different from the income and cost of capital that might be earned by a business enterprise operating on the property, such as a marina, hotel, fitness club, or restaurant. The value of real estate is the value of the real property or the rights inherent in the ownership of real estate or realty and is based on its capacity to support and house economic activities. In essence, real property value is a function of its physical attributes, rights inherent in the ownership of real estate or realty, and its economic location. The property's comparative ability to generate income becomes its basis of value.

Definitions of terms such as *net income* and *cash flow* differ from those used previously in this text. Chapter 9 and this appendix define these terms for real estate valuation; they should not be confused with the terms as defined in financial textbooks.

STEPS IN ESTIMATING REAL PROPERTY VALUE

Value is the present worth of future benefits. The future benefits derived from the ownership of real estate include the cash flow from the real estate plus the proceeds of the resale of the real property, which is often referred to as the reversion or residual. The reversion is defined as "a lump-sum benefit that an investor receives or expects to receive at the termination of an investment which is often called reversionary benefit."[18] Five basic steps are required to estimate value by the income approach:

1. Determine the projection (holding or capital recovery) period.
2. Estimate the future cash flows over the projection (holding or capital recovery) period.
3. Estimate the reversionary or residual value of the property.
4. Select an appropriate yield or discount rate.
5. Discount the expected cash flows, including the reversionary or residual interest to present value.

DETERMINING THE PROJECTION (CAPITAL RECOVERY OR HOLDING) PERIOD

Real property generally is not held indefinitely. Historically, the projection (often called holding or capital recovery period) was tied to the economic life or useful life of the property. Real estate was used in the operation of a business, such as a manufacturing operation. The improvements were considered to be a wasting asset and the investment in the improvements had to be recovered over its useful life and replaced. Subsequently, the income tax laws influenced the maximum holding period due to depreciation benefits. The typical holding period was between 7 and 10 years. The Tax Reform Act of 1986 reduced the tax-sheltered benefits associated with owning real estate, which has affected the holding period.

The most typical projection period applied in the discounted cash flow analysis is 10 years. A different holding period may be justified when it is supported by the actions of market participants. A knowledgeable investor must take into consideration a number of factors in determining the projection or holding period. These factors include, but are not limited to:

- Type of property.
- Tax considerations, such as depreciation benefits.
- Mortgage rollovers.
- Lease rollovers.
- Required capital investment.
- Changes in the conditions of the real estate market.
- Leverage.
- Risk management.
- Portfolio management.
- Changes in corporate strategy.

Typical investors want to maximize their return. Investors may consider selling when the after-tax marginal rate of return falls below the after-tax marginal rate of return that can be achieved on alternative investments.[19] However, if the after-tax

---

[18] Appraisal Institute, *The Dictionary of Real Estate Appraisal*, 4th ed. (Chicago: Appraisal Institute, 2002).

[19] William B. Brueggeman and Jeffrey D. Fisher, *Real Estate Finance and Investment*, 13th ed. (New York: McGraw-Hill, 2006), 420.

marginal rate of return on the investment can be improved by refinancing and/or remodeling, the decision to sell might be postponed. It is also extremely important to consider the level of occupancy at the expiration of the projection period, which can impact the return on the investment, because occupancy will impact the resale price of the property. Ideally, the projected cash flow that provides the basis for the calculation of the resale proceeds should be at or near stabilized occupancy levels. If a projection period other than 10 years is used, the property yield rates may be affected by the shortening or lengthening of the holding period because the market expectations vary with the time period. Regardless, the projection period selected should always be market oriented and reflect the actions of informed buyers and sellers.

Measuring Income

In the valuation of a real estate investment, it is important to develop a reconstructed income and expense statement at stabilized occupancy.

The net operating income (NOI, I_P) is defined as follows: "the actual or anticipated net income that remains after all operating expenses are deducted from effective gross income, but before mortgage debt service and book depreciation are deducted; [it] may be calculated before or after deducting replacement reserves."[20] It is imperative to develop or reconstruct the operating statement based on the methodology utilized by the most probable purchasers. In property analysis, net operating income can be considered as a measure of the productive capacity of the property. The net operating income provides for the payment of the capital structure (debt and equity) and tax implications in the cash flow analysis.

The analysis may be based on one of these:

- Projected income during the first year of ownership.
- Trailing 12 months' income.
- Actual income at the time of the analysis.
- Projected income over the holding or projection period.
- Stabilized income.

The income estimate must reflect the interest being analyzed. If the analyst is estimating the market value of the leased fee interest, the landlord/owner's position, the contract income should be analyzed. This would be the income based on the actual leases in effect as of the date of the analysis and typically reflects the projected income to be received. If the fee simple interest is being analyzed, the appropriate market rents should be considered.

Most often, typical investors forecast the stabilized income that is expected to be received over the next year. The stabilized income is achieved when the real property is at its long-term stabilized occupancy. Stabilized occupancy is defined as

> occupancy at that point in time when abnormalities in supply and demand or any additional transitory conditions cease to exist and the existing conditions are those expected to continue over the economic life of the property;

---

[20] Appraisal Institute, *Dictionary of Real Estate Appraisal.*

the average long-term occupancy that an income-producing real estate project is expected to achieve under competent management after exposure for leasing in the open market for a reasonable period of time at terms and conditions comparable to competitive offerings.[21]

The degree to which the actual net operating income is above or below the stabilized net operating income is one factor that affects the risk associated with a particular real estate investment, and also provides the basis for analyzing comparable sales.[22] This difference or spread is not just essential to reflecting the actual performance of the property relative to its competitive market position, but also when considered within the context of time can be used to address cyclical fluctuations and the time frame required for the value, as is, to converge with the long-term stabilized value. This reconstructed operating statement generally differs from the pro forma cash accounting income statement developed by accountants but is consistent with the accrual accounting procedures they use when annualizing multiperiod capital expenditures and longer-term outlays within a cash flow projection.

Potential gross income includes all income from contractual obligations associated with leases, estimated market rent from vacant space, escalation income, and reimbursements for operating expenses and from services provided to the tenants. A market-derived potential gross income multiplier can be applied to the potential gross income to provide an indication of value.

Effective gross income is defined as the potential gross income minus vacancy and credit loss. Vacancy and credit loss must be market oriented and can be obtained from published surveys, comparable properties, and/or interviews with market participants. Vacancy should include frictional (temporary) vacancy due to lease rollovers, structural (permanent) vacancy, and income loss until stabilized occupancy is achieved. Credit loss is the risk of default by the tenant. Lease concessions must also be considered. A market-derived effective gross income multiplier can be applied to the effective gross income to provide an indication of value.

Operating expenses must be deducted from the effective gross income to estimate the net operating income before capital expenses, such as tenant improvement costs and leasing commissions, annual debt service including interest and amortization, and income taxes. Operating expenses may be classified as fixed, variable, and reserves for replacement. Fixed expenses, such as real estate taxes, do not vary with occupancy. Variable expenses change with occupancy and must be adjusted to reflect actual occupancy over the projection period. Reserves for replacement or a reserve allowance may be necessary in order to replace items that may wear out and are estimated based on the useful life of the item. Building items that may require replacement include carpeting, painting, appliances, roof covering, and parking areas.

The reconstructed income and expense statement should conform to the standard chart of accounts for that particular asset and be based on an analysis of historical income and expenses at the property, a review of comparable properties, and industry standards. Because the valuation must require a focus on the valuation of

---

[21] Ibid.

[22] Richard D. Wincott, "A Primer on Comparable Sale Confirmation," *Appraisal Journal* (July 2002): 274–282.

real estate as a function of its performance capacity, items that are commonly considered in the valuation of a business or an operating enterprise are excluded in the calculation of net operating income. Examples would include book depreciation, income taxes, capital contributions, mortgage interest and amortization, leasing commissions, tenant improvement costs, and major capital expenditures that are nonrecurring.

The total operating expenses are deducted from the effective gross income to indicate the net operating income. As noted with the exclusions just discussed, only property-related expenses are included. A market-derived net income multiplier can be applied to the net operating income to provide an indication of value. This multiplier approach is the preferred or traditional approach used in the United Kingdom. The approach is called the years purchase (YP) technique and is directly equivalent to the net income multiplier method used in the United States, when the valuation period assumes perpetuity. The YP as practiced can also incorporate different time periods into the rate and multiplier calculation. The incorporation of divergent time frames into the factor calculation allows the net income multiplier to incorporate yield capitalization analysis.

Sample Reconstructed Operating Statement

Exhibit 9.10 provides an example of a typical reconstructed operating income and expense statement for a project at stabilized occupancy.

The exhibit provides the basis for analyzing the costs and risks associated with an investment in the real property. The net operating income can be capitalized into value to provide an indication of value at stabilized occupancy by direct capitalization.

If the property is not operating at stabilized occupancy, adjustments might be required to provide an indication of value as is. Adjustments for near-term capital expenditures, such as tenant improvement costs, leasing commissions, and other capital costs, can affect market value. Other adjustments may include the present value of tenant concessions,[23] present value of rent loss until stabilization, present value of below-market rents, and present value of excess rents. In addition, the property discount rate has to reflect the market-perceived risks.

The annual debt service must be deducted to provide the pretax cash flow to the equity position. Usually, a pretax cash flow projection is developed. Pretax cash flow (CF_{pt}) is defined as "the portion of net operating income that remains after total mortgage debt service is paid but before ordinary income tax on operations is deducted; also called before-tax cash flow or equity dividend."[24]

PROJECTING CASH FLOWS

The overall value of the property is equal to the present value of the income stream plus the present value of the reversion of the property at the end of the projection period, as shown in Formula 9.9 repeated here:

---

[23] Tenant concessions are defined as an inducement for a tenant to lease space, usually in the form of free rent, additional tenant improvements, moving costs, and so on.

[24] Appraisal Institute, *Dictionary of Real Estate Appraisal.*

EXHIBIT 9.10 Example Reconstructed Operating Income and Expense Statement

Potential Gross Income		
Leased units	$890,500	
Vacant units	71,000	
Expense reimbursements	48,000	
Concession income	19,000	
Other revenue	10,000	
Total potential gross revenue less vacancy and credit loss		$1,038,500
Vacancy & turnover (5%)	$ 51,925	
Credit loss (1.00%)	$ 10,385	
Total vacancy and credit loss		$ 62,310
Effective gross income		$ 976,190
Operating Expenses		
Fixed Expenses		
Real estate taxes	$195,238	
insurance	20,000	
Total fixed expenses		$215,238
Variable Expenses		
General & administrative	$ 78,000	
Management fees	$ 49,000	
Repairs and maintenance	44,000	
Utilities	34,000	
Trash removal	4,000	
Security	5,900	
Total variable expenses		$214,900
Replacement Allowance		
Carpeting	$ 7,000	
Roof cover	15,000	
Total replacement allowance		$ 22,000
Total operating expenses		$ 452,138
Stabilized net operating income		$ 524,052

Source: MacCrate Associates LLC.

(Formula 9A.1)

$$PV_p = \frac{CF_1}{(1+k_p)} + \frac{CF_2}{(1+k_p)^2} + \frac{CF_3}{(1+k_p)^3} + \cdots \frac{CF_n}{(1+k_p)^n}$$
$$+ \frac{\{(NOI_{n+1}/c_n) - [(NOI_{n+1}/c_n) \times SC\%]\}}{(1+k_p)^n}$$

where: CF = Cash flow for a specific period
       k_p = Property discount rate or overall rate of return on property
  NOI_{n+1} = Net operating income in the year following the projection term
      c_n = Terminal or residual or going-out capitalization rate
    $SC\%$ = Cost of sale

The actual cash flows, including the first year's cash flow, may differ from the stabilized reconstructed income and expense statement presented previously.

Investors usually acquire title to real property subject to the existing leases and other contractual obligations. The projected cash flow takes into consideration the actual contractual obligations specified in the leases. The lease obligations may differ substantially from the market standards that were used to reconstruct the income and operating expense statement.

Projected vacancy is based on lease rollovers and structural vacancy. It will differ from the long-term equilibrium or stabilized vacancy and may vary over the projection period. Credit loss will be based on the creditworthiness of the tenants in place.

The operating expenses must take into account the changes in occupancy over the projection period. Certain expenses are sensitive to changes in occupancy. Other expenses may have to be adjusted to reflect the expected inflation over the projection period.

Certain expenditures are deducted from the net operating income to estimate the cash flow to the property before debt service and income taxes. The cash flow is the actual cash flow to the investors after deducting tenant improvement costs, leasing commissions, capital expenditures, and other nonrecurring anticipated expenses from the net operating income. These deductions may vary over the projection period.

Typically, real estate investors prepare a cash flow including the resale of the property, which usually provides for the recapture of the investment plus a return on the investment if there is an increase in value. The resale price is referred to as the reversion or residual. The future sale price generally is based on capitalizing the income in the first year following the projection period. The rationale is that, at the end of the projection period, the typical buyer will estimate the future benefits that will be received after that point in time.

The net operating income is capitalized by the terminal capitalization rate or the going-out capitalization rate. The terminal capitalization rate is usually, but not always, greater than the going-in capitalization rate. It is reasonable to assume that this rate will be greater because the improvements are older and the economic life may be reduced accordingly. In addition, there is more risk in forecasting the net operating income in the future. Ideally, the building is stabilized at that point in time. If not, adjustments may be required. The costs associated with selling the property must be deducted from the proceeds of sale at the end of the projection period.

The cash flow and the reversion from the sale of the property are developed before deduction for interest, taxes, depreciation, and amortization. These items are considered if the analysts' function is to estimate investment value, not market value.

SUMMARY

The preceding can be summarized into seven steps:

> **Step 1:** Analyze and compare the historical and current income and expenses with competing properties and published industry sources to establish the basis for the forecast going forward.

Step 2: Estimate market rent and the typical lease terms for the different types of tenant spaces, including the probability of lease renewal and downtime between leases.

Step 3: Forecast the potential income over the projection period from all sources, including leased space, vacant space, lease escalations, and expense reimbursements, with a proper allowance for vacancy and credit loss.

Step 4: Forecast and deduct the projected property operating expenses, tenant improvement costs, leasing commissions, and other anticipated capital expenditures from the projected income.

Step 5: Determine the most probable projection period.

Step 6: Estimate the terminal capitalization rate and calculate the projected property reversion.

Step 7: Select the appropriate discount rate and discount the cash flows including the reversion to present value.

The analysis must reflect the expected benefits that would be anticipated by market participants. The most common error is to utilize assumptions to forecast the income and expenses that do not reflect the actions of informed buyers and sellers. The values produced by direct capitalization and the discounted cash flow analysis should be identical with perfect information.

CHAPTER 10

Cost of Capital of Real Estate Entities

Terry V. Grissom
and James R. MacCrate

INTRODUCTION

In Chapter 9, we discussed the development of the cost of capital for direct real property investments. An equity investment in real estate can also be made indirectly by purchasing shares of a company or partnership holding real property interests. In this chapter, we discuss the development and application of the cost of capital for real estate entities that own real property interests to produce income. This chapter

We would like to thank Ronald Donohue, PhD, of The Hoyt Advisory Group and Maureen D. McGoldrick of MDM Appraisals for their assistance. Also, the authors wish to thank Nicholas Arens and William Susott of Duff & Phelps for assistance in assembling certain data and calculations. We appreciate their assistance.

139

is an introduction to the subject; it is not intended to cover all the issues that an analyst might encounter in the process of estimating the cost of capital for real estate entities.

Private real estate markets are often characterized by high transaction costs, illiquidity, lack of diversification and information that is difficult to obtain concerning income, expenses, and cost of capital. These characteristics are often present in open and closed-end real estate funds and privately held real estate entities with just another layer of management that may bring expertise that may increase the value of closely held real estate entities.

This chapter focuses on real estate business enterprises that derive a large percentage of their income from tangible, real property interests, such as equity real estate investment trusts (REITs), partnerships, and real estate operating and/or investment companies. A business enterprise or entity is defined as "any commercial, industrial, service, or investment entity pursuing an economic activity."[1] Because real estate entities are going concerns, or businesses that manage, buy, and sell real estate assets, an investment in this type of company is very different from a single direct investment in real property. Real estate entities can be very complex enterprises that require a thorough knowledge of the various factors that can impact the cost of capital.

The cost of capital for real estate entities can vary substantially based on the characteristics of the entity that owns and controls the real property interest. REITs represent a large portion of the real estate market for which public information is available and can be analyzed. Therefore, we concentrate on REITs in this chapter. It should be pointed out that that real estate entities collect rental revenues which is the primary source of their net operating income. Therefore, the real estate assets and revenue are connected to the local real estate market similar to direct real estate investments. Shares in publicly traded REITs are more liquid and are influenced by the interaction of the supply and demand, the capital market condition, the general market sentiment, and the herd mentality of market participants. This can result in share prices that exceed or fall below the net asset value of the underlying real estate holdings.[2]

DEFINITION OF A REAL ESTATE ENTITY

A real estate entity can be defined as any person including, but not limited to, any partnership, corporation, limited liability company, trust, other entity, or multi-tiered entity that exists or acts substantially for the purpose of holding, directly or indirectly, title to or beneficial interest in real property. The value of a real estate entity includes many components, such as land, buildings, furniture, fixtures and equipment, intangible assets, and the business operation. Real estate related entities enable both direct and indirect ownership interest in real property assets. Real

---

[1] International Valuation Standards Committee, *International Valuation Standards*, 8th ed. (London: International Valuation Standards Committee, 2007), 338.

[2] Jaroslaw Morawski, Heinz Rehkugler, and Roland Füss, "The Nature of Listed Real Estate Companies—Property or Equity Market?" *Financial Markets and Portfolio Management* (March 2008): 101–126.

properties can be owned by individuals, partnerships, corporations, or trusts. These investment vehicles may take many different forms, such as REITs.

A REIT is defined as "a company dedicated to owning and, in most cases, operating income-producing real estate, such as apartments, shopping centers, offices, and warehouses. Some REITs also engage in financing real estate."[3] There can be publicly traded REITs, non–exchange-traded REITs, or private REITs. The characteristics of each type of entity are different with regard to regulatory oversight, liquidity, transaction costs, management, investor control, corporate governance, and taxation.

Real estate entities are extremely diverse, but can be described in general as being engaged in the ownership, acquisition, redevelopment, investment in, and management of income-producing real property. As mentioned, ownership interests may be held in direct investments or indirect investments in joint ventures, syndications, and partnerships. These entities may own real properties that are operated as an ongoing business or held for investment or development or used in various activities. Property interests may be owned through controlled or uncontrolled investments and business enterprises.

Many real estate entities specialize in a specific line of business, such as development of new properties, redevelopment of existing properties, or the operation of existing properties. They may concentrate on buying and selling properties or they may focus on operating properties, or some combination thereof. Some real estate entities are highly specialized in certain areas, such as developing single-family residential communities, marinas, cell towers, prisons, golf courses, timberland, restaurants, theaters, or automobile dealerships, while other real estate entities engage in a broader range of real estate activities. The risk varies by specialization, as well as other factors, such as management, property type, geography, the trends in the economy, and so forth.

It is quite common for real estate entities to specialize by property type, such as industrial, office, multifamily residential, hotel, and health-care related facilities. Other entities diversify across property types or engage in mixed-use development. Real estate entities may also choose to concentrate their investments and activities in specific markets or geographic regions. As a general rule, they acquire and/or develop real property assets to operate as part of a business enterprise that generates income to distribute to shareholders or partners. The extent to which real estate entities are concentrated in a specific property sector or geography can impact their cost of capital as concentration results in nonsystematic risk and can impact credit ratings and required yield spreads.

Real estate entities typically are categorized in the investment community by asset class, type of business, property type, and/or geographical location. These categorizations are useful in helping to identify peer group for analytic and valuation purposes. For example, the National Association of Real Estate Investment Trusts (NAREIT) categorizes REITs as equity REITs, mortgage REITs, and hybrid equity-mortgage REITs. Equity REITs generally own and operate income-producing real estate. Mortgage REITs invest in loans secured by residential or commercial real

---

[3] National Association of Real Estate Investment Trusts, Glossary, www.investinreits.com/learn/glossary.cfm.

estate or in residential or commercial mortgage-backed securities. Hybrid REITs typically own some combination of equity and debt interest in real estate.

Equity REITs represent the majority of the REIT market, as measured by number of companies and market capitalization. Equity REITs can be further segmented into specific real estate subsectors, such as:

- Residential properties.
- Office properties.
- Shopping centers and malls.
- Storage centers.
- Industrial parks and warehouses.
- Lodging facilities, including hotels, motels, and resorts.
- Health care facilities.
- Special use properties.

Real estate companies are going-concern businesses that produce income and may be involved in many different activities, including asset or portfolio management, leasing, property development, and tenant services. Like other types of businesses, real estate entities may be able to create intangible value or franchise value. Franchise value pertains to the ability of management to create value over and above the current value of the existing real property portfolio.[4] Conversely, it is possible to have negative franchise value, in which a collection of assets under management's control is less valuable than current value of the existing real estate portfolio.

The type of properties, the geographical location of the assets, and the business enterprise may influence the cost of capital because the perceived risks vary. The total return on an investment in a real estate entity comes from the distribution of income from the operation of the real property portfolio or development through dividend payments plus long-term appreciation if the real property assets or the entity is sold. Return of capital from depreciation, which is not consistent with accounting standards, represents a significant portion of the distributions from any REIT and other real estate entities. In addition, REITs have refinanced their portfolios to provide sufficient capital to make the required distribution. In 2009 only, IRS guidance provided REITs with the opportunity to payout the required 90% in cash or stock. Revenue Procedure 2009-15 permitted listed REITs to offer shareholders elective stock dividends, which are dividends paid in a mixture of cash and stock (with at least 10 percent of the total distribution being offered as cash), to satisfy their dividend distribution requirements through 2009.[5] Real estate entities other than REITs do not have this characteristic.

Real estate entities are operating businesses that include tangible assets (i.e., real estate) as well as intangible assets, such as the quality and expertise of management and tenant relationships. As a result, the value of a real estate entity can be more or less than the value of the underlying real estate owned by the entity. Equity shares in real estate entities that trade at a premium above the net value of the real estate may have a franchise value. The structure of the entity may create intangible value.

---

[4] Mike Kirby, Warner Griswold, and Jon Fosheim, "Pricing REIT Stocks," REIT University: Core Cirriculum, April 4, 2007.

[5] 26 CFR 601.601: Rules and regulations. (Also: Part I, §§ 301, 305). Part III Administrative, Procedural, and Miscellaneous, http://www.irs.gov/pub/irs-drop/rp-09-15.pdf.

Although the net value of the real estate assets is important, other factors influence share price as well.[6]

Structure of Real Estate Entities

The legal structure of the entity may have an impact on its value and cost of capital. The entity may be a special-purpose entity,[7] sole proprietorship, corporation, partnership, S corporation, or a limited liability company. Pass-through entities that pay no entity level income taxes but pass the earnings through to the investors may have certain tax advantages. For example, REITs and real estate limited partnerships/master limited partnerships make direct investments in real property assets. These entities are pass-through entities. The legal requirements for these entities are quite specific. REITs are required by law to distribute at least 90% of their taxable income to their shareholders each year.[8] REITs are not taxed at the entity level; rather the tax obligation is passed through to the individual investors. REIT dividend distributions typically are derived from various sources. For income tax purposes, distributions usually are allocated to ordinary income, capital gains, and return of capital. The return of capital distribution is not currently taxed, but the investor's cost basis in the investment is reduced by the amount of the distribution. The reduced income tax basis affects the capital gain for tax purposes at the time that the investment is sold. In 2008, 53% of the annual dividends paid by REITs qualified as ordinary taxable income, 10% qualified as return of capital, and 37% qualified as long-term capital gains.[9]

In a partnership, the partnership agreements dictate the timing, character, and amount of distributions to the various partnership interests. Often, distributions and their timing are controlled by the general partner. A real estate partnership may pass through gains, profits, and losses to different investors. Partnerships also have a limited life, whereas corporations generally have an unlimited life.

Many real estate operating companies, public and closely held companies, are not structured as REITs or partnerships and are taxed at the entity level. But they do not face the distribution requirement of a REIT and may have greater opportunity to reinvest earnings. They also do not face the same restrictions on the type of real estate business they conduct.[10]

---

[6] Richard Marchitelli and James R. MacCrate, "REITs and the Private Market: Are Comparisons Meaningful?" *Real Estate Issues* (August 1996): 7–10.

[7] Jalal Soroosh and Jack T. Ciesielski, "Accounting for Special Purpose Entities Revised: FASB Interpretation 46(R)," *CPA Journal Online*, April 5, 2007, describes a special-purpose entity "as an off–balance-sheet entity that is created by a party (the transferor or the sponsor) by transferring assets to another party (the SPE) to carry out a specific purpose, activity, or series of transactions. Such entities have no purpose other than the transactions for which they are created. The legal form for these entities may be a limited partnership, a limited liability company, a trust, or a corporation."

[8] In 2009, the IRS has issued guidance that indicates that the distributions may be in the form of cash or stock in certain instances.

[9] *REITWatch*, October 2009, 2.

[10] *Barron's* refers to a publicly traded real estate company that has opted out of the tax status afforded REITs as a real estate operating company (REOC). Jack P. Friedman, Jack C. Harris, and J. Bruce Lindeman, *Dictionary of Real Estate Terms* (Hauppauge, NY: Barron's Educational Series, 2004).

Other factors to consider in analyzing different ownership structures include different income tax rates, quality and cost of management, diversification, and availability of financing, as well as control and marketability issues. These factors may also have a direct impact on the cost of capital.

Capital Structure

The real estate capital markets are considered to be segmented into four quadrants:

1. Private equity.
2. Public equity.
3. Private debt.
4. Public debt.

The 4-Quadrant model as initially specified by Hudson-Wilson and Fisher allows for property investments and real estate related entities to be placed in combinations of equity ownerships priced in private or public markets or debt positions also occurring in private or public market contexts. This is illustrated in Exhibit 10.1.

Though all sectors have grown since the *ERISA Act of 1974*, public markets have grown in importance throughout the 1990s into the 2000s through the availability of funds from the commercial mortgage-backed securities (CMBS) market, mutual funds, growth in real estate investment trusts, and other investment vehicles. The private and public markets offer alternative investment opportunities to investors in both the debt and equity sectors. The differing combinations of entity ownership positions associated with the different market sectors that they operate creates diverse risk conditions and exposures that result in different pricing issues that

EXHIBIT 10.1   Four Quadrant Model

	Private	Public
Equity	Direct Commingled funds Participating interests Private syndications Limited partnerships Co-investment Development	Equity in operating Cos. Equity REITs Real estate securities Public syndications RE mutual funds Derivatives Development
Debt	Development Mortgages Mortgage pools Synthetic leases Commingled funds Participating marketing Co-investment	Development Mortgage REITs Hybrid REITs Senior/junior positions CMOs Synthetic leases CMBSs

Source: Terry Grissom, "The Four Quadrant Paradigm: Corporate Real Estate Finance," *Journal of Corporate Real Estate of NACORE* (1998).

influence the value and valuation procedures appropriate for different entity structures. These factors may affect the worth of property associated with divergent entity structures, in effect redefining the asset classes that can be linked to underlying real estate assets. In this context, Oppenheimer and Grissom identify REITs not only as real estate entities but argue that they can be denoted as distinct asset classes.[11] This allows for not only an entity specific valuation procedure, but also alters the approach needed to measure the underlying property collateral. Failure to note a link between the entity structure and its effect on the underlying property collateral value has contributed to the mispricing of risk. This mispricing contributed to the 2008-2010 financial crisis in part as a function of underwriting asset collateralized security and debt interests. The mispricing supposed the elimination of risk rather than a reduction or shifting of financial risk that still was not uncoupled from the total risk of the underlying asset collateral.

Prior to the 2008-2010 financial crisis, capital was readily available for debt and equity positions in real estate entities and the cost of capital was relatively inexpensive in comparison to the long-term average cost of capital available for real estate investors. That began to change in 2007 with the collapse of the residential market followed by the commercial real estate market. The lack of credit and declining asset values have forced publicly traded REITs to raise equity capital in the public markets. While the declines in interest rates during 2003-2008 lowered the overall weighted average cost of capital, increases in interest rates can have the reverse impact.[12] The capital may include equity in the form of common stock or preferred stock, partnership interests, convertible debt, secured or unsecured debt, participation loans, and so on. In early 2009, larger well capitalized companies were again able to go to the public markets and raise cash in various forms, while the private market had difficulty restructuring debt.

The debt component may be short, intermediate, or long term, secured or unsecured, fixed or variable rate with different ratings, all of which impact the cost of debt and the perceived risk of the equity and debt components. In many cases, real estate entities have substantial lines of credit, which typically are used as short-term sources of floating rate debt capital until they can be replaced with longer-term debt or equity capital. Other forms of short-term debt may include mezzanine or bridge loans, construction loans, and revolving credit. Debt may or may not be secured. When it is secured, it may be secured by one property or cross-collateralized with multiple properties. For example, Exhibit 10.2 summarizes the total percentages of debt and equity for public REITs as of the end of year and fourth quarter of 2008.

The amount of leverage is extremely important. The greater the leverage, the greater the risk to the equity and debt positions raising required rates of return and the resulting cost of capital. The total debt liability of public REITs increased from the end of the second quarter of 2006 to the end of 2008. The level of debt liability increased over the observed 18 month period from 61.5% to 66.61%. This 5.11% increase may include debt measures of 4.5% mezzanine loans that converted to permanent long term loans.

---

[11] Peter Oppenheimer and Terry Grissom, "Frequency Space Correlation Between REITs and Capital Market Indices," *The Journal of Real Estate Research* 12 (1999): 1.

[12] Pacific Security Capital, "The Impact of Rising Interest Rates on Commercial Real Estate," *Pacific Security Capital, IRETO Report* (May/June 2005).

EXHIBIT 10.2   Percentage of Debt and Equity for Public REITs—4th Quarter/End of Year 2008

Total Liabilities plus Shareholder Equity	
Secured debt	35.83%
Unsecured debt	21.27%
Other liabilities	9.51%
Total liabilities	66.61%
Preferred equity	1.37%
Common equity	32.02%
Total liabilities plus shareholder equity	100.00%

Source: Morningstar EnCorr Analyzer and compiled by Duff & Phelps, LLC.

This observed exposure to financial risk exposures in association with a market downturn requires increased risk management concerns on the part of investors and valuers. Interest rate swaps have become more common to protect against changing interest rates. Interest rate risk is extremely important for a long-term investor in real property interests when debt is placed for shorter periods at variable rates. Some other factors that may affect the cost of debt and associated risk exposure include:

- Position in the real estate and economic cycle.
- Quality and credit rating of tenants.
- Property types and quality held by the entity.
- Total leverage.
- Debt coverage ratio and individual property loan-to-value ratios.
- Bond rating.
- Loan terms.
- Amount of variable rate debt.
- Maturity date of the debt.
- Management reputation and track record.

Public REITs generally have a lower percentage of debt relative to real estate asset value compared to the private property markets, which can have debt to real estate asset value ratios in excess of 70%. This reduced leverage in the public markets lowers the cost of equity capital in comparison to the private markets because of reduced financial risk. During periods of rising interest rates, property values may decline, and this can negatively impact the value of real estate entities. During periods of declining interest rates, similar to the years 2003 to 2006, property values often rise. In turn, the value of real estate entities increases with the collateral value of underlying assets.

Real property transaction prices are influenced by the availability and the flow of funds into the real estate financial markets. After 2001, the construction and real estate markets were positively affected by low interest rates and debt coverage ratios and high loan to value ratios, and the availability of loans from all sources dollars including the explosive growth of the CMBS market.

EXHIBIT 10.3 Changes in REIT Market Capitalization

End of Year	No. of REITs	Market Capitalization (000,000s)	Percent Change	Average Capitalization (000,000s)	Percent Change	Dividend Yield—10 Year Difference
2000	158.0	$134,431		$851		
2001	151.0	$147,092	9.42%	$974	14.49%	2.05%
2002	149.0	$151,272	2.84%	$1,015	4.22%	3.02%
2003	144.0	$204,800	35.39%	$1,422	40.09%	1.25%
2004	153.0	$275,291	34.42%	$1,799	26.51%	0.43%
2005	152.0	$301,491	9.52%	$1,983	10.24%	0.10%
2006	138.0	$400,741	32.92%	$2,904	46.40%	−0.87%
2007	118.0	$288,695	−27.96%	$2,447	−15.75%	0.81%
2008	113.0	$176,238	−38.95%	$1,560	−36.25%	5.14%

Real estate assets were acquired by REITs and new real estate investment companies cropped up in the environment. In September 2002, the dividend yield on REITs was 7.01% while 10 year government treasuries were only yielding 3.97%. This made REITs quite attractive investments and money flowed in. The following chart, Exhibit 10.3, clearly shows the trend in the market capitalization of REITs as the spreads between the REIT dividend yield and the 10 year government bond narrowed.

During the financial crisis that began in 2008, the lack of liquidity adversely affected REITs. REITs that had substantial debt that was maturing were raising cash by issuing more shares, selling assets, or refinancing existing debt. Some companies found it difficult to raise capital and the value of the equity has been reduced or the companies were forced to declare bankruptcy, such as General Growth Properties.

Since the spreads widened during late 2009, the total REIT market capitalization has increased in 2009 but the damage has been done because the demand for real estate is falling, rents are declining, vacancy rates are increasing and capital is difficult to raise except for large, well capitalized public REITs. If the debt was marked to market in 2010, the total capitalization including debt would be significantly less than book values.

Real estate companies tend to be highly leveraged because debt is used to acquire assets during expansion. According to the National Association of Real Estate Investment Trusts (NAREIT), the debt ratio for equity REITs as a group stood at 65.3% at the end of March 2009. By October 2009, the debt ratio had fallen to 49% as REITs raised cash as the financial markets loosened up and market capitalization improved. This shows a significant decline from the 66.61% level of debt at the end of 2008 noted in Exhibit 10.2. Overall this illustrates a needed decline in capital market and financial risk exposures that need to be matched with fundamental property concerns yet to be addressed in the context of endogenous and external events that may impact the cyclical performance of property.

Direct and Indirect Real Estate Cycles

The recent trends and observations since 2002 to present of real estate entities discussed above can be linked to the long-term trends and nature of the performance of

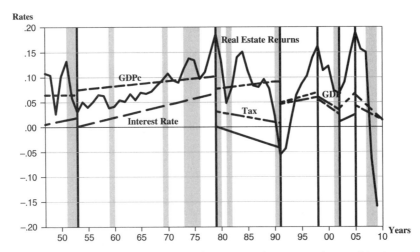

EXHIBIT 10.4   Changes in Real Property Performance Relative to Referenced Business Cycles in Association with GDP, Interest, and Income Tax Effect Trends
Source: Grissom; BERI University of Ulster, Grissom & DeLisle (1999), Ibbotson and Associates, NCREIF and various economic measures.

direct real property and associated entities. The cyclical patterns observed over time assist in identifying the structural associations of investment performance. The changing nature of asset structural relations enables insights into the changing nature of investment performance that is confusing to current decision makers.

Cyclical impacts affecting property related assets and the general economy are a function of real estate market cycles and subject to external impacts. The availability and cost of capital for real estate entities varies substantially over time. The variance may be the result of capital market factors or market for real estate space factors. On the market space side, the availability and cost of capital varies during the real estate cycle. When the supply of space exceeds the demand, the availability of capital decreases and the cost of capital may increase. This requires an understanding of real capital impacts on the performance of real estate markets as well as financial implications.[13]

Exhibit 10.4 illustrates the association of the changes in Gross Domestic Product (GDP) and interest rates as proxies of real and financial capital with the performance of direct investment in property.

The shaded vertical bars illustrate the referenced or officially designated recessions defined by the National Bureau of Economic Research (NBER). The darker vertical lines are inflection points characterizing the real estate return that can be associated with trends developed and observed in measures of changes in gross national/domestic product or annualized real capital change and the proxy risk-free interest rate.

---

[13] Terry Grissom and James DeLisle, "A Multiple Index Analysis of Real Estate Cycles and Structural Change," *The Journal of Real Estate Research* (July 1, 1999) extended by Grissom, "Direct and Indirect Property Performance Cycles and Structural Shifts in Economic Regimes," Built Environment Research Institute and Property Research Institute Working paper, 2009.

Though volatility is observed, the frequency of the change does not define points of major structural change. Inflection points identify key structural shifts where the underlying relationships among the variables change. Property inflection points are not consistent with cyclical phases in all cases, especially recessions. The shifts in the trends specify distinct economic changes that differentiate diverging structural changes in the general economy. These inflection points should correspond with the timing of major shifts in beta measures.

The first point illustrates an economic change at the end of the 1953 recession. The observed relationships after 1954 continue into 1979 with the next economic change preceding the impact of the 1980 recession.

The underlying economic relationship from 1954 to 1979 forms the accepted basis of the traditional understanding of the investment in property. This traditional understanding established over a 30 year period is that property investment is diversified from stocks and bonds specifically in relation to real estate's potential as an inflation hedge and strongly associated with a stable income and capital gain (call on future appreciation). These associations change after the economic efforts of the Reagan administration to deal with the stagflation that defined the end of the 1954–1979 period.

It is interesting to note that this economic phase is consistent with the Fama and French findings discussed in Chapter 12 of *Cost of Capital: Applications and Examples*, 4th ed. on the validity of beta as a significant pricing variable. The period of the slopes in Exhibit 10.4 is consistent with the phases of beta's significance. The shift occurring after 1979 until the present is consistent with the weakening beta studies previously cited. This consistency of findings by different techniques can be observed by the behavior in performance between changes in underlying economic conditions and the increased frequency of the changes after 1979 coincidental with declining frequency of recessionary periods.

The underlying economic shifts observed in Exhibit 10.4 are supported by Exhibit 10.5. Exhibit 10.5 depicts various external events occurring over time as consistent with the cyclical volatility of the property returns and the referenced recession cycles. As Exhibit 10.5 illustrates, the consistent and creeping inflation evolving into stagflation during 1954–1979 created the disintermediation (e.g., deposits leaving banks and savings and loans for money market accounts without fixed interest rates) defining the 1973–1975 recession and an orchestrated oil crisis by OPEC that lead to major financial, banking and monetary reform.

The impact of the inflationary pressures influenced reorganization of the capital structure as represented by the *ERISA Act of 1974* which allowed pension funds and retirement entities to invest in real estate to hedge against inflation affects. Also flexible exchange rates and the dismissal of the gold standard resulting from the repeal of the Bretton Woods Agreement by the Nixon Administration to offset inflationary pressures magnified the very inflation effects it sought to combat.

This inspired major banking and institutional deregulation during the 1980–1990 period which is characterized as a period of declining asset performance except for the stimulating effect of the *1981 Tax Act*. This enabled an accelerated depreciation recapture that initiated after tax investment incentives. These tax incentives created increases in the supply of real estate not supported by market demand. The *1986 Tax Act*, initiated to correct the oversupply generated by the effects of the 1981 act, was the first *ex post facto* legal application of tax law noted in the

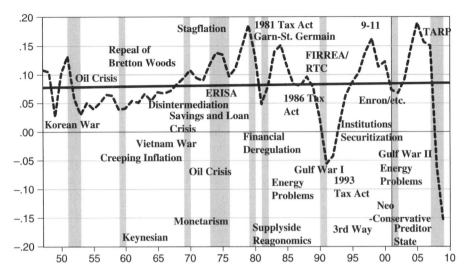

EXHIBIT 10.5 Events Associated with Property Return Cycles and Trends
Source: Grissom, BERI University of Ulster and Grissom Group.

United States in which no phase-out of decisions made under the prior law was allowed. This resulted in significant increases in foreclosure and bankruptcies resulting in major institutional failures, corruption and redistributions of wealth that contributed to the recession of 1990–1991. This recession coincided with the first Gulf War and another oil crisis. The events illustrated in Exhibit 10.5 support the observation depicted in Exhibit 10.4 that the underlying economic relationships from 1980–1990 is the only period of the 62 years studied where the impact of tax effects is significant in explaining property cycle periods. Negative returns were realized by the general index (not just individual properties). This is significant in that more accelerated depreciation rates were allowed prior to the Reagan administration, but the increased impact of deregulation and shift to institutional funding and involvement was unique to the period.

The deregulation initiated in the 1980–90 period offered benefits during the recovery of 1991 through 1998. However, it should be noted that during this period financial growth exceeded real economic growth. This is depicted in Exhibit 10.4 where the slope of the interest rate trend line is above the real growth trend line of the change in the GDP. This inverted relationship occurs only for this period in the 60–70 years covered in the study. In this context it can be noted that regulation during this period supported and favored securitized funding for property and enhanced institutional involvement in property asset markets. This environment has encouraged indirect real estate entities, securitization and institutional investment activity. The influence on structure during this period is a direct extension of the *1986 Tax Act's* creation of real estate mortgage investment conduits (REMIC) and the *ERISA Act of 1974* influence on the *1993 Tax Act*. The 1993 regulation enabled greater institutional participation in property market investment via REITs.

The increased impact of institutional financing on property capital markets is illustrated in the downturn observed in 1998. The 1998 downturn is associated with the Asian capital crisis and capital market fluctuation that correlate with real estate returns, but did not register an impact on the general economy as a defined recession. Observation of Exhibit 10.5 does reflect a declining trend in the periodic change in the GDP trend line following the 1998 inflection point. The trend from 1998 with its emphasis on financial activities and events leads into the 2001 recession. This decline is observed prior to September 11, 2001 ("9-11") and the real economic impact that occurred to commercial real estate.

Though cyclical upturns have occurred over time, the long-term trend has been a decline in both the rate of growth and the interest rate since 1981with convergence expected in 2010 or 2011. This can be observed in the trend of the GDP and interest rate trend lines since 1991. The reduction in the spread between the real rate and the risk-free financial rate coincides with increased volatility in real estate performance. The structural shift in property performance coinciding with financial and monetary deregulation is characterized by increased frequency and magnitude in the volatility of real estate returns.

This increased volatility is further characterized by an increase in the inflection points of the return series over shorter periods of time. The structural changes in property performance occur even though fewer economic cycles/recessions are observed. Two general patterns of structural change are observed. One is that structural shifts and differences have become more frequent over shorter times. The other change is that the magnitude of volatility has increased in both negative and positive shifts.

This increased magnitude of volatility of direct property investment relative to the general economy is observed in a study by Grissom, Lim and DeLisle and has key implications to the performance of real estate related entity investment.[14] This is illustrated in Exhibit 10.6. This exhibit shows the cyclical pattern of REIT performance to direct real estate returns from 1972 to the present. Even though the volatility in underlying changes affecting property has accelerated since 1979 as shown in the previous exhibits, Exhibit 10.6 shows that real estate return volatility pales in relation to the volatility of REITs and by extension other related securities performance for the same period. Over the study period covered by NAREIT data, REIT volatility was greatest in the early 1970s, encompassed by the mortgage REIT failures during this period. The major growth in REITs that followed from the latter 1970s into the 1990s occurred with equity REITs (EREITs). Mortgage and hybrid REIT performance improved along with EREITs after the enactment of the *1993 Tax Act* enabling the increased participation of institutional investors in indirect real estate entities.

In addition to the greater magnitude of REITs volatility relative to property performance, it can be observed that REIT returns tend to increase during recessionary periods. This is counter to the performance observed for direct real estate returns which tend to decline during down markets.

Despite the differences observed in the direction of change observed between real estate entity securities and direct property assets, the relationship between the associations of the asset classes is central to valuation and measurement. The shifts in property asset performance and risk (total and market sensitivity) over time is

---

[14] Terry Grissom, Jasmine Lim, and James DeLisle, "Arbitrage and Cyclical Effects in the Performance of UK and USA Property Markets," Built Environment Research Institute and Property Research Institute Working paper, 2009.

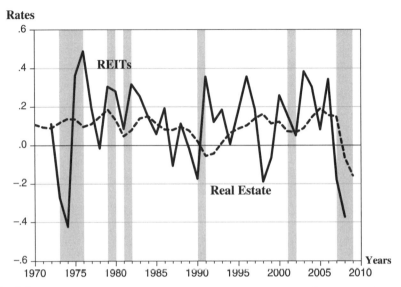

EXHIBIT 10.6   Comparison of REIT (Indirect Real Estate) Entities and Direct Real Estate Returns
Source: Grissom BERI University of Ulster 2009.

essential to the understanding of the income flows, funds from operation (FFO) and dividend returns associated with real estate related entities, especially all forms of REITs. Despite this high correlation of FFO with the performance of the underlying real estate, REIT dividends and property performance, the total return performance of the entities is more highly correlated with securities and equity markets. These divergent correlations are noted in several studies.[15] The consistency in REIT dividends is illustrated in Exhibit 10.7 and can be linked to the direct property total return measures prior to the down turn.

The impact of possible economic cyclical factors leading to reduced earnings, negatively impacting financial ratios, occurred during 2007-2009. When the market deteriorates, rents decline, and the cost of capital for a real estate entity may increase as it becomes more difficult to attract equity and debt investors. Equity investors require a higher return during a crisis as indicated in Exhibit 10.7 which shows the dividend yield from July 2008 through May 2009, with a spike in the dividend yield during the start of the financial crisis.

Consideration of Exhibit 10.7 shows that the REIT dividend yield rose sharply with the collapse of Lehman Brothers in September 2008 reaching a peak at 10.08% in February 2009. It declined as funds moved back into REITs and it became clear that capital was available to larger, well capitalized REITs.

As the real estate market cycle changes, real estate investment companies may have an opportunity to increase earnings and improve their financial ratios as rents increase and the cost of debt continues to decline. When earnings increase, financial ratios improve and capital flow increases into real estate investments, which

---

[15] See footnote 12 and David Hartzell, "REIT Performance Measures," Solomon Research Paper, 1989.

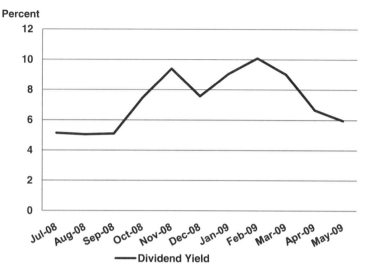

Percent

EXHIBIT 10.7 REIT Dividend Yield Changes during the 2008–2009 Crisis

generally lowers the cost of capital. What is interesting to note is that even though the demand for funds increases, the cost of funds decreases during the cycle as capital flows into real estate.

The implications of the difference in property income and REIT performance and the comparison of total asset performance shows that the impact of market cycles on capital flows and the perception of risk in the marketplace and the premium that investors demand for investing in real estate can increase or decline as a function of the supply and demand for space. This will eventually affect the long term pricing of REITs, especially in down markets. Alternatively, as the cyclical analysis indicates, in the short run capital market expectations can significantly influence the share prices of real estate entities. As such the components comprising real estate related securities entities can impact the nature, pattern and construct delineating the cash flow, earning measures and valuation of property related entities. The difference in short term and long term effects and the tendency for REIT returns to rise during down markets in part explains the counter-intuitive pattern of dividend yields observed in Exhibit 10.7.

The implication of these cyclical relationships of both property assets, real estate entity performance as they relate to the effect of changes in trends of key explanatory cash flow variables supports the time varying nature of beta measures. This requires an investigation of cash flow analysis and the need to apply beta adjustment techniques discussed in Chapter 10 of *Cost of Capital: Applications and Examples*, 4th ed., to the valuation of real estate entities.

MEASURING NET CASH FLOW FOR REAL ESTATE ENTITIES

The estimated net cash flow projection must be matched to the economic income or benefit received. The cash flow may represent net earnings, funds from operations

(FFO), adjusted funds from operations (AFFO), or dividends. The typical equity investor is primarily concerned with the current dividend, the expected future growth in dividends, and expectations with regard to changes in FFO that impact the price and/or capitalization rate accorded to the entity. While FFO is strictly defined by NAREIT, AFFO is not defined by NAREIT and is generally used by analysts and companies. The AFFO may be defined differently by different companies.

FFO or AFFO represent a starting point in the analysis because these estimates are not always developed consistently. An economic unit of comparison similar to FFO or AFFO provides a common point of reference for analyzing guideline companies. The ratio of FFO or AFFO to price is a very common ratio that security analysts use to compare alternative REIT investment opportunities. The dividend yield is also an important consideration. This is discussed in more detail in Appendix 10A.

The cash flow may be affected by other investments, refinancing, and properties developed, renovated, or sold. A land residual analysis may be required to estimate the market value of excess land that has been acquired for development. In the analysis of real estate entities, the prospective cash flow estimate is extremely complicated but is critical to the analysis.

VALUATION OF REAL ESTATE ENTITIES

Even though International Financial Reporting Standards (IFRS) require fair value accounting for income-producing investment property, companies in the United States do not need to comply with these standards at this time. Most real estate entities do not routinely report estimates for real estate asset values, making it necessary for investors and analysts to develop their own estimates. The two primary approaches to value a real estate entity are the underlying asset approach and the capitalization of income.

Net income in accordance with generally accepted accounting principles (GAAP), net cash flow, FFO, AFFO, and other economic benefits that can be capitalized into value are not always consistently developed by Wall Street analysts and brokers, accountants, appraisers, and other financial professionals for publicly traded companies. Further complicating the analysis of publicly traded companies is the fact that these same professionals do not apply the same valuation methods or techniques. Many buy-side and sell-side analysts disagree on the proper methodology.[16] Many of the firms and individuals who provide information to assist in the valuation of real estate entities do not have sufficient information to properly develop the economic benefits that are derived from the ownership of equity interests in real estate operating companies. Many also have biases that are created by conflicts of interest with regard to the net cash flow projections.

The market value of invested capital developed by either approach may have to be adjusted for other assets that might include development projects, land held for future development or sale, other investments in unconsolidated subsidiaries, cash

---

[16] Ross Nussbaum, "Cash Flow Matters—DCF Analysis Suggests REITs Are Fairly Valued . . . For Now," New York University, The REIT Center, February 21, 2006. Available at http://www.scps.nyu.edu/export/sites/scps/areas-of-study/real-estate/reit-center/news-and-commentary/2006.02-ross-nussbaum-cash-flow-matters.pdf.

and cash equivalents, and miscellaneous items. The value of properties under development typically reflects the historical cost as opposed to market value and must be adjusted to reflect potential increases or decreases in value. The value of land held for development or being developed may be estimated based on projected net cash flows and current investor yield requirements for the related assets. Land that is held for development or sale may be similarly valued based on a land residual technique. Any remaining assets, as well as liabilities and preferred stock, usually are included in net asset value (NAV) at historical cost net book value but should be valued separately.

Underlying Assets Approach

The underlying assets approach can be summarized as shown in Exhibit 10.8.

Applying this approach to real estate companies requires a very thorough description of all of the real property assets, liabilities, other investments, equity, service activities, and any unrelated businesses because each asset requires a separate valuation. The real property interests would be valued based on the methodology indicated in Chapter 9.

Real estate companies often own a collection of real property interests that can be valued separately based on private market transactions. The steps applied to estimate the net asset value vary from firm to firm, which makes a direct comparison of information difficult. The assets should be "marked-to-market" by independent analysis. The net operating income developed by each asset can be estimated and divided by a market-derived capitalization rate to provide an indication of the value of each asset as if it was not part of the entity. In addition, a discounted cash flow analysis can be prepared on each asset. The indicated values can be reconciled to estimate the value of the asset. Some analysts apply one capitalization rate to the entire portfolio and/or roll up and discount the cash flows of all the properties. The indicated asset values by the income approach can be compared to the estimated depreciated cost of the improvements plus the site value and comparable sales in the competitive markets.

The property debt should be marked-to-market and can be deducted to provide an indication of the individual net asset value. The net asset values are added to provide an indication of the net asset value contributed by the real property interest.

EXHIBIT 10.8   Underlying Assets Approach

	Net working capital (typically at book value)
+	Fair market value of fixed assets (as appraised)
+	Other assets (typically at book value)
+	Intangible asset value (as appraised)
	Indicated value of assets
−	Long-term debt (at market value, though book value is often used as a proxy)
−	Preferred capital (at market value or redemption value, if redeemable)
−	Other liabilities
	Indicated value of 100% of common stock

Adjustments are required for other business investments, such as management contracts, joint ventures, partnership investments, cash and cash equivalents, land held for development, and existing developments. Other liabilities must be marked to market and deducted to provide an indication of the net asset value. Wall Street analysts estimate net asset value in order to determine the premium or discount paid for an equity interest for comparison purposes.

One of the major problems associated with this approach is that the net asset values are not readily available. As stated, REITs and other publicly traded companies are not required to provide the net asset values. Most analysts do not have access to the required property level detail to estimate value. Because it is extremely time consuming and difficult to secure individual property data on hundreds of assets, some analysts have chosen to develop a weighted average capitalization rate for all of an entity's assets and business operations and apply it to net operating income to estimate value. In addition, some firms take shortcuts in the valuation process and do it incorrectly.

Example of Underlying Assets Approach   For example, one Wall Street analyst stated:

> NAV is an estimate of the private market value of a company's assets.
>
> We first calculate a forward 12-month cash net operating income (NOI) based on annualized GAAP net operating income (real estate NOI plus joint venture NOI, adjusted for partial contributions, less lease termination fees that were included in rental revenue), multiplied by an appropriate growth rate for the next 12 months, minus annualized straight-line rents. In cases in which joint-venture NOI was not available, we used the equity in unconsolidated subsidiaries reported on the company's income statement. (Please note that, for malls and outlets, a rolling four quarters of NOI is used to account for the quarterly fluctuations in revenue driven by percentage rents.) The resultant cash NOI is then capitalized at an appropriate cap rate (adjusted for the quality of a company's assets) to determine the implied value of owned properties. We next add capitalized management fee/service income (using a 20% cap rate, in most cases), cash and cash equivalents, construction in progress at 110% of cost, any land being held for development, other assets, and, in some cases, the value of tax-exempt debt in order to arrive at the gross market value of a company's assets. To determine the net market value of assets, we then subtract all of the company's liabilities and obligations, including preferred stock at liquidation value and the REIT's share of joint venture debt.
>
> Our NAV estimates make no adjustment for any mark-to-market on company debt.

The forward-looking cash flow should take into consideration numerous factors, such as lease rollovers, rent escalations, expense escalations, and more, all of which impact the expected growth rate. In addition, the firm stated that "*construction in progress at 110% of cost, any land being held for development*" was added. The value of construction projects fluctuates during the real estate cycle, and it varies in each real estate market based on demand and supply factors. The value can easily be less than or more than its cost. In the current environment (2009-2010), land values have declined across all markets and land is considered quite speculative. This makes it difficult to compare the net asset values of different companies. The net asset values are reliable only if they are properly developed. The firm stated that the net asset value represented the private market valuation. It may or may not. In order to correctly value a REIT, all assets and debt should be marked to market. While that is not the case in the United States, it would be the case in Europe and the United Kingdom.

The former analysis does not properly address any gains or losses on sales that may have occurred. During the regular course of business, the portfolio of assets may be continuously adjusted for acquisitions, dispositions, and development of properties. Gains on sale may be normal for some entities that are properly managed to create and maintain value over time through increasing the net cash flow. In addition, there are instances, due to poor management and other factors, where the value of the equity is less than the net asset value. Investors may be willing to pay a price for the equity in excess of its net asset value for the intangible value created by good management, access to capital markets, and the ability of management to increase earnings, FFO, and AFFO through internal or external growth.[17] This must be captured in a proper analysis.

Income Capitalization Approach

The income capitalization approach can be implemented through either a direct capitalization or a discounted cash flow method. This approach tends to best reflect the actions of investors when analyzing a real estate entity. Most investors are interested in a company's cash flow and the company's ability to increase cash flow and distribute it to the investors through dividends.

Overall Direct Capitalization In Chapter 4 of *Cost of Capital: Applications and Examples,* 4th ed., the direct capitalization formula for business valuation was presented. We repeat it here as Formula 10.1:

(Formula 10.1)

$$PV = \frac{NCF_1}{c}$$

where: PV = Present value
   NCF_1 = Net cash flow expected in the first period immediately following the valuation date
   c = Capitalization rate

The value of a real estate entity can be estimated using the same formula, but it is extremely important to correctly estimate the net cash flow. If we are valuing equity cash flows, the debt servicing and preferred capital servicing must be deducted from the net cash flow before debt and adjusted for any tax implications.

---

[17] Ralph L. Block, *Investing in REITs—Real Estate Investment Trusts* (New York: Bloomberg Press, 2006).

In Chapter 9, direct capitalization of individual real property assets was accomplished through the basic formula net operating income divided by an appropriate capitalization rate equals value. The basic valuation formula is similar, but the income to be capitalized is not the income to the real property but the income to the real estate entity.

It is possible to separate income stream from owning and operating real estate and other types of income and capitalize each at different rates that are appropriate for the risks inherent in each type of income stream. These values can then be added together to estimate total entity value.

If you choose to develop an overall capitalization rate and apply it to the entity's total net cash flow, that overall capitalization rate must reflect the risks associated with investing in the entity, a business enterprise. It must be based on the weighted average returns required by the market to satisfy the debt and equity capital providers to the real estate entity. This is achieved under UK valuation procedures, for example using the profit approach, which segments the valuation approach into the income directly associated with the property and that linked to the operating enterprise.

Estimating the Capitalization Rate   Capitalization rates can be developed for any of these measures of economic income:

- *Gross* or net revenues.
- Gross income
- Net operating income.
- Net income before tax.
- Net income after tax.
- Operating cash flow.
- Net cash flows to equity or invested capital.
- Funds from operations (FFO).
- Adjusted funds from operations (AFFO).
- Earnings before interest and taxes (EBIT).
- Earnings before interest, taxes, depreciation and amortization (EBITDA).
- Dividends.

Net cash flow, FFO, AFFO, and dividends are the typical measures of economic income that are utilized to develop an indication of value. The overall capitalization rate must be developed in a consistent manner to be relevant and produce a supportable and defensible indication of value. The most appropriate income measure is the net cash flow available to satisfy equity and debt investors. Net cash flow to equity includes the payments made to mortgage holders (reduction in principal balances) as these repayments benefit equity.

An implied capitalization rate can be estimated by dividing a real estate company's net operating income (NOI) by its total market capitalization. Adjustments may be required for non–real estate assets and liabilities and other factors. Capitalization rates developed by dividing the FFO, AFFO, or dividends by the equity or shareholder value provide a better measure of economic performance for real estate entities than a similar ratio using GAAP income. The reciprocal of the FFO or AFFO multiple can provide an indication of the equity capitalization rate based on that measure of economic income of the entity.

Observed market capitalization rates can be analyzed based on market capitalization (market value of equity), property type, projected growth in net cash flow, geographical location, leverage, and other factors that may impact investor expectations developed from guideline companies.

The indicated FFO capitalization rate can then be applied to the subject company to provide an indication of the value of the equity. A similar procedure can be used by substituting the actual dividend payment made to the equity investors. The inferred yield will be higher because the dividend payment would likely be lower than FFO.

One must be careful using capitalization rates developed from REITs or publicly traded real estate entities as a proxy for closely held corporations. The daily share price of REITs may reflect various stock market factors, such as short-term traders entering or exiting a sector or company in response to news or economic factors, as compared to investments made by long term-investors. In addition, the desire to achieve high growth in earnings by publicly traded companies may not match up well with the long-term buy-and-hold strategy employed by private, closely held real estate entities. Finally, public markets are influenced by behavioral finance which is based on emotions and not necessarily logic.[18] Long-term investors are interested in the long-term net asset value because the real property interests generally represent a large percentage of the company's assets. However, long-term investors also consider:

- Quality of management.
- Quality of assets.
- Quality of tenants.
- Entity structure.
- Potential growth in earnings.
- Anticipated total return: net cash flow plus capital appreciation.
- Potential growth in dividend.
- Current dividend yield.
- Dividend-paying capacity.
- Debt coverage ratios.
- Leverage ratios.
- Current real estate market cycle.
- Corporate governance.

Capitalization rates similar to earnings-to-price ratios can be developed from guideline companies. However, earnings-to-price ratios are based on earnings after deducting depreciation and other items, while FFO and AFFO are calculated prior to deducting for depreciation and adjusted for other items. For publicly traded REITs, it is quite common for analysts to compare the share price to the dividend yield, FFO, or AFFO per share. It is preferable to use AFFO if the information is readily available and has been developed correctly. Many security firms have developed an estimate for AFFO based on their individual adjusted cash flows and models. As a result, inconsistencies exist in the calculation of AFFO and the respective

---

[18] See Behavioral Finance Research Initiative at Yale University, http://icf.som.yale.edu/research/behav_finance.shtml.

capitalization rates. In addition, public companies are not required to provide a calculation for AFFO and may choose not to do so to avoid potential litigation.

Public financial information and ratios can be obtained from several companies, such as Bloomberg, Green Street Advisors, SNL Financial, and Standard & Poor's (S&P) *CapitalIQ*. Many brokerage companies and stock analysts rely on these databases for real estate company information. The financial information in this chapter is based on data from S&P and Bloomberg. The information can be exported to a spreadsheet for additional analysis. Market data, including guideline companies, can also be assembled quickly into a spreadsheet. One major underlying assumption is that the databases are built on correct and unbiased information from reliable sources with no conflicts of interest.

This basic direct capitalization formula can be modified to analyze the financial or economic interest in the entity if the appropriate income streams can be estimated, as previously discussed. The analysis can be based on comparable or guideline companies. Exhibit 10.9 summarizes the value measures of several guideline companies providing indications of capitalization rates and other information that can be used for comparative purposes. The items listed are not inclusive of all comparative measures, but provide the basis for evaluating a public or private entity with additional information that may be deemed appropriate by the analyst.

EXHIBIT 10.9   Comparative Ratio Analysis for Guideline REITs

Company	1	2	3	4	5
Market capitalization of equity ($ in millions)	$8,112	$4,671	$2,057	$1,878	$1,669
Premium/discount to net asset value (5)	92.61	109.13	77.49	69.38	65.99
Dividend payout/FFO (%)	81.25	87.13	63.99	85.31	87.94
FFO/share growth 2007–2008 (%)	−14.43	−12.33	4.33	−16.59	−22.14
Historical five year average dividend yield (%)	4.87	3.76	3.80	6.00	5.52
Current dividend yield (%)	6.47	5.89	5.32	9.57	8.93
Forward annual dividend yield (%)	6.52	5.89	5.28	10.43	9.06
Historical five-year average total return (%)	5.03	9.48	7.53	0.81	−1.79
Total debt (book value)/total capitalization (debt + equity) (%)	54.86	43.98	41.69	60.78	60.40
Total equity (market value)/total capitalization (debt + equity) (%)	45.14	56.02	58.3	39.22	39.60
Weighted average cost of debt (%)	4.71	4.24	3.54	5.04	4.98
GAAP income/total capitalization (debt + equity) (%)	2.19	4.93	1.55	13.12	1.51
FFO/total capitalization (debt + equity) (%)	3.38	3.78	4.05	3.91	3.62
GAAP income/market capitalization (equity) (%)	5.18	8.81	3.18	37.64	4.25
FFO/market capitalization (equity) (%)	7.97	6.76	8.31	11.22	10.16

Note: Data as of end of 2008.
Source: NAREIT, Morningstar *EnCorr Analyzer*, compiled by Duff & Phelps, LLC.

It is interesting to note that the annual dividend yield (2008) is well above the five-year historical average dividend yields reflecting the increased perceived risks in the real estate market at that time (price reduced in anticipation of problems with underlying real property). Equity investors are demanding a higher yield reflecting a higher risk premium to reflect the uncertainty of the recent economy. This is consistent with the cyclical patterns and trends discussed earlier and illustrated in Exhibits 10.4, 10.5 and 10.6.

The observed greater dividends are further supported by the studies that note greater returns are required for securities exhibiting relatively greater volatility compared to the performance of their underlying assets and alternative equity investments such as smaller firms (the Size Effect) and real estate entities. See Chapter 13 of *Cost of Capital: Applications and Examples,* 4th ed. Several studies illustrated a high correlation between small firm performance and REITs.[19]

Often "Same Property NOI Change" is provided which refers to the change in net operating income at the property level for the same properties held in the portfolio year over year. Wall Street analysts often refer to this item as same store NOI, which is somewhat misleading for real property.

Exhibit 10.9 could be expanded, if need be, to include an analysis on a per-share basis and various statistical measures, such as measures of central tendency and dispersion. The information clearly indicates a wide range in the historical earnings-to-price ratios between the companies. As the historical FFO to price ranges narrow, adjustments are required for the earnings to properly reflect the economic benefits derived from the investments. In this example the level of total debt affects the ratios indicated for companies 4 and 5 in Exhibit 10.9. This is adjusted to reflect their greater risk exposures.

Observed capitalization rates (FFO to price, AFFO to price, net cash flow to price, etc.) are influenced by risk and the expected growth in the respective FFO, AFFO, net cash flow, or dividend. Different levels of exposure require an assessment of the relative risks between different entities. Differentiating factors that might be considered include size, property sector, and geographical distribution of the assets, type of structure and management, share liquidity, corporate overhead, leverage, and future trends in the real estate markets. In addition, Exhibit 10.9 clearly indicates differences in the dividend to FFO payout ratio.

In addition to analyzing the comparative ratios, it is important to consider the potential growth from investments and from internal operations. The impact of floating rate debt and maturing debt should be considered. During periods of increasing interest rates, the net cash flow can be affected negatively. It is also important to consider the cash retention by the firm and the recovery of capital, which affects the investor's cost basis.[20]

The typical time periods utilized to develop the economic benefits are:

- Trailing 12 months.
- Last fiscal year.
- Straight average for some number of years.

[19] Brent W. Ambrose, Michael J. Highfield and Peter D. Linneman, "Real Estate and Economies of Scale: The Case of REITs," *Real Estate Economics* 33 (2005): 323–350.

[20] William B. Brueggeman and Jeffrey D. Fisher, *Real Estate Finance and Investment,* 13th ed. (New York: McGraw-Hill, 2006), 642–643.

- Trend over some number of years.
- Weighted average for some number of years.
- Projected estimate for next fiscal year.
- Projected estimate for next 12 months.
- Projected estimate for some number of years.

Discounted Cash Flow Method

The value of a real estate entity also can be estimated using a discounted cash flow method based on the expected returns required by investors. The formula for the discounted cash flow method is:

(Formula 10.2)

$$PV = \frac{NCF_1}{(1+k)} + \frac{NCF_2}{(1+k)^2} + \cdots + \frac{NCF_n}{(1+k)^n}$$

where: PV = Present value
$NCF_1 \ldots NCF_n$ = Net cash flow expected in each of the periods 1 through n, n being the last period of the discrete cash flow projections
k = Discount rate (cost of capital)

If the expected net cash flows over the projection period to the entity or equity can be estimated and the price or value of the entity or equity is known, the discount rate or cost of capital can be estimated through an iterative process (discussed in Chapters 5 and 6). The future net cash flows must be projected in order to develop a reliable estimate of the cost of capital for equity. This is not always feasible.

If the cash flows grow evenly in perpetuity from the valuation date, the Constant Dividend or Gordon Growth Model can be employed. This is also referred to as a single-stage growth model. The formula is:

(Formula 10.3)

$$PV = \frac{NCF_1}{k-g}$$

where: PV = Present value
NCF_1 = Net cash flow expected in period 1, the period immediately following the valuation date
k = Discount rate (cost of capital)
g = Expected long-term sustainable growth rate in net cash flow to investor

In solving for k, Formula 10.3 is rearranged to be:

(Formula 10.4)

$$k = \frac{NCF_1}{PV} + g$$

where the definitions of the variables are the same as in Formula 10.3.

This model makes one major assumption that the dividend and value are constantly growing. That is not the case as the FFO changes overtime, the dividend may also change.

Computing the Weighted Average or Overall Cost of Capital

The weighted average cost of capital can be estimated for public companies from component costs derived from market information. For example:

	No. of Shares or Face Value	Price/Share or % of Face Value	Component Value	Component Weight
Common stock	17,666,667	$30.00	$530,000,000	53.00%
Preferred stock	1,500,000	$13.33	$20,000,000	2.00%
Debt	$450,000,000	100%	$450,000,000	45.00%
Market value of invested capital			$1,000,000,000	100.00%

Assume that cost of the common equity is estimated at 7.75%. The preferred stock's cost is estimated at 7.25%. The bonds pay 6.25% on their face value. No discount has been applied. In this example, it is further assumed that all the debt is similar, but in actuality it may include convertible debt, variable rate debt, and mezzanine debt with various maturities.

If the entity itself were a taxable entity and not a pass-through entity, we would adjust the cost of debt for the tax shield resulting from interest payments on the debt capital. REITs are pass-through entities. All operating cash flows are measured pretax without subtracting a hypothetical income tax. If one was valuing equity capital directly, the interest expense would be subtracted in total and no income taxes would be subtracted.

The preceding information can be substituted into Formula 10.5 to compute the weighted average cost of capital for a REIT:

(Formula 10.5)
$$\begin{aligned} WACC &= (k_e \times W_e) + (k_p \times W_p) + [k_{d(pt)} \times W_d] \\ &= (7.75\% \times 53.0\%) + (7.25\% \times 2.0\%) + [6.25\% \times 45.0\%] \\ &= 4.10\% + 0.145\% + 2.8125\% \\ &= 7.0575\% \end{aligned}$$

The valuation of pass-through entities and their cost of capital is discussed in Chapter 29 of *Cost of Capital: Applications and Examples,* 4th ed. If the analyst makes an adjustment to income taxes paid by investors to the REIT operating cash flows, the analyst must make a similar adjustment to the pretax cost of debt in Formula 10.5, that is, $k_d = k_{d(pt)}(1 - t)$.

Closely held real estate companies have often been more highly leveraged than public REITs. Many entities started using shorter term debt for financing rather than long term debt (given the upward sloping yield curve). That financing structure lowered the current cost of capital but increased the refinancing risk in the future if inflation occurs. Unless short-term interest rates remain relatively low and REITs are able to continue to roll-over these loans, the cost of debt capital will increase. Financing at low interest rates lowers the cash outflow for the REIT but, because REITs are pass-through entities, this method of financing also reduces the tax deductions of the equity investors. This may increase the cost of equity capital.

But the most highly leveraged REITs found rolling-over financing to be problematic during the financial crisis of 2008-2010. Because interest rates have remained relatively low, making debt investments relatively unattractive for many institutional investors compared to equity, REITs turned to the equity markets. In 2009 public REITs raised approximately $24 billion in equity, almost double their 2008 total. REITs are deleveraging.

An iterative process also is required to estimate the weighted average cost of capital for closely held real estate companies or partnerships. The procedure is outlined in Chapters 5 and 6.

The cost of capital may be different for the entity than the cost of capital for an individual property owned by the entity. For example, if a REIT specializing in hotels sold one asset, the capitalization and/or discount rate applicable to estimate the market value of that asset may be different from the rates applied to a pool of assets that are part of an entity. Torto Wheaton Research reported that REITs may have an "accretion edge—selling their public equity capital at a low cap rate and buying private equity at higher cap rates."[21]

Estimating the Cost of Equity Capital as if Publicly Traded   The information on rates of return of publicly traded investment in real estate operating companies is limited. The best information currently available is based on REITs, which have certain special characteristics that can impact the expected or forward-looking returns. According to Morningstar, the available information dates back to 1972 (see Exhibit 10.6). Exhibit 10.10 summarizes the annual total returns on equity capital for REITs in comparison to other investments from 1972 through 2008.

EXHIBIT 10.10   Returns on Equity Capital, 1972–2008[22]

	Geometric Mean (%)	Arithmetic Mean (%)	Standard Deviation (%)
U.S. Small Stock	12.52	15.10	23.84
FTSE NAREIT Equity REITS	**11.21**	**12.98**	**19.15**
S&P 500	9.50	11.20	18.65
U.S. Long-term government	9.13	9.71	11.65
U.S. Long-term corporates	8.64	9.11	10.53
U.S. Intermediate government	8.09	8.28	6.56
U.S. 30 30-day Treasury bill	5.86	5.90	2.97
U.S. inflation	4.51	4.56	3.20

---

[21] CB Commercial/Torto Wheaton Research, "Wall Street vs. Main Street, Real Estate Pricing and New Development," *Market Watch* 9(1) (Spring 1997): 3.
[22] *SBBI 2009 Classic Yearbook* (Chicago: Morningstar, 2009), 56.

EXHIBIT 10.11 Total Equity REIT Returns for Various Periods

Total Return	Arithmetic Average, %	Geometric Average, %	Moving Average (from 1972), %
5-year	5.08	0.91	15.48
10-year	10.20	7.42	15.03
15-year	10.57	8.21	14.78
20-year	11.10	8.99	14.60
25-year	11.64	9.86	14.99
30-year	13.65	11.99	15.30
Average	10.37%	7.90%	15.03%

Source: NAREIT. Calculations by MacCrate Associates LLC.

The historical returns are based on the dividends paid plus capital appreciation. They may not accurately reflect the *expected* returns required by equity investors going forward. The historical returns from REITs do form the basis for estimating the equity returns that are expected on other real estate operating companies. The historical returns reflect what has occurred.

REITs have had a declining correlation to stocks and bonds during the 1990s. The correlation between REITs and long term government bonds has been negative during the last decade. As the asset class has gained in importance and became more volatile during the later 2000s, the correlation to small and large growth company stocks increased.

Exhibit 10.11 summarizes the total equity returns from REITs for the last 5, 10, 15, 20, 25, and 30 years and the moving average for each period from 1972 through 2008. The data could be further segregated by property type.

The 5-year arithmetic average and geometric average were affected by the low returns experienced during 2007 and 2008 while the moving average is smoothed by the high returns from 2004–2006 and appears more consistent over the long term. No one would enter a real estate investment expecting the low returns indicated over the last five years. Nor, would an investor expect the higher returns experienced from 2004 through 2006. It is preferable to look at longer returns, which would approximate a long-term investor's position in a closely held company. In addition, the cost of debt has been well below the historical cost of debt because of the Federal Reserve Board's monetary policy.

Implied FFO Yield

The expected long-term growth rates in income and value are likely to follow changes in inflation over a long period of time. The inferred *ex ante* FFO yield can be calculated based on solving for k utilizing a discounted cash flow model:

(Formula 10.6)

$$PV = \frac{NCF_1}{(1+k)} + \frac{NCF_2}{(1+k)^2} + K + \frac{NCF_n}{(1+k)^n} + \frac{\frac{NCF_n(1+g)}{k-g}}{(1+k)^n}$$

EXHIBIT 10.12   Inferred FFO Cost of Equity Capital for Period 2009

Property Type	Market Capitalization (000s)	Two-Year Growth Rate	Inferred Capitalization Rate	Terminal Capitalization Rate	Inferred FFO Equity Yield
Apartments	$25,544,084	−8.58%	9.43%	7.11%	9.61%
Industrial buildings	$8,504,900	5.59%	13.00%	13.88%	16.38%
Office buildings	$21,397,786	6.44%	13.14%	14.26%	16.76%
Retail	$40,682,535	−4.22%	11.72%	10.02%	12.52%
Healthcare	$25,217,313	−3.79%	9.02%	7.72%	10.22%
Public storage	$15,452,854	−0.68%	9.73%	9.02%	11.52%

Source: NAREIT, MacCrate Associates.

where: PV = Present value

$NCF_1 \ldots NCF_n$ = Net cash flow expected in each of the periods 1 through n, n being the last period of the discrete cash flow projections

k = Discount rate (cost of capital)

g = Expected long-term sustainable growth rate in net cash flow, starting with the last period of the discrete projections as the base year

Exhibit 10.12 based on FFO (not dividends), summarizes the estimated growth rate in FFO for two years reverting to the long term average, inferred FFO capitalization rate and FFO yield to the equity position by property type based on the formula that the FFO yield rate is equal to the capitalization rate plus the long-term average rate of growth ($k = c + g$) and assuming that the growth rate is into perpetuity.

There are some important observations based on the above calculations based on historical data. Risk does vary by property type as indicated above. It has been assumed that the negative growth rates will continue for another two years based on historical analysis of the recessions in 1973–1974 and 1989–1991 and the data illustrated in Exhibit 10.6. Thereafter, the growth rate in income will increase based on inflation of, say, 2.5%. Restructurings may occur over the next two years or companies will be forced into bankruptcies. The inferred FFO cost of capital brackets the long term historical cost for all equity REITs referred to in Exhibit 10.12.

The inferred FFO equity yield indicates that apartments are the safest investment, followed by healthcare and public storage. Industrial buildings and office buildings have the highest risk. This situation is a function of the forecasted growth in FFO, which is extremely high. The projections reported by the sampled companies observed comprising this average may be atypical. In fact, those risks are clearly evident in 2009 because preliminary indications are that the FFO for these two sectors is falling as rental rates decrease, vacancies increase and net operating income is declining. FFO will be down thus resulting in a probable decline in the market capitalization. This is consistent with the patterns observed in Exhibits 10.4 and 10.6.

Estimating growth rates is complicated given the cyclical patterns observed. However, recognition of cyclical patterns and, more specifically, changes in the underlying economics of owning real property are critical in the analysis. This technical skill requires judgment based on experience or forecasting abilities in an uncertain market.

As can be observed, the terminal capitalization rate is greater for office and industrial properties than the observed current capitalization rate. This can be attributed to the need to consider the added incurable obsolescence that grows for the depreciating assets over time. This is necessary given that these assets are older than the other property types observed. As such, forecasting of the performance of older assets into the future may be more speculative or uncertain. Alternatively, the terminal capitalization rate for apartments and healthcare is lower because the market anticipates that those sectors will improve over the next five years.

One must also consider asset attributes relative to the preferences of the market in addition to the financial characteristics of property assets to fully value the performance of real estate entities as well as the underlying collateral assets.

One must also analyze the timing of required refinancing relative to the underlying cycle. It is far easier to refinance in the upward part of the cycle than in the downward part. The failure to link timing of refinancing to the risk characteristics and value of the underlying assets (the collateral) explains a major problem and cause of failure of REITs in the current economic situation.

Dividends

Historical information regarding AFFO is not easily obtainable. Many analysts rely on FFO and/or the actual dividend yield because historical information is available that provides support for the analysis. Historical dividend growth per share is readily available, which permits an analysis by either a discounted cash flow analysis or dividend growth models. Dividends are useful because they represent the net cash flow to investors. As long as the dividend does not exceed the FFO or AFFO, this offers an appropriate measure of the economic return to consider for analyzing shareholder value. The analyst must be cognizant of the dividend payout ratio. Exhibit 10.13 shows the historical per share growth in dividends from 1987 through 2008 for REITs.

It is interesting to note that REIT dividend growth dropped substantially between 1989 and 1991 during the last recession but rebounded sharply in 1992 and 1993 (see Exhibit 10.6 and discussion). The same was true between 2000 and 2002 followed by increases through 2007 as the growth cycle came to an end. We would expect to see a sharp decline through 2009 into 2010.

Exhibit 10.14 is a summary of the average dividend yield per year plus the compound change per year for the last 30 years through 2008 based on returns for public equity REITs.

The dividend yield has been falling while the total dividends have been increasing. The dividend yield has increased going into 2009, but that is caused by the fact that the market capitalization of REIT companies has declined. It is important to note that in 2008, the Internal Revenue Service ruled that public REITs can satisfy the tax requirement provided that they distribute at least 90% (legislatively reduced from 95%) of their taxable income to shareholders by paying cash as well as stock. As of year-end 2008, only a few companies exercised this option.

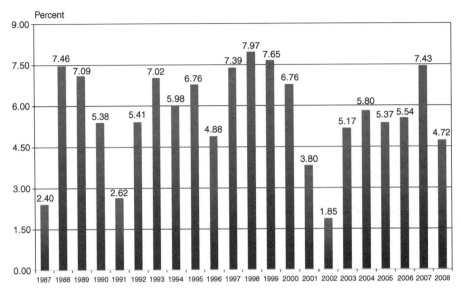

EXHIBIT 10.13   REIT Dividend Growth per Share, 1987–2008
Source: NAREIT, SNL Financial.

If an analyst was estimating the cost of equity for a publicly traded REIT that has a share price of $34.00 that was expected to pay a $2.00 dividend per year and it was expected to grow in perpetuity at 2%, the cost of equity would be estimated using

(Formula 10.4)

$$k = \frac{NCF_1}{PV} + g$$

where: $NCF_1 = \$2.00$ per share
$\qquad PV = \$34.00$ per share
$\qquad g = 2.0\%$ per year

$$k = \frac{\$2.00}{\$34.00} + 2.00\%$$
$$= 5.88\% + 2.00\%$$
$$= 7.88\%$$

EXHIBIT 10.14   Average Public Equity REITs Dividend Yield per Share

	Arithmetic Average, %	Geometric Average, %
5-year	5.08	5.07
10-year	6.13	6.12
15-year	6.36	6.35
20-year	6.78	6.77
25-year	7.02	7.01
30-year	7.15	7.14
Average	6.42	6.41

Source: NAREIT, MacCrate Associates.

The indicated cost of equity would be 7.88%. It is extremely important that the forecasted expected growth rate is correct. It is quite common for REITs and other entities to pay dividends from other sources, such as reserve funds, the sale of assets, refinancing of assets, and/or one-time earnings from a large-scale development project. The dividend-paying ability is critical along with the forecasted compound change in the dividend over the projection period. This model does not permit the growth rate to exceed the cost of equity or capital. It is important to also note that companies may choose to cut or suspend their dividends. SNL Financial reported that in 2008, 43 companies cut or suspended their dividends.

Some investment analysts apply a two- or three-stage growth model to estimate the value of real estate entities.

The projection period should be reasonable and based on the time period for which reasonable forecasts can be made. It generally ranges from 3 to 10 years. The net cash flow, which is often assumed to be the dividend, should be projected for each year in the projection period. The net cash flow may be based on earnings per share, adjusted funds from operations, or dividends. Consistent application in the development of the information is most important. The last part of the equation provides an indication of the residual or terminal value based on capitalizing the income into perpetuity. No deduction for transaction costs is included as it is assumed that the entity is not being sold but held indefinitely.

The long-term growth rate in perpetuity should be supportable and defensible. The last part of the formula represents the constant growth or Gordon Growth Model and is used to estimate the terminal or residual value at the end of the projection period. Each year's net cash flow is discounted back to present value, including the terminal value that is assumed to be received in the last year of the projection period.

For illustration purposes, assume that the following table summarizes the information that has been developed from analyzing a real estate company and the general market information.

Projection Period	Annual Dividend
1	$2.00
2	$2.06
3	$2.14
4	$2.25
5	$2.29
Terminal value	$37.81
Expected future growth	2.00%
Current share price	$34.00

Through the iterative process, the inferred discount rate or equity cost of capital is approximately 8.19% based on a current share price of $34.00. The next table shows the calculation.

The analyst must be cognizant of the relationships that develop based on the assumptions that are made concerning the cash flows. The current capitalization rate is 5.88% while the terminal capitalization increased to 6.19%, reflecting the lower forecasted growth in the net cash flows. The terminal value discounted represents approximately 75% of the present value of $34.00.

Projection Period	Annual Dividend	Expected Growth, %	Net Cash Flow	Present Value Factor@ 8.19%	Present Value
1	$2.00		$2.00	0.9243	$1.85
2	$2.06	3.00	$2.06	0.8543	$1.76
3	$2.14	4.00	$2.14	0.7897	$1.69
4	$2.25	5.00	$2.25	0.7299	$1.64
5	$2.29	2.00	$40.10	0.6746	$27.06
6	$2.34	2.00	Thereafter		
Terminal value	$37.81		Total Present Value		$34.00

Terminal capitalization rate	6.18%
Future growth	2.00%
Current share price	$34.00
Inferred yield	8.19%

If it was assumed that the current capitalization rate and the terminal rate were the same (5.88%), the indicated discount rate or equity cost of capital would be increased to 9.12%. The next table supports the calculations.

Projection Period	Annual Dividend	Expected Growth, %	Net Cash Flow	Present Value Factor@ 9.12%	Present Value
1	$2.00		$2.00	0.9164	$1.83
2	$2.06	3.00	$2.06	0.8398	$1.73
3	$2.14	4.00	$2.14	0.7697	$1.65
4	$2.25	5.00	$2.25	0.7053	$1.59
5	$2.29	2.00	$42.08	0.6464	$27.20
6	$2.34	2.00	Thereafter		
Terminal value	$39.79		Total Present Value		$34.00

Terminal capitalization rate	5.88%
Future growth	2.00%
Current share price	$34.00
Inferred yield	9.12%

The preceding examples were based on annual payments of dividends. Usually dividends are paid quarterly, and the cash flows should reflect quarterly discounting.

The five apartment guideline REITs selected (data displayed in Exhibit 10.15) can be analyzed based on the expected dividends to be paid in the future. The true return to the equity investors is the dividend yield and expected long-term growth rate in dividends. Using the same two-stage model formula, but applying it to the dividends expected to be paid over the long term, the next chart indicates the implied equity yield based on the assumption that the short and long-term growth expected varies for each company over five years.

EXHIBIT 10.15 Apartment REIT Dividends

REIT	1	2	3	4	5
Forward dividend yield, %	6.52	5.89	5.28	10.43	9.06
Expected dividend growth, %	5.00	5.00	5.00	−8.00	−3.00
Long term growth, %	2.50	2.50	2.50	2.50	2.50
Implied equity yield, %	9.57	8.89	8.26	10.81	10.05

For illustration purposes, it was assumed that the first three companies operate in stable markets with the potential to increase income while the last two companies are negatively affected by local market conditions that will have an adverse impact on revenues. In fact, the dividends could be at risk. One of the problems encountered deals with the source of forward looking dividends and the expected dividend growth. Many times, these figures are provided by analysts who do not have sufficient information to properly make a forecast. The information may have also been provided by management with a potential for bias.

The table provides a better indication of the cost of equity capital because it is based on the actual expected earnings to be received by the equity investor if the sources are reliable and unbiased. In certain instances, the market expects the dividends will decrease because debt has to be restructured at a higher cost and/or cash flows from operations will decline. As a result, the outlook for guideline companies 4 and 5 are not favorable. Guideline companies 1, 2 and 3 may have the potential to develop new product and/or less competition which can improve earnings long range.

Applying the Build-up Method

In valuing real estate companies similar to REITs, many analysts utilize the 10-year U.S. government bond because it has the longest continuity in the public markets. The yield on 10-year U.S. government bonds provides a reasonable estimate for the risk-free rate if a 10-year cash flow has been used to prepare the discounted cash flow model. Most investors analyze real estate holdings over 10 years, and the termination value is based on the reversionary net asset value to be received at the end of 10 years. Generally, the real property assets owned by a real estate operating entity may have been individually analyzed and real property cash flows for 10 years or longer have been prepared. Therefore, the 10-year Treasury bond more closely matches the typical projection period used by analysts. In addition, the longer time period reflects the longer investment horizon associated with investments in similar companies and compensates for inflation risk.

An adjustment for size may be required based on studies completed by Morningstar and Duff & Phelps and a study by Brent W. Ambrose, Michael J. Highfield, and Peter D. Linneman.[23]

The total return indicated by REITs indicates that REITs act like small stocks; however, a large percentage of the return comes from dividends, which is more

[23] Brent W. Ambrose, Michael J. Highfield and Peter D. Linneman, "Real Estate and Economies of Scale: The Case of REITs," *Real Estate Economics* 33 (2005): 323–350.

comparable to a high-yielding investment than to small stocks. Additional risk is inherent in small-company stocks in comparison to larger stocks. See Chapter 13 of *Cost of Capital: Applications and Examples,* 4th ed. for a discussion of the size effect.

The *SBBI Yearbook* displays an industry premium for real estate investment trusts. In 2008, the adjustment was 2.18%. The problem with using this data is that it includes many types of REITs: equity, hybrid and mortgage. Beginning in 2006, mortgage and hybrid REITs showed extreme volatility because of the "residential bubble" that resulted in the collapse of the residential market. Mortgage and hybrid REITs were affected with several declaring bankruptcy in the years that followed. This repeats the performance of mortgage and hybrid REITs observed in the latter 1970s continuing into the 1990s. EREITs have been the major growth sector of the REIT vehicle from the 1980s through the current market.

Example of Applying the Build-up Method   Combining the risk-free rate, equity risk premium, size premium, and industry premium to provide an indication of the cost of equity for a mid-cap real estate investment trust, the formula would be:

(Formula 10.7)
$$E(R_i) = R_f + RP_m + RP_s \pm RP_u$$

Assume the following variables:

Risk-free rate $= 4.5\%$

Equity risk premium $= 6.0\%$

Size premium $= 1.0\%$

Company-specific risk premium $= 2.18\%$

Substituting into the formula the estimated cost of equity is:

$$\begin{aligned} E(R_i) &= R_f + RP_m + RP_s \pm RP_u \\ &= 4.5\% + 6\% + 1\% + 2.18\% \\ &= 13.68\% \end{aligned}$$

Applying the Capital Asset Pricing Model

Example of Applying CAPM   For illustration purposes, if we assume that you have been asked to analyze a closely held REIT, the cost of equity can be estimated based on these variables:

Risk-free rate $= 4.5\%$

Expected equity premium $= 6.0\%$

REIT Industry beta $= 0.92$

Size premium $= 1.0\%$

The expected return is based on the assumption that the total capitalization and the capital structure of the company being analyzed are comparable to the industry average. If the actual financial leverage at the company is substantially different, the beta would be calculated based on unlevered betas (discussed previously) and relevered to reflect the actual risks based on the capital structure of the firm. See Chapter 11 for a discussion of formulas to unlever betas and Chapter 12 on beta estimation issues in *Cost of Capital: Applications and Examples*, 4th ed.

Substituting the risk-free rate, beta, the equity premium, and size premia indicated previously, the estimated cost of equity would be:

$$E(R_i) = R_f + B(RP_m) + RP_s$$
$$= 4.5\% + 0.92(6\%) + 1\%$$
$$= 11.02\%$$

Adjusting Cost of Equity Capital for Closely Held REIT The investment in a closely held REIT is subject to added risk compared to an otherwise identical investment in a public REIT. The market favors liquidity and the cost of equity capital is greater for the illiquid investment in the closely held REIT. We discuss adjusting the "as if public" cost of equity capital (or the "as if public value") in Chapters 27 and 28 of *Cost of Capital: Applications and Examples*, 4th ed.

Analysis of Long-Term Dividend and Total Return Many investors and analysts compare the total return on REITs to the 10-year bond return to capture the risks associated with real estate companies in the public market. Real property is frequently analyzed using a 10-year discounted cash flow analysis. The 10-year bond approximates the risk-free investment of a similar investment period. Exhibit 10.16 summarizes the 10- to 30-year total return to the same return on the 10-year bond for a similar time frame. A long-run average historical risk premium is often used as an indicator of the expected risk premium of a typical equity investor. The measure of REIT returns below is based on dividend income plus capital appreciation and represents returns before corporate taxes because REITs are pass-through entities.

The exhibit indicates that the equity risk premium over the 10-year U.S. government bond for an investment in a public REIT is between 5% and 6% over a long investment horizon. The equity risk premium has been declining in the short term, which may indicate that the market has a greater understanding of REIT returns and risks. It could also be a function of the lower cost of debt capital that flowed into equity REITS. The long-term risk premium could be added to the current 10-year bond yield to provide an indication of the equity cost of capital.

Historically, there is a strong tendency for most equity returns to revert to the mean. This was illustrated by the convergence in the trend lines illustrated for direct

EXHIBIT 10.16 Comparison of Public REIT and 10-Year U.S. Government Bond Returns

Total Return	REIT, %	10-yr Treasury, %	Difference, %
10-year	10.20	5.19	5.01
15-year	10.57	5.76	4.81
20-year	11.10	6.41	4.68
25-year	11.64	7.58	4.06
30-year	13.65	7.79	5.86

Source: MacCrate Associates.

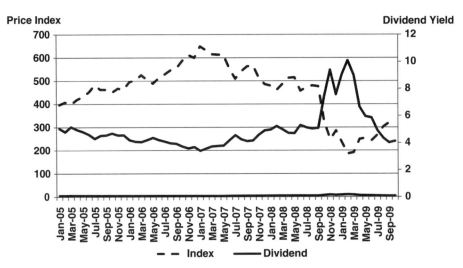

EXHIBIT 10.17   Relationship between REIT Dividends and Price Appreciation
Source: MacCrate Associates.

property returns depicted in Exhibit 10.4. By association (see Exhibit 10.6), the same is true with REIT total equity returns and the equity dividends returns illustrated below. For example, equity dividends averaged 7.33% from June 1998 through June 2003 and began to decline as interest rates were lowered increasing the value of the underlying net asset value, which provided for appreciation. A high was reached in February 2009 at 10.08%, but it has quickly fallen back down with the monthly average for the last 12 months estimated at 6.80% which is in the range indicated by the 10- and 25-year averages. In the meantime, over 10 to 25 years, the difference between the total equity return and the 10-year U.S. government bond has held fairly constant as well. Exhibit 10.17 clearly shows the relationship that exists between dividends and appreciation.

This same pattern was witnessed during the 1970s and late 1980s recession when interest rates were higher. The net asset value was driven higher by lower interest rates and capital inflows into real estate, which resulted in lower dividends. This tends to support the view that, over the long term, the correct equity premium should reflect long-term averages.

Exhibit 10.18 displays a comparison between the 10-year bond and the average dividend yield for REITs. The trend for both is downward and the spread historically is quite narrow.

Based on the preceding analysis, the majority of the risk associated with REITs appears to be in the long-term appreciation in value.

Discount rates can also be estimated by analyzing publicly held real estate limited partnerships, which sell in the informal secondary markets.[24] This method is similar to the build-up method based on REIT total returns. Partnership Profiles'

---

[24] Bruce A. Johnson, Spencer J. Jefferies, and James R. Park, *Comprehensive Guide for the Valuation of Family Limited Partnerships*, 3rd ed. (Fort Worth, TX: Partnership Profiles, 2006), 44.

EXHIBIT 10.18 Returns on 10-Year U.S. Government Bonds versus REIT
Dividend Yields

	Dividend Yield, %	10-Year Treasury Bond, %	Difference, %
5-year	5.08	4.33	0.75
10-year	6.13	4.70	1.44
15-year	6.36	5.25	1.11
20-year	6.78	5.82	0.96
25-year	7.02	6.58	0.45
30-year	7.15	7.44	−0.29

Source: MacCrate Associates.

Rate of Return Study analyzes the sale of publicly held limited partnership interests.
Additional adjustments may be required based on the type of entity being analyzed,
leverage, and other factors.

The example provided in this chapter was based on a REIT that will distribute
90% of its income to equity investors. This is not always the case. The dividends
that are paid may be lower or nonexistent, as with nondistributing partnerships.
REITs also have relatively low debt in comparison to private companies and partnerships that use leverage to maximize the return to equity investors.

REIT shares are relatively liquid in comparison to investments in restricted
stock, partnership interests, and closely held corporations.

SUMMARY

This chapter introduced the methods and applications utilized to develop the appropriate returns on real estate entities, focusing on REITs for valuation application.
The basic concepts are quite similar to business valuation concepts, but additional
factors must be considered in the analysis of real estate entities. Valuation of real
estate related enterprises requires a link and focus on the performance and valuation
of underlying and collateral property performance. The specification of property asset valuation as a foundation then allows the valuation of the entities structured
around property assets and their financing instruments. Failure to make this link,
especially in down markets with forced liquidation required, explains a major problem experienced in the current and previous recessions. Though the problems arise
with the bailout positions acquired in the down market context, the failure to recognize these relationships in growth and more normally functioning market environ-
ments have contributed to the mispricing of real estate entities and property itself
that can be offset with the use of the structure, tools, and strategies presented in
this book.

It should be noted that the estimated required rates of return on REIT equity
have been derived from equity rates of return for publicly traded companies. If the
real estate equity investment of the subject company is not publicly traded, the indicated required rates of return may need further adjustment for a discount for lack of
marketability because publicly traded shares (stock) are more liquid.

ADDITIONAL READING

Arsenault, Marcel and Liang Peng. "Mortgage Fund Flows, Capital Appreciation, and Real Estate Cycles." Working paper, Social Science Research Network, August 2009. Available at http://ssrn.com/abstract=1458188.

Block, Ralph L. *Investing in REITS—Real Estate Investment Trusts*. New York: Bloomberg Press, 2006.

Clayton, Jim, David C. Ling, and Andy Naranjo. "Commercial Real Estate Valuation: Fundamentals versus Investor Sentiment." Working Paper, Social Science Research Network, October 2007. Updated April 2008. Available at http://ssrn.com/abstract=1132361.

Diermeier, Jeffrey, Roger Ibbotson, and Laurence Siegel. *"The Supply of Capital Market Returns." Financial Analysts Journal* (March–April 1984): 74–80.

Erickson, John, Su Han Chan, and Ko Wang. *Real Estate Investment Trusts: Structure, Performance, and Investment Opportunities, Financial Management Association Survey and Synthesis Series*. Oxford: Oxford University Press, 2002.

Fass, Peter M., Michael E. Shaff, and Donald B. Zief. *Real Estate Investment Trusts Handbook*, 2009–2010 ed. Eagan, MN: Securities Law Handbook Series, 2009.

Grissom, Terry. "The Four Quadrant Paradigm: Corporate Real Estate Finance." *Journal of Corporate Real Estate of NACORE* (1998).

Grissom, Terry. "The Economic Structure of Real Estate Syndication and Its Impact on Real Estate Assets." *The Real Estate Securities Journal* (1985).

Grissom, Terry. "Real Estate Syndication: An Analysis of Real Estate Investments with Multiple Equity Problems." *Appraisal Journal* 50(3) (1986).

Grissom, Terry. "Direct and Indirect Property Performance Cycles and Structural Shifts in Economic Regimes." Built Environment Research Institute and Property Research Institute Working Paper, University of Ulster.

Grissom, Terry, Jasmine Lim, and James DeLisle. "Arbitrage and Cyclical Effects in the Performance of UK and USA Property Markets." Built Environment Research Institute and Property Research Institute Working Paper, University of Ulster, 2009.

Hatzell, David. "REIT Performance Measures." Research Paper, Solomon Brothers, 1989.

Ibbotson, Roger, Jeffrey Deirmeier, and Laurence Siegel. "The Demand for Capital Market Returns: A New Equilibrium Theory." *Financial Analysts Journal* (January–February 1984): 22–33.

Lee, Ming-Long, Ming-Te Lee, and Kevin C.H. Chiang. "Real Estate Risk Exposure of Equity Real Estate Investment Trusts." Working paper, July 6, 2006. Available at http://ssrn.com/abstract=1020058.

Parsons, John, Richard T. Garrigan, and John F.C. Parsons. *Real Estate Investment Trusts: Structure, Analysis and Strategy*. New York: McGraw-Hill, 1997.

Oppenheimer, Peter and Terry Grissom. "Frequency Space Correlation Between REITs and Capital Market Indices." *The Journal of Real Estate Research* 12 (1999): 1.

Van Hemert, Otto. "Testing the Efficiency of the Commercial Real Estate Market: Evidence from the 2007–2009 Financial Crisis." Working Paper, Social Science Research Network, November 2009. Available at http://ssrn.com/abstract=1470249.

Valuing Real Estate Entities

Introduction
Measuring Net Cash Flow for Real Estate Entities
Projected Cash Flow from Real Estate Operations
Projected Net Cash Flow for Real Estate Entity
Funds from Operations and Adjusted Funds from Operations

INTRODUCTION

Estimating the net cash flow associated with real estate entities is the focus of this appendix. Some real estate entities use their own set of definitions that parallel those used in business valuation. This appendix introduces the reader to the accounting measures that may be encountered in real estate entity valuations.

MEASURING NET CASH FLOW FOR REAL ESTATE ENTITIES

The anticipated financial benefits that come from investing in a real estate entity are no different from any other enterprise. The three sources of these benefits are:

1. Earnings or cash flow (from operations or investments).
2. Liquidation or hypothecation of assets.
3. Sale of the interest.[25]

Real estate entities are going concerns engaged in a real estate-related business enterprise. Generally, the value of a going concern has been defined as the value of a business enterprise that is expected to continue to operate into the future. The intangible elements of going concern value result from factors, such as having a trained work force, an operational plant, and the necessary licenses, systems, and procedures in place.[26]

---

[25] Shannon P. Pratt, *Valuing a Business: The Analysis and Appraisal of Closely Held Companies*, 5th ed. (New York: McGraw-Hill, 2008), Chapter 3.
[26] American Society of Appraisers, *Business Valuation Standards—Glossary* (Herndon, Va.: American Society of Appraisers, 2006), 5.

The value of a going concern includes the tangible assets as well as the intangible assets.

Most real estate entities prepare consolidated financial statements in accordance with generally accepted accounting principles (GAAP). Income statements and cash flow statements prepared in accordance with GAAP must be adjusted by the analyst to provide a basis for forecasting future cash flows from operations and other investments as well as the potential residual or terminal interest if the entity is sold. Taxable income does not indicate the dividend-paying ability of real estate entities. The projected net cash flow that can be distributed to shareholders or partners is most important to investors. In addition, the book value of the real property assets does not generally reflect the actual net asset value of the assets. Because most real estate entities have a large percentage of fixed assets that are depreciated, the accounting statements may not properly reflect the actual operating results of a real estate entity.

PROJECTED CASH FLOW FROM REAL ESTATE OPERATIONS

The projected operating income and expenses for each asset must be estimated in order to produce the total cash flows from the real property interests. The items considered in the analysis of individual assets in Chapter 9 must be considered for all the assets to produce a consolidated reconstructed income and operating expense statement. Projected capital expenditures such as nonrecurring expenditures, leasing commissions, and tenant improvement costs must be deducted. The annual debt service must be deducted for each asset to provide an indication of the cash flow to the entity before depreciation and taxes. Exhibit 10.19 provides a sample projected cash flow statement from the real property operations of an entity prior to depreciation and taxes.

The estimated total projected cash flow from real property operations before interest, taxes, depreciation, and amortization must take into consideration the potential changes in income and expenses at the property level and dispositions, acquisitions, exchanges, or refinancings that may have occurred at the property level or are expected over the projection period.

Further adjustments are required for debt service, depreciation, interest, and taxes at the property level, if any. Exhibit 10.20 provides a basic summary of the adjustments to provide an indication of the total projected after-tax cash flow from the real property operations.

Additional items that must be modeled at the property level over the projection period may include:

- Projected re-leasing assumptions upon lease expiration including leasing costs.
- Capital expenditures.
- Tenant improvement costs.
- Redevelopment costs.

This type of analysis provides a good indication of the contribution made by the tangible assets to the projected before- and after-tax cash flows to the

EXHIBIT 10.19 Sample Projected Cash Flow Statement from Real Estate Operations

Projected Gross Revenue
Potential rental revenue
  – Loss due to absorption and turnover vacancy
  – Base rent abatements
  = **Projected scheduled base rental revenue**
  + Expense reimbursement revenue
  + Other income
  = **Projected total gross revenue**
  – General vacancy
  – Collection loss
  = **Projected effective gross revenue operating expenses**
  Real estate taxes
  Insurance
  Utilities
  Cleaning
  Repairs and maintenance
  Management fee
  Payroll and benefits
  Ground rent
  Recurring capital expenditures for replacement
  – **Total operating expenses**
  = **Projected net operating income from real property operations**
  – **Leasing and replacement capital expenditures**
  Tenant improvements
  Leasing commissions
  Nonrecurring capital expenditures for replacement
  – **Total leasing and replacement capital expenditures**
  = **Total projected cash flow from real property**
Operations before debt service, depreciation, and taxes
  – **Debt service (principal plus interest payments)**
  = **Total projected net cash flow from real property**
Operations before depreciation and taxes

EXHIBIT 10.20 Calculating After-Tax Cash Flow from Real Property Operations

Net cash flow income from real property operations before depreciation and taxes
  – Interest
  – Other taxes
  – Depreciation and amortization
= **Taxable income**
Total net cash flow from real property operations before depreciation and taxes
  – Taxable income × Tax rate (if applicable)[1]
= **Total after-tax cash flow from real property operations before depreciation and taxes**

[1]There would not be federal taxes at the entity level for real property interests owned by pass-through entities.

entity, which has a direct bearing on the cost of capital. Cash flows for other types of properties, such as development properties or assets held for sale, can be developed separately or combined. Assets held in joint ventures may also be accounted for separately. Additional risks are associated with real property developments; these risks can impact the cost of capital as well as the expected net cash flow growth.

PROJECTED NET CASH FLOW FOR REAL ESTATE ENTITY

Additional adjustments are required for corporate or partnership expenses, depreciation, and amortization that are not allocated to a specific real property asset. There may also be additional income from other investments, such as a minority interest in other partnerships. Additional income may be generated by providing management or development services or other property services to related or unrelated entities. A real estate entity may incur another layer of expenses, such as management and advisory fees, that are not incurred by an individual property owner. Other adjustments that may be required to provide the total projected net cash flow to the entity may include:

- Projected net proceeds from the sale of assets.
- Projected net proceeds from refinancing.
- Income from unconsolidated entities.
- Other nonoperating income.
- Other nonoperating expenses.
- Adjustments for asset dispositions.
- Adjustments for new asset acquisitions.
- Adjustments for new or completed real property developments.

    Exhibit 10.21 provides a basic formula to estimate the net cash flow to a real estate entity.

    If it is a pass-through entity, there would not be any adjustment for federal taxes at the entity level.

EXHIBIT 10.21   Calculating Net Cash Flow

Total after-tax cash flow (real property operations before depreciation and taxes)
+ Net income from other sources
= Net income to common stock or partnership (after tax, if any)
+ Noncash charges at the entity level (depreciation, amortization, and deferred taxes)
− Capital expenditures at the entity level to support projected operations
− Required additions to net working capital or retained earnings to support projected
   operations at the entity level
+ Interest expense at the entity level (net of the tax deduction, if any)
+ Dividends on preferred stocks
Net cash flow to invested capital

FUNDS FROM OPERATIONS AND ADJUSTED FUNDS FROM OPERATIONS

Currently there is disagreement within the real estate community concerning the analysis of financial statements prepared in accordance with GAAP for real estate entities. Analysts must be keenly aware that real estate companies report earnings differently. Terminology in the industry also differs from Wall Street to Main Street. The calculation of the projected net cash flow is critical and must be clearly defined. It provides the basis for consistent comparative analysis.

In order to promote an industry-wide standard measure of operating performance, the National Association for Real Estate Investment Trusts (NAREIT) adopted additional measures that analysts may consider for comparative purposes for real estate investment trusts (REITs).[27]

One measure is known as funds from operations (FFO). FFO is defined as

net income (computed in accordance with generally accepted accounting principles), excluding gains (or losses) from sales of property, plus depreciation and amortization, and after adjustments for unconsolidated partnerships and joint ventures. Adjustments for unconsolidated partnerships and joint ventures will be calculated to reflect funds from operations on the same basis.[28]

Depreciation and amortization should reflect the amounts that are associated with the real estate assets. Exhibit 10.22 summarizes the formula developed by NAREIT for the calculation of FFO.

In a study completed by Tsang and Fortin, the authors concluded that the GAAP earnings per share (EPS) measures have higher absolute forecast errors than the non-GAAP funds from operations measures. According to the study, EPS measures have higher forecast errors than FFO because:

- Managers are more likely to manipulate EPS.
- Analysts exert larger positive biases on EPS forecasts.
- The number of analysts following analysis of the EPS measure for REITs is less than that for other types of companies, making EPS forecasts less accurate.[29]

A study completed by Downs and Guner provides additional support for the conclusions developed by Tsang and Fortin. The study indicated that a very high percentage of income on real estate is contractually obligated through lease obligations and known to REIT management and analysts. The study went on to say that

---

[27] National Association of Real Estate Investment Trusts, Inc., "Funds from Operations," *NAREIT White Paper* (April 2002): 2.

[28] Ibid.

[29] Desmond Tsang and Steve Fortin, "Analyst Forecast Accuracy on GAAP vs. Non-GAAP Financial Measures: Case of Real Estate Investment Trust," Working Paper, November 2005.

EXHIBIT 10.22   Calculating FFO

Gross revenues
– Operating expenses
– Depreciation and amortization
– Interest expense
– <u>General and administration expenses of the entity</u>
Net income
– Net proceeds on sale of ssets
+ <u>Depreciation and amortization associated with real estate assets</u>
Funds from operations

the income and expense streams are less volatile and income streams are more predictable than for many other types of businesses.[30]

Many analysts use FFO to estimate the equity or shareholder value of REITs. Some critics maintain that FFO may not be representative of the true operating profitability of an entity because the entity may not properly account for leasing commissions, tenant improvements, recurring capital expenditures, and other items.[31] If proper adjustments are made to FFO, cash flow estimates, such as adjusted funds from operations (AFFO)—also known as cash or funds available for distribution (CAD or FAD)—can be developed for valuation purposes. These measures are used as benchmarks for valuing the equity interest in REITs. AFFO is usually calculated by subtracting from FFO:

- Normalized recurring expenditures that are capitalized by the REIT and then amortized, but which are necessary to maintain a REIT's properties and its prospective cash flow.
- "Straight-lining" of rents.
- Other noncash items.

The basic formula would be as shown in Exhibit 10.23.

Straight-line rent is the average rental revenue received over the life of the lease, not the actual rent received in a particular year.[32]

EXHIBIT 10.23   Calculating AFFO

Funds from operations
– Recurring capital expenditures
+ Other noncash items
– <u>Adjustment for rent straight-lining</u>
Adjusted funds from operations

---

[30] David H. Downs and Z. Nuray Guner, "On the Quality of FFO Forecasts," *Journal of Real Estate Research* 28(3) (2006): 257–274.

[31] Richard Marchitelli and James R. MacCrate, "REITs and the Private Market: Are Comparisons Meaningful?" *Real Estate Issues* (August 1996): 7–10.

[32] Jonathan Litt, "Gaming FFO," *Property* (Fall 2001).

Adjustments may be required when rents have been straight-lined in accordance with GAAP because this adjustment may result in the reported income being overstated in the early years of the actual lease term.

FFO or AFFO can provide analysts with a starting point in their analysis, but this information should be used with caution because companies may use different methods to estimate these measurements. It is important to develop a common point of reference to make comparisons by the type of entity or across the different types of entities.

Many analysts use FFO or AFFO as a measure of the real estate company's ability to pay dividends. Other analysts rely solely on the historic dividend payment and trend. The ratio of price to FFO or AFFO is a very common ratio that security analysts use to compare alternative REIT investment opportunities, in a manner that is similar to how price/earnings ratios are used in the broader equity market. Some analysts also use the dividend yield as a basis for estimating equity value. Regardless, the net cash flow projections must be indicative of the future operating performance for the entity and must take into consideration all recurring charges against gross revenues. The cost of capital developed must be matched conceptually and empirically to the definition of the economic income or benefit that will be capitalized or discounted.[33] In the case of REITs, the cost of equity capital is generally a function of the current dividend return, the expected future growth in dividends, and expectations with regard to changing FFO multiples accorded to the entity.

Real estate entities often create or have an interest in subsidiaries that can provide additional services to tenants or own or have an interest in development or other real estate companies and/or partnerships that may have a positive or negative influence on the entity's net cash flow. During the real estate cycle, properties can be refinanced, renovated, or sold during the normal course of business, which will affect the net cash flow that should be considered. In some cases, excess land is purchased as part of the development process and held until developed or sold, often resulting in gains. Although this potential source of income typically is excluded from FFO, it should not be ignored. The analyst must develop a consistent framework to analyze real estate entities. In the normal course of valuation, the prospective free cash flow or net cash flow is critical.

---

[33] Pratt, *Valuing a Business*, Chapter 9.

Three

Learning Objectives, Questions, and Problems

Learning Objectives, Questions, and Problems

CHAPTER 1: DEFINING COST OF CAPITAL

After reading the chapter and completing this exercise, the reader will be able to:

- List and identify the components of a capital structure.
- List and identify the basic components of the cost of capital.
- Explain the difference between nominal and real terms and when to use each.
- Explain the different standards (definitions) of value in common usage.
- Explain alternate terms for cost of capital and the difference between these and a capitalization rate.

1. The cost of capital is also referred to as the:
   a. Discount rate.
   b. Capitalization rate.
   c. Required rate of return.
   d. a and c above.
2. If one uses the cost of capital for a particular investor, the resulting value would be:
   a. Fair market value.
   b. Investment value.
   c. Fair value.
   d. Either b or c above.
3. Cost of capital is based on:
   a. Past observed returns.
   b. Current returns.
   c. Expected future returns.
   d. a and c above.
4. The base against which cost of capital is measured is:
   a. Cost.
   b. Cost adjusted for inflation.
   c. Book value.
   d. Market value.
5. The time value of money reflects:
   a. A real rate of return.
   b. Inflation.
   c. Risk.
   d. a and b above.

6. In an economy in which inflation is reasonably predictable, cost of capital is usually stated in:
   a. Real terms.
   b. Nominal terms.
   c. Either a or b above.
   d. None of the above.

CHAPTER 2: INTRODUCTION TO COST OF CAPITAL APPLICATIONS: VALUATION AND PROJECT SELECTION

After reading the chapter and completing this exercise, the reader will be able to:

- Explain what is the preferred income measure to use in valuation and project selection.
- Explain what a discount rate is.
- Given certain information about a security, compute its present value by the income approach.

1. What is the preferred income measure to use in the income approach in connection with valuation and project selection?
   a. Net income.
   b. EBITDA.
   c. Net cash flow.
   d. Gross cash flow.
2. In developing a discount rate for a firm's overall capital, the relative weights of debt and equity most widely used in practice are:
   a. Dollars the firm has raised in the past.
   b. Dollars the firm plans to raise in the current year.
   c. The existing proportions of debt and equity.
   d. The proportions of debt and equity that the firm targets for its capital structure over the long-term planning period.
3. Given the following information, compute the present value of the XYZ Corp's bond:

   Face value of bond $1,000.

   Interest rate on face value: 7%.

   Bond pays interest once a year at the end of the year.

   Bond matures exactly 4 years from valuation date.

   As of the valuation date, bonds of comparable risk are selling to yield 10% to maturity.
     a. $904.9
     b. $1000.0
     c. $857.1
     d. $946.6

4. When evaluating a new investment, the company should discount the expected cash flows from the investment at:
   a. The company's cost of borrowing for the new investment.
   b. The company's overall cost of capital.

c. The cost of capital relative to the risk of the new investment.

d. The company's overall cost of borrowing.

CHAPTER 3: NET CASH FLOW: PREFERRED MEASURE OF ECONOMIC INCOME

After reading the chapter and completing this exercise, the reader will be able to:

- Compute net cash flow to equity and to invested capital from a set of financial statements.
- Compute the expected value from a probability distribution.
- Explain the economic income measure most preferred in business valuations and why.

1. What is the *expected value* of the following distribution of possible cash flow in period 1: _____

Amount	Probability
$1,500	.10
$1,200	.20
$1,000	.30
$800	.20
$500	.20

2. When using a discounting model, the preferred income measure to discount is:
   a. Reported GAAP earnings
   b. Adjusted GAAP earnings
   c. Net cash flow
   d. EBITDA

3. Given the following income statement for 2008, calculate Apex Widget Company's net cash flow to invested capital for 2008:

Apex Widget Co., Inc.

Income Statement

Year Ended December 31, 2008

Revenues	$100,000,000
Cost of goods sold	$ 70,000,000
Gross profit	$ 30,000,000
Selling, general & administrative expenses	$ 5,000,000
EBITDA	$ 25,000,000
Depreciation & amortization	$ 3,000,000
EBIT	$ 22,000,000
Interest expenses	$ 2,000,000
Taxable income	$ 20,000,000
Federal & state income taxes (30%)	$ 6,000,000
Net Income	$ 14,000,000
Capital expenditures	$ 4,000,000
Additions to net working capital	$ 1,000,000

4. When starting with net income to common equity, net cash flow to invested capital is computed by:

   a. Adding interest expense (net of tax), adding dividends on preferred stock, subtracting additions to net working capital, subtracting capital expenditures, and adding noncash charges.

   b. Adding interest expense (net of tax), subtracting dividends on preferred stock, subtracting additions to net working capital, subtracting capital expenditures, and adding noncash charges.

   c. Adding interest expense (net of tax), adding dividends on preferred stock, subtracting additions to net working capital, subtracting capital expenditures, and subtracting noncash changes.

   d. Adding interest expense (net of tax), subtracting dividends on preferred stock, subtracting additions to net working capital, adding capital expenditures, and adding noncash charges.

CHAPTER 4: DISCOUNTING VERSUS CAPITALIZING

After reading the chapter and completing this exercise, the reader will be able to:

- Explain the difference between discounting and capitalizing.
- Given a discount rate and a growth rate, compute a capitalization rate and vice versa.
- Given certain information, compute the value using the Gordon Growth Model.
- Explain the term *midyear convention* and use it to compute a value using both the discounting method and the capitalizing method.

1. What is the value of an annuity in perpetuity of $1,000 per year capitalized at 5%?

2. Given the following information:

   Normalized cash flow in the year immediately prior to the valuation date: $1,000

   Discount rate: 15%

   Growth rate of expected cash flow in perpetuity: 3%

   Compute the present value of this investment. _____

3. What is the value of the following set of expected net cash flows? _____

   Year 1: $1,000

   Year 2: $1,100

   Expected rate of growth in perpetuity beyond Year 2: 4%

   Discount rate: 20%

4. Given the same assumptions:

   a. The discounting method will produce a higher value than the capitalization method.

   b. The capitalization method will produce a higher value than the discounting method.

  c. The discounting method will produce the same value as the capitalization method.

  d. The values produced by the two methods may differ depending on the assumptions.

5. Given the same annual cash flows:

  a. The midyear convention will always produce a higher value than the year-end convention.

  b. The year-end convention will always produce a higher value than the mid-year convention.

  c. The year-end convention will produce the same value as the midyear convention.

  d. The value produced depends on whether the discounting or the capitalization method is used.

6. Given the following information about XYZ Corp's cash flow, what is the value using the midyear capitalization convention? _____

  Next year's expected cash flow: $1,000

  Discount rate: 20%

  Growth rate in perpetuity: 4%

CHAPTER 5: RELATIONSHIP BETWEEN RISK AND THE COST OF CAPITAL

After reading the chapter and completing this exercise, the reader will be able to:

- Explain FASB's Concept Statement 7 position regarding discount rates with respect to cash flows.
- Understand the different elements of risk (e.g., market risk, unique risk) and explain the implications of each.
- Explain skewed and symmetric distributions of probable future cash flows and their implications for discount rates.

1. Which of the following statements about the risk-free rate is FALSE?

  a. It is a nominal rate.

  b. It contains horizon risk (interest rate risk).

  c. Both a and b above.

  d. None of the above.

2. Which of the following statements about risk is TRUE?

  a. Risk is measured relative to the most likely forecast of the expected cash flow for a given period.

  b. Risk can be eliminated by developing an expected value probability distribution of the expected cash flow for each future period.

  c. Both a and b.

  d. Neither a nor b.

3. Which of the following is a TRUE statement?

  a. The risk-free rate is observable in the market.

  b. The risk-free rate is not observable in the market.

    c. The equity risk premium is observable in the market.

    d. Expected net cash flows are observable in the market.

4. Which of the following is/are a TRUE statement(s)?

    a. In a symmetrical distribution of expected cash flows, the most likely value equals the expected value.

    b. In a skewed distribution the expected value can be greater or less than the expected value.

    c. a and b are both true.

    d. Neither a nor b is true.

5. TRUE or FALSE:

FASB's Concept Statement 7 advocates discounting at the risk-free rate when the expected value of the probability distribution is used in the numerator.

---

6. Interest rate risk is also called:

    a. Horizon risk.

    b. Maturity risk.

    c. Either a or b above.

    d. Neither a nor b above.

7. Market risk is also called:

    a. Systematic risk.

    b. Undiversiable risk.

    c. Either a or b above.

    d. Neither a nor b above.

8. Unsystematic risk is also called:

    a. Unique risk or residual risk.

    b. Unique risk or company-specific risk.

    c. Residual risk or company-specific risk.

    d. Any of the above.

9. Capital market theory assumes:

    a. Efficient markets.

    b. Liquidity of investment.

    c. A lack of risk aversion.

    d. Both a and b above.

CHAPTER 6: COST COMPONENTS OF A BUSINESS'S CAPITAL STRUCTURE

After reading the associated chapter and completing this exercise, the reader will be able to:

■ Identify each component in a company's capital structure and compute the cost of capital applicable of that component.

■ Describe and interpret a "yield curve."

■ Given the coupon rate, yield to call, and maturity date, select which is the most relevant market yield rate for a bond.

■ Given certain information, select which rate is the appropriate cost of capital for debt to use in the WACC.

■ Select which categories of debt to include when computing WACC.

- Categorize convertible securities as components of the capital structure;
- Categorize options and warrants as components of the capital structure.
- Describe the term *duration* and explain its implications in the context of cost of capital.

1. The yield curve for a debt instrument is based on:
   a. The number of years to maturity.
   b. The relative volatility of cash flows among firms.
   c. Both a and b above.
   d. None of the above.
2. The coupon rate (interest rate based on face value) of Company A is 6% and the coupon rate for Company B is 12%. The current cost of borrowing for both companies is 9%. What is the relevant market "yield" for each company?
   a. Company A yield to call, Company B yield to maturity.
   b. Company A yield to maturity, Company B yield to call.
   c. Yield to maturity for both companies.
   d. Yield to call for both companies.
3. Duration is:
   a. Another name for yield to maturity.
   b. Another name for yield to call.
   c. The weighted average number of years the debt is outstanding based on the present value of the cash outflows to service the debt in each year.
   d. None of the above.
4. In estimating the after-tax cost of debt most corporate finance theoreticians recommend using:
   a. The current marginal tax rate.
   b. The current effective tax rate.
   c. The marginal tax rate over the life of the investment.
   d. The effective tax rate over the life of the investment.
5. When calculating the total amount of debt for a company the analyst should:
   a. Not include any leases.
   b. Include only capitalized leases.
   c. Include both capitalized and operating leases.
   d. None of the above.
6. When a company has personal guarantees on its debt, the estimated cost of the guarantees:
   a. Should not affect the company's cost of capital.
   b. Should be added to the cost of debt.
   c. Should be added to the cost of equity.
   d. Should be allocated between the cost of debt and the cost of equity.
7. Employee stock options should be treated as:
   a. Common equity.
   b. Preferred equity.
   c. Debt.
   d. Some combination of a, b, and/or c.
8. TRUE or FALSE:

   Convertible preferred and convertible debt can both be thought of as a combination fixed income instrument and a warrant. _____

CHAPTER 7: BUILD-UP METHOD

After reading the chapter and completing this exercise, the reader will be able to:

- Given certain information, estimate the cost of capital by the build-up method using both *SBBI* and Duff & Phelps *Size Study* data.
- Identify the most commonly used length of maturity for the U.S. Government security for the risk-free rate and why.
- Critique an analyst's estimation of the discount rate by the build-up method.

1. Which of the following subcomponents for the premiums for risk is NOT generally used in the build-up method?
   a. General equity risk premium.
   b. Beta.
   c. Small company premium.
   d. Company specific risk premium.
2. Which of the following maturities of government securities is used to match SBBI's equity risk premium?
   a. 30 days, 5 years, and 20 years.
   b. 1 year, 5 years, and 20 years.
   c. 30 days, 5 years, and 10 years.
   d. 30 days, 5 years, and 30 years.
3. Which of the following is NOT a component of the risk-free rate?
   a. The real return for foregoing consumption.
   b. Inflation.
   c. Investment risk.
   d. Duration.
4. Which of the following are combined into one number in the Duff & Phelps data for use in the build-up method?
   a. A general equity risk premium and a proxy for stock's volatility.
   b. A general equity risk premium and a size premium.
   c. A size premium and a proxy for the stock's volatility.
   d. A size premium and a proxy for beta.
5. The predominant consensus of financial analysts today is to use which of the following maturities of government obligations as the basis for the risk-free rate?
   a. 30 days
   b. 5 years
   c. 10 years
   d. 20 years
6. What are the components of return to investors for public company stocks?
   a. Distributions or withdrawals.
   b. Realized capital gains or losses.
   c. Capital gains or losses whether realized or not.
   d. a and/or c above.
7. Which of the following statements about the Morningstar industry risk variable is NOT true?

a. It attempts to make the build-up method more closely approximate CAPM.

b. The industries are based on SIC codes and use full-information betas.

c. The weights accorded to each company's beta in the computed industry adjustment are based on segment sales as reported in the company's 10-K filing.

d. a, b, and c above are ALL true.

8. For which of the following has Morningstar's industry adjustments NOT been criticized?

a. Use of full-information beta.

b. Weighing the company's contribution by segment sales.

c. The risk factors in the companies making up the SIC code selection may not be similar to the subject company.

d. The Morningstar industry adjustments have been criticized for ALL of the above.

9. Which of the following components of the discount rate derived from the build-up model is most controversial?

a. The risk-free rate.

b. The equity risk premium.

c. The small company risk premium.

d. The specific-company adjustment.

10. Given the following information, calculate the estimated discount rate for XYZ Company by the build-up method using Morningstar data: _____

30-day T-bill yield rate	4%
20-year bond yield to maturity	5%
Beta	.90
Equity risk premium	6%
Small stock premium (10th decile)	5.8%
Company-specific adjustment	3.0%

11. Using the information from Question 10 and the following data from the Duff & Phelps *Size Study*, estimate the discount rate for Company XYZ using the build-up method and Duff & Phelps data. _____

Size as measured by	Risk Premium
Book value of common equity	11.32%
5-year average net income	12.18%
Total assets	11.65%
5-year average EBITDA	11.86%
Sales	10.90%
Number of employees	11.08%
Risk-free rate	4.00%

CHAPTER 8: CAPITAL ASSET PRICING MODEL

After reading the chapter and completing this exercise, the reader will be able to:

- Explain the difference between the Capital Asset Pricing Model (CAPM) and the build-up method for estimating the cost of equity capital.
- Explain *systematic risk* and *unsystematic risk*.
- Understand the assumptions underlying CAPM.
- Given certain information, compute the estimated cost of equity for a company using both the "pure" (original) CAPM and the expanded CAPM.
- Critique an analyst's estimate of the cost of equity by CAPM.

1. The main difference between CAPM and the build-up model is:
   a. Including beta as a separate factor.
   b. Including beta as a modifier to the general equity risk premium.
   c. Including a measure of systematic risk as a modifier to the general equity risk premium.
   d. b and c above.
2. Beta measures which of the following:
   a. Systematic risk.
   b. Diversifiable risk.
   c. Unique risk.
   d. a and b above.
3. The formula $E(Ri) = Rf + B(RPm)$ is:
   a. The unmodified CAPM formula.
   b. The build-up model formula.
   c. The modified CAPM formula.
   d. None of the above.
4. The security market line is:
   a. A portrayal of the general relationship between returns on stocks and returns on bonds.
   b. A portrayal of the relationship between stocks and bonds at a given point in time.
   c. A portrayal of the expected rate of return–beta relationship.
   d. A portrayal of the expected rate of return-risk relationship under the expanded CAPM formula.
5. If a nondividend-paying stock tended to move 75% as much as the market, that would indicate:
   a. Beta > 1.0.
   b. Negative beta.
   c. B < 1.0.
   d. Beta = 1.0.
6. Given the following information, what is the estimated cost of equity for XYZ Company under the original (pure) capital asset pricing model formula? _____

Movement in market	−10%
Beta for XYZ Company	.7

General equity risk premium	5%
Size premium for companies the size of XYZ	6%
Risk-free rate	4%
Company-specific risk	0

7. Given the following information, compute the estimated cost of capital for XYZ Company using Morningstar data: _____

Market movement last 12 mos. (CPM)	+10%
General equity risk premium	5%
Beta for XYZ Company	.70
Size premium for XYZ Company	.08
Co. specific risk for XYZ Company	.01
Risk-free rate	4%

8. Which of the following is NOT an assumption underlying the Capital Asset Pricing Model?
   a. There are no brokerage commissions or bid-asked spreads.
   b. Investors need to hold at least 16 positions in order to have a fully diversified portfolio.
   c. All investors have identical time horizons (expected holding periods).
   d. The rate received for lending money is the same as the cost of borrowing money.

CHAPTER 9: EQUITY RISK PREMIUM

After reading the chapter and completing this exercise, the reader will be able to:

- Define the equity risk premium (ERP).
- Explain what sources to use to estimate the ERP and the strengths and weaknesses of each.
- Explain the difference between the conditional ERP and the unconditional ERP.
- Critique an analyst's estimate of the ERP.

1. The equity risk premium (ERP) is:
   a. The cost of equity capital for a company.
   b. The differences between a company's cost of equity capital and the same company's cost of debt capital.
   c. The difference between expected returns on an index of market equities and the expected returns on so-called risk-free securities of the U.S. government.
   d. The difference in the rate of return expected on a company's equity over the expected market return on debt of a comparably rated company.
2. The proxy for the market in the context of the equity risk premium (ERP) can be:
   a. The Standard & Poor's (S&P) 500.
   b. The New York Stock Exchange (NYSE) composite stock index.

    c. Either a or b above.

    d. Neither a nor b above.

3. Which of the following is a true statement about past ERP data?

    a. Such data represent the ERP expected in prior periods.

    b. Such data represent the ERP expected in the current period.

    c. Both a and b above.

    d. Neither a nor b above.

4. Which of the following statements is correct for the period 1942–1951?

    a. Average inflation was higher than the income return on U.S. government bonds.

    b. The Federal Reserve publicly committed itself to maintaining a ceiling on interest rates on U.S. government bonds.

    c. Both a and b above.

    d. Neither a nor b above.

5. Which of the following statements is TRUE?

    a. Studies have shown that it is unlikely that the 1926–present arithmetic average figures on which Morningstar's historical ERP is based are representative of current expectations about the future ERP.

    b. Morningstar also publishes what it calls a "supply side" equity risk premium, which is lower than the historical ERP.

    c. Both a and b are true.

    d. Neither a nor b is true.

6. Which of the following statements is TRUE?

    a. The conditional ERP tends to be highest at market tops.

    b. The conditional ERP tends to be lowest at market bottoms.

    c. Both a and b are true.

    d. Neither a nor b is true.

7. Assume the following as of September 30, 2009:

    20-year U.S. government bond yield = 4.03%

    S&P 500 index = 1,057

    Cash flows expected to companies comprising the S&P 500 (dividends plus stock buy backs):

      Year 1 = $48.52

      Year 2 = $51.00

    Annual rate of growth in cash flows years 3 and thereafter = 3.5%

    What is the implied *ERP* (relative to a 20-year U.S. government bond)?

    a. 2.20%.

    b. 10.27%.

    c. 4.13%.

    d. 12.42%.

CHAPTER 10: BETA: DIFFERING DEFINITIONS AND ESTIMATES

After reading the chapter and completing this exercise, the reader will be able to:

■ Use beta correctly in the Capital Asset Pricing Model formula.

- Understand what beta measures and differences among published sources and practitioners in procedures for measuring it.
- Understand the various modifications of beta, how each is calculated, and when each is useful.

1. Which of the following statements is TRUE?
   a. Beta is used as a modifier to the equity risk premium in CAPM.
   b. Beta is used as a modifier to the equity risk premium in the build-up model.
   c. Both a and b are true.
   d. Neither a nor be are true.
2. Beta measures:
   a. Systematic risk.
   b. Financial risk.
   c. Business risk.
   d. None of the above.
3. What length of a look-back period do most services that calculate beta use?
   a. 1 to 2 years.
   b. 1 to 3 years.
   c. 2 to 3 years.
   d. 2 to 5 years.
4. The most commonly used frequency of measurement when calculating betas is:
   a. Daily.
   b. Weekly.
   c. Monthly.
   d. Quarterly.
5. The ordinary least squares (OLS) beta:
   a. Works about the same regardless of the size of the company.
   b. Tends to overstate the beta for large companies
   c. Tends to understate the beta for large companies.
   d. Tends to understate the beta for small companies.
6. When using guideline companies to develop proxy betas:
   a. Use of different sources won't make any difference because they all use the same procedures.
   b. Use of different sources is good because it leads to a more accurate beta estimate.
   c. They should all come from the same source in order to be comparable.
   d. Any of the above is a correct answer.
7. For an index to be representative of the market, it must be:
   a. Market-capitalization weighted.
   b. Revenue weighted.
   c. Earnings weighted.
   d. Any of the above.
8. The S&P 500 comprises 70% of the total value of which of the following indexes?
   a. NYSE.
   b. NYSE and AMEX.
   c. NYSE and NASDAQ.
   d. NYSE, AMEX, and NASDAQ.

CHAPTER 11: UNLEVERING AND LEVERING EQUITY BETAS

After reading the chapter and completing this exercise, the reader will be able to:

- Determine when levering and unlevering betas is important.
- Know the various formulas for levering and unlevering betas (the student is not required to memorize the formulas, but should learn that each formula is appropriate when certain assumptions are met).
- Know how to implement the formulas when given the formulas and the necessary information.

1. Which of the following statements is true about most published betas?
   a. They are unlevered.
   b. They are levered.
   c. They reflect the company's capital structure at market value.
   d. b and c above.
2. Levered betas reflect which of the following types of risk?
   a. Business risk.
   b. Financial risk.
   c. Both a and b above.
   d. Neither a nor b above.
3. Which of the following risks is removed by unlevering the beta?
   a. Business risk.
   b. Financial risk.
   c. Both a and b above.
   d. Neither a nor b above.
4. In which of the following situations would unlevering and relevering beta be most appropriate?
   a. Valuing a minority interest where business risk differs significantly among subject and guideline companies.
   b. Valuing a controlling interest where financial risk differs significantly among subject and guideline companies.
   c. Valuing a controlling interest where business risk differs significantly among subject and guideline companies.
   d. Valuing a minority interest where financial risk differs significantly among subject and guideline companies.
5. The Hamada formulas are consistent with the assumption of:
   a. A constant capital structure measured by components' percentages at market value.
   b. A constant capital structure measured by components' capital structure at book value.
   c. A constant dollar level of debt.
   d. A gradually changing capital structure until it reaches a specified target capital structure measured by components' percentages at market value.
6. Compute the unlevered beta for XYZ Company by the Hamada formula for unlevering: _____

$$B_U = \frac{B_L}{1 + (1 - t)\,W_d/W_e}$$

Levered (published) beta	1.10
Tax rate	30%
Debt	$10 million at face value
	$8 million at market value
Coupon on debt	6%
Common shares	10 million at $1 par value, $2 market value

7. Compute a relevered beta for XYZ Company (question 6 above) by the Hamada formula for relevering: _____

$$B_L = B_U(1 + [1 - t]W_d/W_e)$$

assuming debt capital equals 50% of the capital structure.

CHAPTER 12: CRITICISM OF CAPM AND BETA VERSUS OTHER RISK MEASURES

After reading the chapter and completing this exercise, the reader will be able to:

■ Understand the limitations of CAPM and their implications for beta.
■ Be able to explain expanded CAPM.
■ Be able to explain risk measures other than beta.

1. How many stocks does it take to reach the point that little added diversification can be gained?
   a. 16.
   b. 30.
   c. 50.
   d. More than c.
2. When are betas most reliable?
   a. In periods of low market volatility.
   b. In periods of average market volatility.
   c. In periods of high market volatility.
   d. Market volatility is not a factor that influences the reliability of betas.
3. Which of the following are typically included in the expanded CAPM?
   a. Size factor.
   b. Company specific risk factor.
   c. Book to market factor.
   d. a and b above.
4. What measure of risk did Shannon Pratt use in his doctoral dissertation titled "The Relationship Between Risk and Rate of Return for Common Stocks"?
   a. Beta.
   b. Standard deviation of 3 years of quarterly total returns.
   c. Volatility.
   d. None of the above.
5. The following are measures of downside risk:
   a. Downside beta.
   b. Variance.

   c. Value at risk.
   d. a and c above.
   e. b and c above.
   f. all of the above
6. Which fundamental accounting variable(s) does the Duff & Phelps *Risk Study* use to measure risk?
   a. Standard deviation of total return.
   b. Operating margin.
   c. Coefficient of variation in operating margin.
   d. b and c above.

CHAPTER 13: SIZE EFFECT

After reading the chapter and completing this exercise, the reader will be able to:

▪ Incorporate the size effect into the cost of equity capital using either CAPM or the build-up method and either Morningstar or Duff & Phelps data.

   Given the following information and the attached exhibits, compute the cost of equity for G&P Book Publishers and Printers, Inc. (SIC code 2731).

1. By the build-up method using Morningstar data _____.
2. By the build-up method using Duff & Phelps data _____.
3. By the CAPM using Morningstar data _____.
4. By the CAPM using Duff & Phelps data _____.

U.S. Treasury 20-year yield to maturity	4.5%
Specific-company risk premium	1.0%
Book value of equity	$425,000,000
Common shares outstanding	50,000,000
Price per share	$14
Equity risk premium	6.0%
Beta	.90
Industry Risk Premium	2.36%

EXHIBIT 13.1   Returns in Excess of CAPM with S&P 500 Benchmark

Term Returns in Excess of CAPM Estimation for Decile Portfolios of the NYSE/AMEX/NASDAQ, 1926–2008

Decile	Beta*	Arithmetic Mean Return	Realized Return in Excess of Riskless Rate[†]	Estimated Return in Excess of Riskless Rate[‡]	Size Premium (Return in Excess of CAPM)
1—Largest	0.91	10.75%	5.56%	5.91%	−0.36%
2	1.03	12.51%	7.31%	6.69%	0.62%
3	1.10	13.06%	7.87%	7.13%	0.74%
4	1.12	13.45%	8.25%	7.28%	0.97%
5	1.16	14.23%	9.03%	7.49%	1.54%
6	1.18	14.48%	9.28%	7.65%	1.63%

EXHIBIT 13.1 (*continued*)

Term Returns in Excess of CAPM Estimation for Decile Portfolios of the NYSE/AMEX/NASDAQ, 1926–2008

Decile	Beta*	Arithmetic Mean Return	Realized Return in Excess of Riskless Rate[†]	Estimated Return in Excess of Riskless Rate[‡]	Size Premium (Return in Excess of CAPM)
7	1.24	14.84%	9.65%	8.03%	1.62%
8	1.30	15.95%	10.76%	8.41%	2.35%
9	1.35	16.62%	11.42%	8.71%	2.71%
10—Smallest	1.41	20.13%	14.93%	9.12%	5.81%
Mid-cap, 3–5	1.12	13.37%	8.18%	7.24%	0.94%
Low-cap, 6–8	1.22	14.86%	9.66%	7.92%	1.74%
Micro-cap, 9–10	1.36	17.72%	12.52%	8.79%	3.74%

*Betas are estimated from monthly portfolio total returns in excess of the 30-day U.S. Treasury bill total return versus the S&P 500 total returns in excess of the 30-day U.S. Treasury bill, January 1926-December 2008.

[†]Historical riskless rate is measured by the 83-year arithmetic mean income return component of 20-year U.S. government bonds (5.20 percent).

[‡]Calculated in the context of the CAPM by multiplying the equity risk premium by beta. The equity risk premium is estimated by the arithmetic mean total return of the S&P 500 (11.67 percent) minus the arithmetic mean income return component of 20-year government bonds (5.20 percent) from 1926–2005.

Source: Ibbotson Stocks, Bonds, Bills, and Inflation® 2009 Valuation Yearbook. Copyright © 2009 Morningstar, Inc. All rights reserved. Used with permission. (Morningstar, Inc. acquired Ibbotson Associates in 2006.) Calculated (or derived) based on CRSP® data, © 2009 Center for Research in Security Prices (CRSP®), University of Chicago Booth School of Business.

EXHIBIT 13.2 Size-Decile Portfolios of the NYSE/AMEX/NASDAQ, Largest Company and Its Market Capitalization by Decile

Decile	Market Capitalization of Largest Company (in thousands)	Company Name
1—Largest	$465,651,938	Exxon Mobil Corp.
2	18,503,467	Waste Mgmt Inc. Del
3	7,360,271	Reliant Energy
4	4,225,152	IMS Health Inc.
5	2,785,538	Family Dollar Stores Inc.
6	1,848,961	Bally Technologies Inc.
7	1,197,133	Temple Inland Inc.
8	753,448	Kronos Worldwide Inc.
9	453,254	SWS Group Inc.
10—Smallest	218,553	Beazer Homes USA Inc.

Source: Ibbotson Stocks, Bonds, Bills, and Inflation® 2009 Valuation Yearbook. Copyright © 2009 Morningstar, Inc. All rights reserved. Used with permission. (Morningstar, Inc. acquired Ibbotson Associates in 2006.) Calculated (or derived) based on CRSP® data, © 2009 Center for Research in Security Prices (CRSP®), University of Chicago Booth School of Business.

Historic Equity Risk Premium: Average Since 1963
Data for Year Ending December 31, 2008

Equity Risk Premium Study: Data through December 31, 2008
Data Smoothing with Regression Analysis
Dependent Variable: Average Premium
Independent Variable: Log of Average Book Value of Equity

Regression Output:

Constant	15.965%
Std Err of Y Est	0.917%
R Squared	79%
No. of Observations	25
Degrees of Freedom	23
X Coefficient(s)	-2.863%
Std Err of Coef.	0.303%
t-Statistic	-9.44

Smoothed Premium = 15.965% - 2.863% *Log(Book Value)

Smoothed Premium vs. Unadjusted Average

Portfolio Rank by Size	Average Book Val. ($mils)	Log of Average Book Val.	Number as of 2008	Beta (SumBeta) Since '63	Standard Deviation of Returns	Geometric Average Return	Arithmetic Average Return	Arithmetic Average Risk Premium	Smoothed Average Risk Premium	Average Debt/ MVIC
1	37,502	4.57	38	0.81	16.42%	10.10%	11.35%	4.31%	2.87%	24.52%
2	11,465	4.06	34	0.85	16.64%	10.37%	11.64%	4.60%	4.34%	29.42%
3	7,877	3.90	35	0.90	17.85%	12.01%	13.46%	6.42%	4.81%	30.55%
4	5,622	3.75	33	0.92	17.11%	10.50%	11.82%	4.78%	5.23%	29.87%
5	4,184	3.62	36	1.01	18.50%	10.92%	12.54%	5.50%	5.60%	27.52%
6	3,055	3.49	33	1.01	19.33%	10.31%	11.99%	4.95%	5.99%	27.39%
7	2,447	3.39	38	1.04	18.44%	10.99%	12.61%	5.57%	6.26%	26.21%
8	2,016	3.30	39	1.08	18.63%	11.05%	12.68%	5.64%	6.50%	25.81%
9	1,739	3.24	35	1.05	19.44%	12.01%	13.73%	6.69%	6.69%	25.49%
10	1,551	3.19	36	1.07	19.06%	11.52%	13.17%	6.13%	6.83%	26.43%
11	1,368	3.14	44	1.07	18.74%	10.96%	12.54%	5.50%	6.99%	26.88%
12	1,157	3.06	45	1.06	20.61%	12.46%	14.39%	7.35%	7.19%	27.11%
13	1,029	3.01	42	1.09	20.43%	12.41%	14.31%	7.27%	7.34%	25.90%
14	923	2.97	49	1.11	20.27%	13.23%	15.03%	7.99%	7.47%	25.32%
15	825	2.92	44	1.10	20.28%	13.30%	15.13%	8.09%	7.61%	24.82%
16	736	2.87	46	1.17	20.50%	12.56%	14.47%	7.43%	7.76%	25.73%
17	640	2.81	49	1.18	21.23%	11.99%	14.06%	7.02%	7.93%	24.26%
18	553	2.74	59	1.18	20.83%	12.70%	14.65%	7.61%	8.11%	25.11%
19	482	2.68	45	1.20	21.53%	11.77%	13.91%	6.87%	8.28%	26.53%
20	430	2.63	56	1.23	22.60%	14.36%	16.64%	9.60%	8.43%	26.05%
21	382	2.58	61	1.21	21.58%	14.25%	16.33%	9.29%	8.57%	25.42%
22	312	2.49	84	1.21	24.28%	13.63%	16.13%	9.09%	8.82%	24.70%
23	235	2.37	112	1.24	25.13%	12.87%	15.56%	8.52%	9.17%	25.53%
24	162	2.21	142	1.26	26.01%	15.19%	18.14%	11.10%	9.64%	25.67%
25	60	1.77	394	1.30	31.70%	15.06%	19.04%	12.00%	10.88%	25.71%
Large Stocks (Ibbotson SBBI data)						9.39%	10.88%	3.84%		
Small Stocks (Ibbotson SBBI data)						13.07%	15.96%	8.92%		
Long-Term Treasury Income (Ibbotson SBBI data)						7.01%	7.04%			

EXHIBIT 13.8 Duff & Phelps *Size Study*: Risk Premiums for Use in Build-up Method: Companies Ranked by Book Value of Equity

Source: © 200902 CRSP®, Center for Research in Security Prices. University of Chicago Booth School of Business used with permission.

Historical Equity Risk Premium: Average Since 1963
Data for Year Ending December 31, 2008

Portfolio Rank by Size	Average Book Val. ($mils.)	Log of Size	Beta (SumBeta) Since '63	Arithmetic Average Return	Arithmetic Average Risk Premium	Indicated CAPM Premium	Premium over CAPM	Smoothed Premium over CAPM
1	37,502	4.57	0.81	11.35%	4.31%	3.11%	1.20%	-0.16%
2	11,465	4.06	0.85	11.64%	4.60%	3.26%	1.34%	0.91%
3	7,877	3.90	0.90	13.46%	6.42%	3.45%	2.97%	1.25%
4	5,622	3.75	0.92	11.82%	4.78%	3.55%	1.23%	1.55%
5	4,184	3.62	1.01	12.54%	5.50%	3.89%	1.61%	1.82%
6	3,055	3.49	1.01	11.99%	4.95%	3.88%	1.07%	2.11%
7	2,447	3.39	1.04	12.61%	5.57%	3.99%	1.58%	2.31%
8	2,016	3.30	1.08	12.68%	5.64%	4.15%	1.49%	2.48%
9	1,739	3.24	1.05	13.73%	6.69%	4.05%	2.64%	2.61%
10	1,551	3.19	1.07	13.17%	6.13%	4.12%	2.01%	2.72%
11	1,368	3.14	1.07	12.54%	5.50%	4.13%	1.38%	2.83%
12	1,157	3.06	1.06	14.39%	7.35%	4.08%	3.27%	2.98%
13	1,029	3.01	1.09	14.31%	7.27%	4.20%	3.07%	3.09%
14	923	2.97	1.11	15.03%	7.99%	4.25%	3.73%	3.19%
15	825	2.92	1.10	15.13%	8.09%	4.24%	3.85%	3.29%
16	736	2.87	1.17	14.47%	7.43%	4.50%	2.93%	3.39%
17	640	2.81	1.18	14.06%	7.02%	4.55%	2.47%	3.52%
18	553	2.74	1.18	14.65%	7.61%	4.52%	3.09%	3.65%
19	482	2.68	1.20	13.91%	6.87%	4.62%	2.25%	3.77%
20	430	2.63	1.23	16.64%	9.60%	4.71%	4.89%	3.88%
21	382	2.58	1.21	16.33%	9.29%	4.69%	4.63%	3.98%
22	312	2.49	1.21	16.13%	9.09%	4.65%	4.45%	4.16%
23	235	2.37	1.24	15.56%	8.52%	4.74%	3.78%	4.42%
24	162	2.21	1.26	18.14%	11.10%	4.86%	6.24%	4.76%
25	60	1.77	1.30	19.04%	12.00%	4.99%	7.00%	5.66%

Large Stocks (Ibbotson SBBI data)				10.88%	3.84%			
Small Stocks (Ibbotson SBBI data)				15.96%	8.92%			

Long-Term Treasury Income (Ibbotson SBBI data) 7.04%

Equity Risk Premium Study: Data through December 31, 2008
Data Smoothing with Regression Analysis
Dependent Variable: Premium over CAPM
Independent Variable: Log of Average Book Value of Equity

Regression Output:

Constant	9.353%
Std Err of Y Est	0.953%
R Squared	65%
No. of Observations	25
Degrees of Freedom	23
X Coefficient(s)	-2.080%
Std Err of Coef.	0.315%
t-Statistic	-6.60

Smoothed Premium = 9.353% - 2.080% * Log(Book Value)

Smoothed Premium vs. Unadjusted Average

Premium over CAPM
Log of Average Book Value of Equity

EXHIBIT 13.14 Duff & Phelps *Size Study*: Risk Premiums for Use in CAPM: Companies Ranked by Book Value of Equity: Premium over CAPM

Source: © 200902 CRSP®, Center for Research in Security Prices. University of Chicago Booth School of Business used with permission.

All rights reserved. www.crsp.chicagobooth.edu Calculations by Duff & Phelps LLC. © Duff and Phelps, LLC.

CHAPTER 14: CRITICISMS OF THE SIZE EFFECT

After reading the chapter and completing this exercise, the reader will be able to:

- Describe what effect using the sum beta has on the reported size premium.
- Describe what *SBBI* offers for information on the 10th (smallest) decile.
- Describe the differences between the information available on the size effect between *SBBI* and the Duff & Phelps *Risk Premium Report*.
- Discuss the relationship between size and liquidity.

1. Which of the following Morningstar categories is likely to have the most distressed companies?
   a. 10th decile.
   b. 10a.
   c. 10b.
   d. Microcaps.
2. Which of the following is NOT a difference between the Morningstar data and the Duff & Phelps data?
   a. The Morningstar data starts with 1926, whereas the Duff & Phelps data starts with 1963.
   b. The Morningstar data are broken down into 10 size categories and the 10th decile is further broken down by market capitalization, while Duff & Phelps data is broken down by 25 size categories plus distressed companies.
   c. Morningstar's only size measure is market value of equity, while Duff & Phelps has 8 size measures.
   d. All of the above are differences.
3. The so-called "size effect"
   a. Is reduced by using sum beta.
   b. Is an empirically derived correction to the textbook CAPM.
   c. Does not exist.
   d. Both a and b.
4. Which of the following is a TRUE statement?
   a. Small stock premiums tend to run in cycles.
   b. Periods in which small firms have outperformed large firms have generally coincided with periods of economic growth.
   c. Company size and variance of returns are highly correlated.
   d. All of the above.
5. Liquidity risk is/are
   a. Part of the size premium.
   b. Related to but separate and in addition to the size premium.
   c. Systematic
   d. Both b and c.

CHAPTER 15: COMPANY-SPECIFIC RISK

After reading the chapter and completing this exercise, the reader will be able to:

- Tell what "company-specific" risk is
- Explain the contents of the Duff & Phelps *Risk Premium Report*.

- Use the Duff & Phelps *Risk Premium Report* to estimate a cost of equity for a company.
- Explain the contents and implications of the Butler-Pinkerton model.

1. Company-specific risk is also called
   a. Unsystematic risk.
   b. Idiosyncratic risk.
   c. Market risk.
   d. Either a or b.
2. Average risk premiums corresponding to company accounting data are found in
   a. SBBI.
   b. Duff & Phelps *Risk Premium Report*.
   c. Both a and b.
   d. Neither a nor b.
3. Which of the following is NOT a fundamental risk measure in the Duff & Phelps *Risk Study?*
   a. Operating margin.
   b. Coefficient of variation (CV) of operating margin.
   c. Return on book value of equity.
   d. Coefficient of variation of return on book value of equity.
4. Using Exhibit 15.1 (reproduced on the following page) and the following, what is the cost of equity by the build-up method for XYZ Co.? _____

XYZ sales	$400 million
XYZ beta	1.10
XYZ operating margin	10.1%
Your estimated equity risk premium	5.5%
Yield on valuation date for 20-year U.S. Treasury bond	4.0%

5. The Butler-Pinkerton model
   a. Is based on total beta.
   b. Is based on downside beta.
   c. Is based on measures which do not reflect beta.
   d. Always produces some indication of fair market value.

Historical Equity Risk Premium: Average Since 1963
Data for Year Ending December 31, 2008

Portfolio Rank	Median Operating Margin	Log of Median Op Margin	Number as of 2008	Beta (SumBeta) Since '63	Standard Deviation of Returns	Geometric Average Return	Arithmetic Average Return	Arithmetic Average Risk Premium	Smoothed Average Risk Premium	Average Debt/ MVIC
1	39.7%	-0.40	55	0.85	17.98%	11.07%	12.50%	5.46%	4.42%	26.93%
2	30.0%	-0.52	65	0.78	17.35%	9.31%	10.67%	3.63%	5.23%	29.58%
3	24.5%	-0.61	60	0.83	17.55%	11.09%	12.51%	5.47%	5.81%	28.00%
4	21.8%	-0.66	51	0.94	17.33%	11.53%	12.93%	5.89%	6.16%	24.44%
5	19.7%	-0.71	62	0.99	18.10%	11.54%	13.04%	6.00%	6.45%	20.85%
6	17.7%	-0.75	67	1.06	19.55%	12.54%	14.24%	7.20%	6.76%	17.75%
7	16.4%	-0.79	66	1.13	19.42%	11.53%	13.19%	6.15%	6.08%	17.76%
8	15.0%	-0.82	57	1.13	19.74%	11.41%	13.25%	6.21%	7.23%	19.55%
9	14.0%	-0.85	51	1.15	20.47%	13.83%	15.63%	8.59%	7.44%	19.22%
10	13.0%	-0.89	49	1.18	22.38%	13.21%	15.37%	8.33%	7.65%	21.09%
11	12.2%	-0.91	58	1.21	21.07%	11.51%	13.49%	6.45%	7.83%	21.49%
12	11.4%	-0.94	61	1.14	19.87%	12.26%	14.03%	6.99%	8.03%	21.90%
13	10.8%	-0.97	54	1.21	22.05%	12.51%	14.76%	7.72%	8.20%	21.91%
14	10.1%	-0.99	64	1.19	22.88%	13.38%	15.79%	8.75%	8.38%	22.96%
15	9.4%	-1.03	66	1.22	23.47%	14.30%	16.75%	9.71%	8.59%	23.56%
16	8.8%	-1.06	60	1.15	22.32%	14.59%	16.83%	9.79%	8.80%	25.30%
17	8.3%	-1.08	60	1.26	25.02%	13.96%	16.65%	9.61%	8.66%	25.85%
18	7.7%	-1.11	65	1.23	24.02%	14.04%	16.64%	9.60%	9.18%	26.10%
19	7.2%	-1.14	58	1.28	25.09%	14.00%	16.83%	9.79%	9.37%	27.56%
20	6.5%	-1.19	66	1.26	25.84%	14.75%	17.61%	10.57%	9.66%	29.28%
21	5.8%	-1.24	84	1.24	25.73%	15.76%	18.52%	11.48%	10.00%	29.94%
22	5.0%	-1.30	72	1.26	26.20%	14.12%	17.09%	10.05%	10.44%	30.21%
23	4.1%	-1.39	81	1.30	26.54%	15.10%	18.20%	11.16%	11.00%	31.75%
24	3.2%	-1.49	83	1.32	27.63%	15.39%	18.73%	11.69%	11.67%	32.34%
25	2.0%	-1.70	114	1.28	28.87%	14.39%	18.09%	11.05%	13.08%	31.38%
Large Stocks (Ibbotson SBBI data)						9.39%	10.88%	3.84%		
Small Stocks (Ibbotson SBBI data)						13.07%	15.96%	8.92%		
Long-Term Treasury Income (Ibbotson SBBI data)						7.01%	7.04%			

Equity Risk Premium Study: Data through December 31, 2008
Data Smoothing with Regression Analysis
Dependent Variable: Average Premium
Independent Variable: Log of Median Operating Margin

Regression Output:

Constant	1.744%
Std Err of Y Est	0.965%
R Squared	82%
No. of Observations	25
Degrees of Freedom	23
X Coefficient(s)	-6.669%
Std Err of Coef.	0.647%
t-Statistic	-10.31

Smoothed Premium = 1.744% - 6.669% * Log(Operating Margin)

Smoothed Premium vs. Unadjusted Average

EXHIBIT 15.1 Duff & Phelps *Risk Study*

Source: Compiled from data from Center for Research in Security Prices. © 200902 CRSP® Graduate School of Business, The University of Chicago used with permission. All rights reserved. www.crsp.chicagobooth.edu. Calculations by Duff & Phelps LLC. © Duff & Phelps, LLC.

CHAPTER 16 DISTRESSED BUSINESSES

After reading the chapter and completing this exercise, the reader should:

- Recognize the names of bankruptcy prediction models.
- Be able to explain the effect of distress on the accuracy of published betas.
- Be able to use the Duff & Phelps *Risk Premium Report* and the related section for high-financial-risk companies to value distressed companies and to present and/or critique testimony on how this is done.

1. Which of the following is/are (a) model(s) to predict bankruptcy?
   a. Altman z score.
   b. Ohlsen O score.
   c. Black-Scholes-Merton.
   d. All the above.
2. Published betas for distressed companies:
   a. Tend to overstate the risk.
   b. Tend to understate the risk.
   c. Tend to represent the risk relatively accurately.
   d. Tend to over- or understate the risk about equally.
3. Starting in 2010 (figures through 12/31/09), Part III of the Duff & Phelps *Risk Premium Report* for High-Financial-Risk companies contains:
   a. One portfolio for distressed companies.
   b. Two portfolios for distressed companies, as measured by Altman's z score.
   c. Four portfolios for distressed companies, as measured by Altman's z score.
   d. Ten portfolios for distressed companies as measured by Altman's z score.
4. Which of the following is/are a correct statement(s) about Altman's z score?
   a. Altman's z score uses market value of common equity/book value of debt
   b. Since private companies do not have a market value of common equity, Altman developed a z score that uses book value of common equity
   c. Both a and b.
   d. None of the above.
5. The Duff & Phelps *Risk Premium Report*:
   a. Can be used to estimate a cost of capital in the CAPM but not in the build-up method.
   b. Can be used to estimate the cost of capital in the build-up method but not he CAPM.
   c. Can be used to estimate the cost of capital in either the CAPM or build-up methods.
   d. Is not appropriate to use to estimate the cost of capital in either the CAPM or build-up method.

CHAPTER 17: OTHER METHODS OF ESTIMATING THE COST OF EQUITY CAPITAL

After reading the chapter and completing this exercise, the reader will be able to:

- Tell what variables are included in the Fama-French three-factor method.
- Describe the Arbitrage Pricing Theory (APT).

- Work out an implied cost of capital for a public company using the DCF method.

1. Which of the following is NOT a factor in the Fama-French model?
   a. Beta.
   b. Small minus big risk premium (difference between historical average annual returns on the small-cap and large-cap portfolios).
   c. High minus low risk premium (difference between historical average annual returns on high book-to-market and low book-to-market portfolios).
   d. Volatility.
2. Which of the following is NOT true of the Arbitrage Pricing Theory (APT) model?
   a. It is a multivariate (multiple regression) model.
   b. Most formulations of the APT theory consider only pervasive macro-economic variables.
   c. It is widely used.
   d. Beta may or may not be one of the factors in the model.
3. Using the single-stage DCF model and the following information, what is the implied cost of equity for ABC Manufacturing (a public company)? _____

NCF_0	$100/share
g	6%
PV (Stock Price)	$12/share

4. TRUE or FALSE: _____
   The multistage DCF model usually produces a more accurate result than the single-stage DCF model.
5. Where can single-stage and multistage DCF models for various industries be found?
   a. SBBI.
   b. Cost of Capital Yearbook.
   c. Duff & Phelps *Risk Premium Report*.
   d. Beta Book.

CHAPTER 18: WEIGHTED AVERAGE COST OF CAPITAL

After reading the chapter and completing this exercise, the reader will be able to:

- Explain WACC.
- Compute a WACC.
- Explain where a hypothetical (versus actual) capital structure should be used.
- Explain where a variable (versus constant) capital structure should be used.

1. In computing WACC, one should use:
   a. The market value of equity and the book value of debt.
   b. The book value of equity and the market value of debt.

   c. The market values of both equity and debt.

   d. The book values of both equity and debt.

2. Given the following information, compute the WACC for Company XYZ: _____

Shares common stock outstanding	1,000,000
Per share market price of common stock	$12
Shares preferred stock outstanding	100,000
Per share price of preferred stock	$50
Market value of debt outstanding	$3,000,000
Interest rate on debt at market value	7.5%
Income tax rate	20%
Cost of equity capital	20%
Cost of preferred capital	10%

3. Assume that state taxes can be deducted from Federal taxes. Given the following facts, what is the effective tax rate for calculating the WACC? _____

Federal rate	30%
State rate	10%

4. TRUE or FALSE? _____

   It is necessary to use an iterative process to compute the WACC for a private company given its existing capital structure.

5. Which of the following is most likely to be used as a capital structure when computing WACC?

   a. Actual capital structure when valuing either a control or a minority interest.

   b. Hypothetical capital structure when valuing either a control or a minority interest.

   c. Actual capital structure when valuing a control interest, and hypothetical capital structure when valuing a minority interest.

   d. Hypothetical capital structure when valuing a control interest, and actual capital structure when valuing a minority interest.

CHAPTER 19: GLOBAL COST OF CAPITAL MODELS

After reading the chapter and completing this exercise, the reader will be able to:

- Describe the various global cost of equity models.
- Describe the rationale and justifications for country risk adjustments.

1. Which of the following is NOT a legitimate reason for country risk adjustments?

   a. Financial risks.

   b. Economic risks.

   c. Political risks.

   d. All the above are legitimate reasons.

2. Which model is the best to use in estimating the cost of capital in developing countries, according to a consensus among both academics and practitioners?
   a. Global version of CAPM.
   b. Local, single-country version of the CAPM.
   c. Country credit rating method.
   d. There's no consensus about which is the best model.
3. When expressing expected returns from an investment in a foreign country in U.S. dollars, how should the exchange risk be treated?
   a. In the expected cash flows.
   b. As an adjustment to the discount rate.
   c. Either a or b.
   d. Neither a nor b.
4. Most global cost of capital formulas can be expanded to include:
   a. Size premium but not company-specific risk.
   b. Company-specific risk but not size premium.
   c. Neither a nor b.
   d. Both a and b.
5. Which of the following is a FALSE statement?
   a. When estimating cost of capital in the current economy for developed countries, there is often little justification for large country risk premiums.
   b. Any systematic country risk should be treated in the cash flows.
   c. Country risk premiums tend to have large standard errors.
   d. All of the above are TRUE statements.

CHAPTER 20: USING MORNINGSTAR COST OF CAPITAL DATA

After reading the chapter and completing this exercise, the reader should be able to:

- Describe Morningstar's four basic publications and summarize their content.
- Have a general knowledge of what is included on Morningstar's web site beyond what is in their four basic publications.
- Identify when an analysis is using Morningstar's data incorrectly, and make the correction(s).

1. In their *Stocks, Bonds, Bills and Inflation*, Morningstar bases the ERP on three maturities of U.S. government bonds. Which of the following do they NOT use for a basis for ERP?
   a. 30-day.
   b. 5-year.
   c. 20-year.
   d. 30-year.
2. The Morningstar data covers what period?
   a. 1921–present.
   b. 1926–present.
   c. 1953–present.
   d. 1963–present.

3. The *SBBI*'s position is that the best estimate of the ERP is:
    a. The long-term arithmetic average returns of stocks over government bonds using the NYSE as a representative of the market.
    b. The long-term arithmetic average returns of stocks over government bonds using the S&P 500 as a representative of the market.
    c. The long-term geometric average returns of stocks over government bonds using the NYSE as a representative of the market.
    d. The long-term geometric average return of stocks over government bonds using the S&P 500 as a representative of the market.
4. The *SBBI* uses which of the following measures when classifying firms by size:
    a. Market value of invested capital.
    b. Book value of invested capital.
    c. Market value of common equity.
    d. Book value of common equity.
5. The 10z size category contains what percentage of the NYSE stocks?
    a. 10%.
    b. 5%.
    c. 4%.
    d. 2.5%.
6. *SBBI*'s industry risk premium is:
    a. Determined by SIC code, with each stock receiving equal weight.
    b. Determined by SIC code, with each stock weighted by its contribution to operating profits.
    c. Determined by SIC code, with each stock weighted by its contribution to sales.
    d. Determined by SIC code, with each stock weighted by its contribution to gross profit.
7. What does Morningstar say about whether their data leads to a minority or a controlling interest?
    a. Because their data is all from the public markets, which, by definition, are minority interests, the result of using Morningstar data is minority interest value.
    b. Controlling interest values; otherwise somebody would take over the companies.
    c. It may be either a control or minority value, depending on the cash flows.
    d. It may be either a control or minority value, depending on the discount rate.
8. Which of the following is NOT included in the *Ibbotson Cost of Capital Yearbook*?
    a. Individual company data.
    b. Industry capital structure.
    c. Levels of profitability by industry.
    d. WACC measures by industry.
9. Which of the following is NOT true of the Fama-French three-factor model?
    a. It is a multiple linear regression model.
    b. The dependent variable is the company's monthly excess return on the stock market over Treasury bills.
    c. One of the variables is the difference in the monthly return on small-cap stocks and large-cap stocks.
    d. One of the variables is the change in GDP (Gross Domestic Product) by industry.

10. Which of the following is true about the implied cost of equity (Ibbotson calls them the discounted cash flow models) presented in the *Ibbotson Cost of Capital Yearbook*?
    a. The single-stage model is presented and considered most accurate.
    b. The two-stage model is presented and considered most accurate.
    c. The three-stage model is presented and considered most accurate.
    d. The four-stage model is presented and considered most accurate.
11. Which of the following is NOT included in the *Ibbotson Beta Book* for each stock?
    a. CAPM OLS levered beta.
    b. CAPM OLS unlevered beta.
    c. Fama-French beta.
    d. Sum beta.
12. Which of the following is NOT included in the Ibbotson Cost of Capital Resources web site?
    a. Individual company betas.
    b. International Cost of Capital Reports.
    c. International Risk Premium Reports.
    d. International Liquidity Analysis.

CHAPTER 21: CAPITAL BUDGETING AND FEASIBILITY STUDIES

After reading the chapter and completing this exercise, the reader will be able to:

■ Use cost of capital to make capital budgeting decisions that maximize value to shareholders.

1. Which is the appropriate variable on which to focus in making capital budgeting decisions?
   a. Earnings (net income).
   b. Net cash flow.
   c. EBITDA.
   d. Any of the above, assuming the appropriate matching cost of capital is used.
2. What is the appropriate cost of capital to focus on for capital budgeting decisions?
   a. The firm's overall current WACC.
   b. The firm's overall target WACC.
   c. The current WACC for the project.
   d. The target WACC for the project.
3. The best corporate decision model has been demonstrated to be:
   a. Ratio analysis, because ratios provide a direct, simple link to the market.
   b. Formulas, because they are straightforward and simple to use.
   c. DCF.
   d. None of the above has been demonstrated to be superior to the others.
4. What should be the target returns for a capital budgeting project in order for it to add to shareholder value?

    a. The company's overall cost of capital.

    b. Above the company's overall cost of capital.

    c. The project's overall cost of capital.

    d. Above the project's overall cost of capital.

5. What should be the time horizon for capital budgeting decisions?

    a. Perpetual time horizon.

    b. The estimated life of the company.

    c. The life of the proposed project.

    d. Any of the above.

CHAPTER 22: COST OF CAPITAL FOR DIVISIONS AND REPORTING UNITS

After reading the chapter and completing this exercise, the reader will be able to:

- Identify tools that can be useful in estimating the value of divisions and reporting units.
- Tell what standard of value and on what basis divisions and reporting units should be valued according to ASC 820, Fair Value Measurements and Disclosures (formerly FASB Statement 157).
- Describe the times that goodwill impairment testing is required.

1. Which of the following tools is NOT useful in estimating a division or reporting unit's cost of equity capital?

    a. Duff & Phelps *Risk Premium Report*.

    b. Full information betas.

    c. Pure play guideline companies.

    d. RMAs Annual Statement Studies.

2. Reporting units are usually valued under which of the following standards?

    a. Fair market value.

    b. Fair value.

    c. Investment value.

    d. Fundamental value.

3. Reporting units should be valued under which of the following notions?

    a. Cost.

    b. Cost less depreciation and obsolescence.

    c. Exit price.

    d. Value of tangible assets and goodwill.

4. Which of the following times must goodwill impairment be tested?

    a. Must be made at least annually.

    b. At interim times when an event renders the goodwill impairment more likely than not.

    c. both a and b.

    d. neither a nor b.

5. Cost of capital for a division or reporting unit should be:

    a. The parent company's cost of equity capital.

   b. The parent company's WACC.
   c. Measured against other firms operating in the same line of business and with similar risks.
   d. None of the above.

CHAPTER 23: COST OF CAPITAL FOR FAIR VALUE REPORTING OF INTANGIBLE ASSETS

After reading the chapter and completing this exercise, the reader will be able to:

■ Explain the definition of "fair value" in the context of financial reporting.
■ Identify those items that are and are not identifiable intangible assets in the context of fair value for financial reporting.

1. Fair value for financial reporting is based on:
   a. The cost of the asset.
   b. The most recent transaction in the asset.
   c. An exit price (i.e., what the asset could be sold for).
   d. None of the above.
2. Fair value is based on what might be paid by:
   a. Market participants.
   b. The type of potential buyers who would maximize the value.
   c. Both a and b.
   d. Neither a nor b.
3. Fair value is based on the cost of capital of:
   a. Market participants.
   b. The market participants' perceptions of the subject entity's risks and attributes.
   c. The industry average cost of capital.
   d. Either a or b.
4. TRUE or FALSE _____

   In a fair value measurement, buyer-specific synergies should be eliminated.

5. For fair value reporting, which of the following is NOT considered an identifiable intangible asset?
   a. Customer lists.
   b. Assembled workforce.
   c. Broadcasting rights.
   d. Literary and musical works.

CHAPTER 24: COST OF CAPITAL IN EVALUATING MERGERS AND ACQUISITIONS

After reading the chapter and completing this exercise, the reader should be able to:

■ Discuss the record of successes and failures of mergers and acquisitions in recent decades.
■ Identify the major reasons for failure.
■ Avoid leading a company into an acquisition that will fail.

1. Which of the following is NOT a common mistake when assessing the value of an acquisition?
   a. Doing a DCF using the acquiring firm's overall cost of capital.
   b. Assessing the price on the basis of premiums paid for comparable acquisitions.
   c. Doing a DCF using the target's estimated stand-alone WACC.
   d. Using an earnings per share accretion/dilution test to assess the value.
2. What is the appropriate discount rate and level of cash flow to use to assess the value of an acquisition?
   a. Acquirer's WACC applied to expected cash flows including synergies.
   b. Estimated target's WACC applied to expected cash flows including synergies.
   c. Acquirer's cost of equity applied to target's cash flow including synergies.
   d. Estimated target's WACC applied to expected cash flow without synergies.
3. When is contingent consideration classified as a liability recognized in an acquisition?
   a. When the contingency is resolved.
   b. It is measured only on the acquisition date.
   c. It is recognized on the acquisition date and remeasured on each reporting date following until it is resolved.
   d. Either a or c above is acceptable accounting treatment.
4. What's the most frequent cause of loss of value to the acquiring company's shareholders?
   a. Overpaying.
   b. Failure to merge cultures.
   c. Failure to efficiently integrate systems.
   d. Poor business strategy.
5. What is considered by most practitioners the best corporate decision model for assessing a potential acquisition?
   a. The cost to replace (replicate).
   b. DCF.
   c. The market approach using guideline mergers and acquisitions.
   d. The market approach using guideline publicly traded companies.

CHAPTER 25: COST OF CAPITAL IN TRANSFER PRICING

After reading the chapter and completing this exercise, the reader will be able to:

- Describe situations in which transfer pricing is most commonly applied for tax purposes.
- Describe the commonly accepted methods for valuation in transfer pricing, especially transfers of intangible assets.

1. Transfer pricing analysis is used most frequently when goods or services:
   a. Are transferred between affiliated entities in different taxing jurisdictions.
   b. Are transferred between unaffiliated entities in different taxing jurisdictions.
   c. Are transferred between affiliated entities in the same taxing jurisdiction.
   d. Are transferred between unaffiliated entities in the same taxing jurisdiction.

2. Which of the following is (are) the most common approach(es) to valuation in transfer pricing?
    a. Cost.
    b. Market.
    c. Income.
    d. b and c.
3. Transfer pricing analysis is used for transfer of
    a. Commodities.
    b. Fixed assets.
    c. Intangible assets.
    d. All the above.
4. Which of the following was found to be the most appropriate rate of return for intangible assets?
    a. WACC.
    b. Unlevered cost of equity capital.
    c. Levered cost of equity capital.
    d. Either b or c.
5. Which of the following is/are income approach(es) to valuation for transfer pricing?
    a. Profit split method.
    b. Relief from royalty.
    c. Comparable uncontrolled transaction (CUT).
    d. a and b.

CHAPTER 26: CENTRAL ROLE OF COST OF CAPITAL IN ECONOMIC VALUE ADDED

After reading the chapter and completing this exercise, the reader will be able to:

- Explain what the EVA program means and how it works.
- Explain the mechanics of how the employees are incentivized by this program.
- Explain what the recommended WACC is for use in EVA and the income variable to which it is applied.

1. Which of the following best describes Economic Value Added (EVA)?
    a. NOPAT less a charge for capital.
    b. EVA uses CAPM with capital structure weighted at the actual proportion of the company or division.
    c. EVA uses CAPM with the capital structure weighted at the company's or division's target proportions.
    d. Both a and c.
2. In applying EVA, which of the following are recommended criteria for adjusting GAAP financial statements?
    a. Is the required information relatively easy to track or derive?
    b. Can the operating people readily grasp it?
    c. Can the managers influence the outcome?
    d. All the above.
3. Under the EVA leveraged stock options (LSOs):

a. The employees are given in-the-money stock options.
b. The employees buy in-the-money stock options.
c. The employees buy at-the-money stock options.
d. The employees are given out-of-the-money options.

CHAPTER 27: HANDLING DISCOUNTS FOR LACK OF MARKETABILITY AND LIQUIDITY FOR MINORITY INTERESTS IN OPERATING BUSINESSES

After reading the chapter and completing this exercise, the reader will be able to:

- Describe the primary methods of reflecting the discount for lack of marketability in the final value.
- Recognize the names of the main restricted stock and pre-IPO empirical studies used to support DLOMs for minority interests.
- Distinguish between the concepts of DLOMs for minority v. controlling interests.

1. Which of the following is a correct way to treat the discount for lack of marketability?
   a. Subtract a percentage from the value as if publicly traded.
   b. Build the DLOM into the discount rate.
   c. Either a or b.
   d. Neither a nor b.
2. Which of the following is NOT a restricted stock study?
   a. SEC study.
   b. John Emory studies.
   c. FMV Opinions study.
   d. Trugman Valuations study.
3. Which of the following *is* a pre-IPO study?
   a. Silber study.
   b. *LiquiStat* study.
   c. *Valuation Advisors' Lack of Marketability Discount Study*™.
   d. Columbia Financial Advisors studies.
4. Which of the following is an accurate statement about discounts for lack of marketability for controlling interests?
   a. The U.S. Tax Court has granted discounts for controlling interest in the range of 10–25%.
   b. All practitioners believe that there should be *some* discount for lack of marketability for controlling interests in private companies.
   c. Discounts for lack of marketability for controlling interests are of about the same magnitude as DLOM for minority interests.
   d. All of the above are accurate.
5. How long is the current required holding period for restricted stocks?
   a. 2 years.
   b. 1 year.
   c. 6 months.
   d. There is no longer a required holding period for restricted stocks.

CHAPTER 28: THE PRIVATE COMPANY DISCOUNT FOR OPERATING BUSINESSES

After reading the chapter and completing this exercise, the reader will be able to:

- Discuss the magnitudes of the private company discounts (PCD) in sales of controlling interest in private companies compared to public companies.
- Explain the reasons for PCDs.
- Give the range of PCDs in the U.S. Tax Court.

1. Which of the following statements is true regarding the empirical evidence about. the prices at which private companies have sold compared to prices at which public companies sell?
   a. All five studies presented in *Cost of Capital*, 4th ed. conclude that private companies sell for less.
   b. The evidence is mixed, with the preponderance showing that private companies sell for more than public companies.
   c. The evidence is mixed, with the preponderance showing that private companies sell for less.
   d. All studies conclude that private companies sell for more than public companies.
2. Which of the following statements is true?
   a. The U.S. Tax Court does not recognize discounts for lack of marketability (DLOM) for controlling interests.
   b. The U.S. Tax Court has granted DLOMs for controlling interests between 1% and 9%.
   c. The U.S. Tax Court has granted DLOMs for controlling interests between 10% and 25%.
   d. The U.S. Tax Court has granted DLOM for controlling interests as low as 15% and as high as 45%.
3. Which of the following most accurately describes the results of the Officer Study of private company acquisitions?
   a. Acquisitions for cash were at an average discount of 22% compared to acquisitions of public companies.
   b. Acquisitions for stock were at an average discount of 12% compared to acquisitions of public companies.
   c. Acquisitions of private companies averaged a 17% discount compared to acquisitions of public companies whether they were for cash or stock.
   d. Both a and b are true.
4. Which of the following is NOT a reason given by some researchers for the private company discount?
   a. Quality of accounting data and choice of an audit firm.
   b. Smaller size of most private firms.
   c. Restrictions in the sales process of some closely held firms.
   d. Poorer management of closely held firms.

CHAPTER 29: COST OF CAPITAL OF INTERESTS IN PASS-THROUGH ENTITIES

After completing the chapter and this exercise, the reader should be able to:

- Recognize what forms of entities are pass-through entities.
- Be able to explain the characteristics and risk of owning minority interests in pass-through entities.
- Know what has been the tax treatment of pass-through entities to date (1) by the Tax Court and (2) by the Delaware Court of Chancery.

1. Which of the following is NOT a pass-through entity?
   a. S-corp.
   b. Limited Liability Company (LLC).
   c. Both a general and a limited partnership.
   d. All the above are pass-through entities.
2. Which of the following is NOT a characteristic of a pass-through entity?
   a. There is no federal income tax at the entity level.
   b. The owner pays tax on the income passed through, and the items are classified the same as they would have been at the entity level.
   c. The entities may or may not pass through enough distributions to cover the owners' taxes arising from the entity ownership.
   d. All pass-through entities avoid double taxation.
3. Which of the following is a correct statement about the *Gross* case?
   a. The taxpayer's expert tax-affected the earnings, but the IRS's expert did not.
   b. The IRS's expert tax-affected the earnings, but the taxpayer's expert did not.
   c. Both experts tax-affected earnings.
   d. Neither expert tax-affected earnings.
4. The Chancery Court of Delaware:
   a. Took the same position as the court in the *Gross* case.
   b. Tax-affected the earnings at C-corp rates.
   c. Tax-affected earnings at its estimate of what the recipient would have to pay.
   d. None of the above.
5. Which of the following is NOT a risk/limitation for owners of pass-through entities?
   a. Distribution policies may change.
   b. It is hard to find buyers for minority interests in closely held pass-through entities.
   c. The owner may not receive enough distribution to pay the taxes due.
   d. In some instances there may be a state-level income tax.

CHAPTER 30: RELATIONSHIP BETWEEN RISK AND RETURNS IN VENTURE CAPITAL AND PRIVATE EQUITY INVESTMENTS

After reading the chapter and completing this exercise, the reader will be able to:

- Explain the distinction between venture capital and private equity.
- Explain the definition of PIPEs.

- Give an idea of expected rates of return for venture capital investors at various stages of development.
- Give an idea of the range of realized returns for private equity and venture capital investments.

1. While the terms *private equity* and *venture capital* are sometimes used interchangeably and there is some overlap, the usual distinctions are:
    a. Venture capital primarily invests in public companies, whereas private equity primarily invests in private companies.
    b. Venture capital entities usually have an exit strategy for an investment, whereas private equity entities do not.
    c. Venture capital entities primarily invest in new companies or companies with a limited history, whereas private equity entities tend to invest in more established companies.
    d. Both a and c.
2. A PIPE is:
    a. Public company investments in private equity.
    b. Private company investments in a public company.
    c. Preferred (stock) investment in a public company.
    d. Preferred (stock) investment in a private company.
3. First stage or early development hurdle rates for cost of capital according to the AICPA IPR&D Practices Aid were:
    a. 20–35%
    b. 35–50%
    c. 40–60%
    d. 50–70%
4. According to the Ewens Study (16,849 companies, 1987–2007) what percentage of venture-financed companies eventually had an IPO or were acquired?
    a. 25% had IPOs and 20% were acquired.
    b. 35% had IPOs and 25% were acquired.
    c. 10% had IPOs and 27% were acquired.
    d. 20% had IPOs and 17% were acquired.

CHAPTER 31: MINORITY VERSUS CONTROL IMPLICATIONS OF COST OF CAPITAL DATA

After reading the chapter and completing this exercise, the reader will be able to:

- Explain what determines whether a valuation by the DCF method produces a minority or control value.
- Explain what minority and control owners can and should do.
- Recognize when a control premium should and shouldn't be applied and what drives the percentage.
- Tell the approximate percentage of takeovers that occur at less than the prevailing public market trading prices.

1. Does the DCF method using the build-up or CAPM method for the discount rate produce a minority or a control value?
   a. Minority value, because the data inputs are all from the public stock market, which, by definition, are minority transactions.
   b. A control value, because if the public companies were not selling at control value (apart from synergies) they would be taken over.
   c. It could be either minority or control, depending on the projected cash flows.
   d. It could be either minority or control, depending on the standard of value.
2. Benefits available to minority owners are a function of:
   a. Efficiency of company operations.
   b. Differential benefits, if any, between control and minority owners.
   c. a and/or b.
   d. None of the above.
3. Absent encumbrances of the articles of incorporation, by-laws, or a binding agreement, which of the following can a nonmanager minority owner NOT do?
   a. Sell his or her stock to a private or public entity.
   b. Pledge his or her stock as security for a loan.
   c. Register a public offering to sell his or her stock.
   d. Any owner can do any of the above.
4. A control premium should be applied to the results of the DCF method if:
   a. The projected cash flows do not reflect what a control owner would expect to achieve.
   b. A buyer can achieve strategic or synergistic benefits, and is willing to pay some of those in the acquisition price.
   c. The buyer might want to register a public offering, create an ESOP, or re-purchase outstanding shares.
   d. Any of the above.
5. About what percentage of takeovers of public companies were at less than the pretakeover market price?
   a. Less than 2%
   b. 2–6%
   c. 6–10%
   d. 12–18%

CHAPTER 32: HOW COST OF CAPITAL RELATES TO THE EXCESS EARNINGS METHOD OF VALUATION

After reading the chapter and completing this exercise, the reader should be able to:

■ Describe the origin of the excess earnings method.
■ Describe the IRS' attitude toward the method.
■ Reconcile the implied cost of capital and the value estimated from an application of the excess earnings method with the cost of capital derived by methods in this book and the resulting indicated value.

1. For what purpose was the excess earnings method originally created?
   a. To value small service business.

  b. To compensate brewers and distillers for their loss of goodwill during Prohibition.

  c. To value small retail businesses.

  d. Both a and c.

2. What is the number of the Revenue Ruling that applies to the excess earnings method?

   a. 59–60

   b. 68–609

   c. 89–249

   d. 93–12

3. What is the IRS position regarding use of excess earnings method?

   a. They approve of it, as indicated in the Revenue Ruling about how to use it.

   b. They say the capitalization rate should be 8 percent to 15 percent on tangibles and intangibles, respectively, although 10 percent and 20 percent can be applied to businesses where the hazards are high.

   c. It should be used only if there is no better basis for valuing the intangibles.

   d. It should be applied to the latest 12 months earnings.

4. What economic income variable does the excess earnings revenue ruling direct the analysts to use? _____

   a. Net income.

   b. Net cash flow.

   c. EBITDA.

   d. The Ruling is silent about which economic income variable to use.

   Use the following information for questions 5, 6, 7 and 8:

Return on tangible assets	8%
Cap rate on intangibles	15%
Value of tangible assets	$500,000
Total economic income (as measured by cash flow)	$70,000
Growth rate	5%
Capital structure	100% equity
Risk-free rate	4%
Equity risk premium	6%
Size premium	5%
Specific company risk premium	10%

5. What is the concluded value by the excess earnings method? _____

6. What is the overall cap rate by the excess earnings method? _____

7. What is the overall cap rate by the capitalization method using the build-up method? _____

8. What is the concluded value by the capitalization method using the build-up method? _____

CHAPTER 33: ADJUSTING THE DISCOUNT RATE TO ALTERNATIVE ECONOMIC MEASURES

After reading the chapter and completing this exercise, the reader will be able to:

- Convert a discount or cap rate applicable to net cash flow to a rate applicable to some other economic income variable.
- Convert an after-tax cap or discount rate to a pretax cap or discount rate.
- Identify an incorrect conversion and correct it, providing a rebuttal report and/ or testimony if necessary.

1. Which of the following must hold true in order to convert a discount or cap rate applicable to a measure of economic income other than net cash flow?
   a. The tax rate must be constant over time.
   b. The growth rate must be constant over time.
   c. The relationship between net cash flow and the variable to which the converted rate is applied must be constant over time.
   d. a and c.
2. If the variable for which you wish to convert a capitalization rate applicable to WACC to a capitalization rate applicable to EBITDA, which of the following must hold?
   a. There must be a constant relationship between WACC and EBITDA.
   b. There must be a constant capital structure.
   c. There must be a constant relationship between net cash flow to equity and EBITDA.
   d. a and b.
3. If one converts an after-tax cap rate to a pretax cap rate, which of the following is a (are) true statement(s)?
   a. The tax rate is assumed to be constant in the future.
   b. The pretax cap rate is equal to the pretax discount rate if the variable is constant over time (that is, there is no growth or decline).
   c. Both a and b.
   d. None of the above.

   Use the following information for questions 4 and 5:

Net cash flow expected next year (NCF1)	$100,000
Expected growth rate in perpetuity	5%
Discount rate from build-up or CAPM	25%
Tax rate	20%

4. What is the pretax capitalization rate? _____
5. What is the pretax discount rate? _____

CHAPTER 34: ESTIMATING NET CASH FLOWS

After reading the chapter and completing this exercise, the reader will be able to:

- List the components of net cash flow to equity and net cash flow to invested capital.
- Explain practitioner preferences with respect to their involvement in the preparation of cash flow forecasts.
- Explain the best practices in developing and/or testing cash flow forecasts.

1. Which of the following do NOT directly affect net cash flow to equity?
   a. Repayment of long-term debt principal.
   b. Deferred taxes.
   c. Capital expenditures.
   d. Changes in net working capital.
2. Which of the following DOES directly affect cash flow to invested capital?
   a. Preferred dividends.
   b. Amortization.
   c. Repayment of long-term debt principal.
   d. Deferred taxes.
3. Which of the following statements is TRUE about most professional valuers regarding cash flow forecasts?
   a. They prefer to make their own forecasts.
   b. They prefer to accept management's forecasts as presented.
   c. There prefer to either start with management's forecasts and test them for reasonableness or assist management in preparing forecasts.
   d. Either a or c is acceptable to most.
4. Which of the following are important to understand in forecasting net cash flows?
   a. Estimated capacity utilization of existing production.
   b. Expected volume.
   c. Expected inflation.
   d. All the above.
5. In a company expected to have steady volume (no growth) in perpetuity, what is the reasonable assumption affecting the terminal value?
   a. Capital expenditures will exceed depreciation.
   b. Capital expenditures will equal depreciation.
   c. Depreciation will exceed capital expenditures.
   d. None of the above.

PART Four

Answers and Solutions

Answers and Solutions

CHAPTER 1 SOLUTIONS

1.d A capitalization rate is applied to a *single* element of return, while the cost of capital reflects *all* elements of return.

2.b Investment value is the value to a *particular* investor. Cost of capital is determined by the market as a whole.

3.c Cost of capital is forward looking, based on expectations. Past returns are only sometimes used as a guide as to what to expect in the future.

4.d The base against which cost of capital is measured is market value, regardless of which element of cost of capital is being measured.

5.d The combination of the real rate of return and expected inflation are the components of the "risk-free rate," also called the time value of money.

6.b Both the projections and the discount rate should include expected inflation.

CHAPTER 2 SOLUTIONS

1.c The income approach uses a measure of net cash flow. It is what the owner can take out of the business without jeopardizing operations.

2.d The proper weights of the components of the capital structure are the firm's long-term target weights.

3.a
$$PV = \frac{\$70}{(1+.10)} + \frac{\$70}{(1+.10)^2} + \frac{\$70}{(1+.10)^3} + \frac{\$1,070}{(1+.10)^4}$$
$$= \$63.64 + \$57.85 + \$52.59 + \$730.82$$
$$= \$904.9$$

4.c Each investment should be evaluated in light of its own risk.

CHAPTER 3 SOLUTIONS

1.
$$\$1,500 \times .10 = \$150$$
$$\$1,200 \times .20 = \$240$$
$$\$1,000 \times .30 = \$300$$
$$\$800 \times .20 = \$160$$
$$\$500 \times .20 = \underline{\$100}$$
$$\$950$$

2.c Net cash flow is the amount that the investor can take out of the business consistent with the assumptions on which the forecast is based.

3.   Net income to common equity $14,000,000

    +Non-cash charges (depreciation & Amortization) $3,000,000

    −Capital expenditures $4,000,000

    −Additions to working capital $1,000,000

    +Interest expense (net of tax effect)

        $2,000,000\,(1 − .30) $1,400,000

                                       $13,400,000

4.a Preferred stock is part of invested capital, so preferred dividends must be included in the returns to invested capital.

CHAPTER 4 SOLUTIONS

1. $\dfrac{\$1,000}{.05} = \$20,000$

2. $\dfrac{NCF_0(1+g)}{k-g}$

$= \dfrac{\$1,000(1+.03)}{.15-.03}$

$= \dfrac{\$1,000(1.03)}{.12}$

$= \dfrac{\$1,030}{.12}$

$= \$8,583.33$

3. $= \dfrac{NCF_1}{(1+k)} + \dfrac{NCF_2}{(1+k)^2} + \dfrac{\dfrac{NCF_2(1+g)}{k-g}}{(1+k^2)}$

$= \dfrac{\$1,000}{(1+.20)} + \dfrac{\$1,100}{(1+.20)^2} + \dfrac{\dfrac{\$1,100(1+.04)}{.20-.04}}{(1+.20)^2}$

$= \dfrac{\$1,000}{1.20} + \dfrac{\$1,100}{1.44} + \dfrac{\dfrac{\$1,100(1+.04)}{.16}}{1.44}$

$= \dfrac{\$1,000}{1.20} + \dfrac{\$1,100}{1.44} + \dfrac{\$7,150}{1.44}$

$= \$833 + \$763.89 + \$4,965.28$

$= \$6,562.17$

4.c The capitalization method is just a shortcut form of the discounting method.

5.a The midyear convention always produces a higher value because it assumes that the cash flows are received earlier.

6. $$= \frac{\$1,000(1+.20)^{.5}}{.20-.04}$$
$$= \frac{\$1,000(1.095)}{.16}$$
$$= \frac{\$1,095}{.16}$$
$$= \$6,846$$

CHAPTER 5 SOLUTIONS

1.d It is nominal because it reflects inflation expectations. It contains interest rate risk because the values rise and fall with changes in the level of interest rates.

2.d Risk is measured relative to the expected value of the probability distribution. This does not eliminate risk; it just confines risk to something measurable.

3.a The risk-free rate can be observed as the yield to maturity on a government bond of appropriate maturity.

4.c The symmetrical distribution has equal amounts on both sides of the center. In the skewed distribution, the expected value depends on whether the distribution is skewed left or right.

5. FALSE
Concept Statement 7 is sometimes misinterpreted to advocate this.

6.c Interest rate risk is the risk that the value of the investment can change with changing levels of interest rates. The longer the term of the investment, the higher this risk, thus the alternative terms *horizon risk* or *maturity risk*.

7.c Market risk is that risk related to sensitivity to some broad index of stocks. As such it is systematic and undiversifiable, that is, it cannot be avoided by diversification.

8.d Unsystematic risk is that risk arising from factors other than the level of returns in the broad stock market.

9.d Capital market theory assumes efficient markets, complete liquidity, and risk-averse investors. Smaller public companies tend to be less aligned with capital market theory than larger public companies.

CHAPTER 6 SOLUTIONS

1.a Although volatility of a firm's cash flows are an important factor affecting the firm's cost of debt, the term *yield curve* applies only to the length of time to maturity.

2.b Company B is likely to call at the call date and refinance at the lower market rate, whereas Company A is likely to take advantage of its lower-than-market rate and let its debt run to maturity.

3.c See Exhibit 6.3 for illustrative calculation.

4.c The marginal tax rate over the life of the investment is what will be incurred as a result of the investment.

5.c Both are forms of financing. Standard & Poor's Rating Service routinely capitalizes both capital and operating leases when calculating comparative ratios.

6.b   Personal guarantees should be treated as an additional cost of the debt.

7.a   Employee stock options will generate equity capital for the company when exercised (and consequent dilution).

8.   TRUE
      Both have attributes of a fixed obligation and an option on the company's equity.

CHAPTER 7 SOLUTIONS

1.b   Beta is used in the CAPM method, but not in the build-up method. This is the primary difference between the two methods.

2.a   The length of time to maturity matches *SBBI's* short-term, intermediate term, and long-term general equity risk premiums.

3.d   The first three are all components of the risk-free rate.

4.b   The Duff & Phelps data for use in the build-up method combines the historic realized risk premium for the market and the size premium.

5.d   The 20-year maturity most closely matches the often-assumed perpetual lifetime horizon of an equity investment, and the yields fluctuate less than shorter-term yields.

6.d   Capital gains or losses are included, regardless of whether they are realized because it is assumed that the public stock is liquid and the investor has the choice of selling it or not at any time.

7.d   The list of companies for each industry segment and its weight in the computed industry adjustment are available for downloading free from Morningstar's web site.

8.a   The proportionate contribution to earnings (also available in the segment information on the 10-K) would be better because stock returns are a function of profit, not revenue. Also, most of the industries are not so homogenous as to represent the risk factors of any given company.

9.d   The specific company adjustment because it lacks empirical studies for estimating the amounts attributable to the various factors that make it up.

10.   19.8%

20-year bond	5.0%
Equity risk premium	6.0%
Small stock premium	5.8%
Company-specific risk	3.0%
	19.8%

11.   19.5%

20-year bond	5.0%
Duff & Phelps risk premium (average of 6 risk factors)	11.5%
Company-specific risk	3.0%
	19.5%

CHAPTER 8 SOLUTIONS

1.d Beta is the commonly used term for the measure of systematic risk in CAPM.

2.a Systematic risk measures *undiversifiable* risk.

3.a The CAPM formula is a single regression formula with RP_m as the variable and B(beta) the coefficient.

4.c The "Security market line" schematically portrays the relationship between expected rate of return and beta.

5.c Beta less than 1.0 means that, when the market moves, the stock tends to move in the same direction but to a lesser magnitude.

6. 7.5%

$$E(R_i) = R_f + B(RP_m)$$
$$= .04 + .7(.05)$$
$$= .04 + .035$$
$$= .075$$

7. 16.5%

$$E(R_i) = R_f + B(R_m) + RP_s + RP_u$$
$$= .04 + .7(.05) + .08 + .01$$
$$= .04 + .035 + .08 + .01$$
$$= .165$$

8.b The CAPM assumptions do not address the number of positions. Research has indicated that an investor needs to have far more than 16 positions in order to have a fully diversified portfolio.

CHAPTER 9 SOLUTIONS

1.c Analysts usually use the return on U.S. Government securities as the risk free rate.

2.c *SBBI* contains estimates of the ERP relative to both the S&P 500 and also the NYSE index.

3.d To the extent that past events are not expected to reoccur, past data should be adjusted to remove the effects of such events in order for the past to be a proxy for future expectations.

4.c Eliminating the effect of the 1942–1951 so called "Federal Reserve accord" lowers the historical ERP by about a half a percentage point.

5.c The authors of this book conclude that the true unconditional ERP is lower than either Morningstar's historical ERP or Morningstar's supply side ERP.

6.d The conditional ERP tend to be lowest at market tops and highest at market bottoms.

7.c Implied ERP = 4.13%
Implied rate of return on S&P 500 = 4.13% + 4.03% = 8.16%

$$
\begin{aligned}
\$1,057 &= \frac{\$48.52}{(1.0816)} + \frac{\$51.00}{(1.0816)^2} + \frac{\$51.00 \times 1.035}{(.0816 - .035)} \frac{1}{(1.0816)^2} \\
&= \frac{\$48.52}{(1.0816)} + \frac{\$51.00}{(1.1699)} + \frac{\$52.79}{(.0816 - .035)} \frac{1}{(1.1699)} \\
&= \$44.86 + \$43.59 + \$1,132.83 \frac{1}{(1.1699)} \\
&= \$44.86 + \$43.59 + \$968.31 \\
&= \$1,057
\end{aligned}
$$

CHAPTER 10 SOLUTIONS

1.a The primary difference between CAPM and the build-up model is CAPM's use of beta as a modifier to the equity risk premium.

2.a Beta measures the sensitivity of returns on the stock or portfolio to returns on some measure of the market. This is call systematic risk.

3.d Most services that calculate betas use a two- to five-year sample period.

4.c Monthly is the most common. Morningstar uses 5 years of monthly observations, but Value Line uses 5 years of weekly observations.

5.d For smaller companies, especially those without an active market, their betas tend to be underestimated using OLS betas.

6.c Betas from different sources vary as to the length of the look-back period, the frequency of measurement, the choice of a market index, and the choice of a risk-free rate.

7.a The weight for each company in the index is determined by the market value of its equity.

8.d The S&P 500 comprises about 70% of the value of all the major indexes listed.

CHAPTER 11 SOLUTIONS

1.d They are *levered*, meaning that, if the company has debt, they reflect the degree of systematic risk that results from the debt.

2.c Business risk is also called operating risk. Financial risk is also called capital structure risk. Both bear on the company's systematic risk.

3.b Unlevering the beta leaves the effect of business risk only.

4.b Minority interests usually cannot change the capital structure even if that would result in a higher value.

5.c The Hamada formulas are based on a constant amount of debt.

6.   1.2783

Cap structure (levered)
Debt $8,000,000
10 million shares stock @ $2 $20,000,000
                                        $28,000,000

$$W_d = \frac{\$8,000,000}{\$28,000,000} = .2857$$

$$W_e = \frac{\$20,000,000}{\$28,000,000} = .7153$$

$$B_U = \frac{1.10}{1 + (1 - .30)\left(\frac{.2857}{.7153}\right)}$$

$$= \frac{1.10}{1 + .70(.3976)}$$

$$= \frac{1.10}{1 + .2783}$$

$$= \frac{1.10}{1.2783}$$

$$= 0.8605$$

7. 1.46

$$\begin{aligned}
B_L &= B_U(1 + [1 - t]W_d/W_e) \\
&= .8605(1 + [1 - .3].5/.5) \\
&= .8605(1.7).5/.5 \\
&= .8605(1.7) \\
&= 1.46
\end{aligned}$$

CHAPTER 12 SOLUTIONS

1.d Research has shown that investors need to have at least 164 stocks to have at most a 1% chance of underperforming government bonds.

2.a Research has shown that estimating betas during periods of high market volatility will generally provide less reliable estimates of beta.

3.d Both the size and company-specific risk factors are included in most versions of the expanded CAPM.

4.b This measures "total risk," and turned out to be a good predictor of future returns except in the highest risk quintile.

5.d The shorter the duration for a given amount of total return over the life of the investment, the higher the present value.

6.d The Duff & Phelps *Risk Study* measures:
  1. Operating margins.
  2. Coefficient of variation in operating margin.
  3. Coefficient of variation in return on equity.

CHAPTER 13 SOLUTIONS

1. 16.21% (round to 16.2%)

    20-year T-bond YTM   4.50%

General equity risk premium	6.00%
Industry adjustment (SIC 2731)	2.36%
Size premium	
50,000,000 shares × $14 = $700,000,000 (8th decile)	2.35%
Specific company risk premium	1.00%
	16.21%

2. 16.09% (round to 16.1% or 16%)

20-year T-bond YTM	4.50%
Equity risk premium (20th portfolio)	
(6.00 − 3.84 = 2.16)	
8.43 + 2.16 =	10.59%
Specific company risk premium	1.00%
	16.09%

3. 13.25%

20-year T-bond YTM	4.50%
ERP	
6.00% × beta .90 =	5.40%
Size premium (8th decile)	2.35%
Specific company risk premium	1.00%
	13.25%

4. 14.78% (round to 14.8%)

20-year T-bond YTM	4.50%
ERP	
6.0% × beta .90 =	5.40%
Size premium	3.88%
Company specific risk	1.00%
	14.78%

CHAPTER 14 SOLUTIONS

1.c 10b has the smallest companies by market capitalization of the categories listed. This category has many large companies whose prices have been depressed by poor performance. Morningstar will further break down 10b into 10y and 10z.

2.d Duff & Phelps data has 8 different size measures.

3.d The magnitude of the size effect, which is an empirically derived correction to the textbook CAPM, is reduced when using sum betas.

4.d These factors are part of the reason that small firms are more risky.

5.d Liquidity costs tend to increase with declining sizes but not necessarily. Liquidity risk changes with overall market conditions.

CHAPTER 15 SOLUTIONS

1.d Market risk is systematic risk.

2.b The *SBBI* contains data relating only to market value of equity.

3.c The return on book value of equity is not included because Duff & Phelps research showed that it was not as strong an indicator of risk as the other three fundamental measures.

4. 14.04%

Yield on U.S. 20-year Treasury bonds		4.0%
Risk premium		
Smoothed average risk premium		8.38%
Plus: Adjustment to risk premium		
Your estimated equity risk premium	5.50	
Historic risk premium embedded in D&P data	3.84	
		1.66%
		10.04%
Estimated cost of equity for XYZ Company		14.04%

5.a It implies the assumption of a nondiversified investor.

CHAPTER 16 SOLUTIONS

1.d The three listed are all designed as predictors of bankruptcy.

2.b Betas for distressed companies tend to understate the risk and thus lead to overvaluation of distressed companies.

3.b There is one portfolio with z scores between 1.8 and 2.99 called the gray zone and one portfolio with z scores < 1.8 called the distress zone. Companies with z scores over 3.0 are grouped together.

4.c Altman revised the formula so that it could be used to measure the risk of closely held companies.

5.c The Duff & Phelps *Risk Premium Report* gives both the estimates of the total risk premium and the premium over CAPM.

CHAPTER 17 SOLUTIONS

1.d The Fama-French three-factor model does not have volatility as a factor.

2.c The variables are not specified and there is no universal consensus about what they should be.

3. 14.83%

$$
\begin{aligned}
k_e &= \frac{NCF_0(1+g)}{PV} + g \\
&= \frac{\$100(1+.06)}{\$12} + .06 \\
&= \frac{\$106}{\$12} + .06 \\
&= 8.83 + .06 \\
&= 14.83\%
\end{aligned}
$$

4. TRUE

Multistage models use more years of forecasts and usually produce more accurate results than the single-stage model.

5.b The *Cost of Capital Yearbook* gives average results for single-stage and multistage DCF models for over 300 industries.

CHAPTER 18 SOLUTIONS

1.c However, some services use the market value of equity and the book value of debt, and some even use the book value of both. (Banks almost never make inquiry into the market value of equity for private companies.)

2.

1,000,000 common shares @ $12	$12,000,000
100,000 preferred shares @ $50	5,000,000
Market value of debt	3,000,000
Market Value of Invested Capital (MVIC)	$20,000,000

$$
\frac{\$12,000,000}{\$20,000,000} = .60 \text{ (proportion of common stock)}
$$

$$
\frac{\$5,000,000}{\$20,000,000} = .25 \text{ (proportion of preferred stock)}
$$

$$
\frac{\$3,000,000}{\$20,000,000} = .15 \text{ (proportion of debt)}
$$

$$1.00$$

$$.20 \times .60 = .12$$

$$.10 \times .25 = .025$$

$$.15 \times [.075(1-.20)] = .15(.075 \times .80)$$

$$= .15 \times .06 = .009$$

$$WACC = .154(15.4\%)$$

3. $.10 \times .30 = .03$

    $.30 - .03 = .27(27\%)$
4. TRUE

    We need to have the weight of the market value of the equity, which is unknown. Therefore, an iterative process is necessary in order to compute the weight to apply to the common equity.
5.d The control interest has the ability to change the capital structure, but the minority interest does not.

CHAPTER 19 SOLUTIONS

1.d Financial, economic, and political risks are all legitimate reasons for country risk adjustments, especially in countries with developing economies.
2.d Each model has strengths and weaknesses.
3.c The exchange risk in most or all of the models can be treated either in the cash flows or in the discount rate.
4.d Most or all of the country risk formulas can be expanded to include both size and specific company risk, but the criteria for either to avoid double-counting may be different in some instances than the criteria for companies in the United States.
5.b Any systematic risk should be treated in the discount rate.

CHAPTER 20 SOLUTIONS

1.d There was no 30-year government bond when the series started.
2.b It contains information for any subperiod of years within that time period that is of interest to the user.
3.b They show the arithmetic average both relative to the NYSE and the S&P 500 but they prefer the S&P 500.
4.c The number of common shares and common share equity equivalents outstanding times the price of each.
5.d There are 10 deciles, representing 10% of the NYSE each by size. The 10th decile is further broken down by 10a and 10b (5% each), and 10a and 10b are further broken down by 10w (2.5%), 10x (2.5%), 10y (2.5%) and 10z (2.5%).
6.c Thus a low margin company gets the same weight as a high margin company in the same industry as determined by SIC code. The SIC codes were last updated in 1987, and there can be a wide variety of companies in an SIC code.
7.c The discount rate is not the determining factor; it's the cash flows. If somebody thinks they can make more money with the company, either by synergies or by more efficient operations, a takeover bid will probably occur.
8.a The *Cost of Capital Yearbook* is strictly by industry, containing data for about 300 SIC codes.
9.d Changes in GDP is more likely to be one of the variables in APT (Arbitrage Pricing Theory).
10.c The two-stage model is not presented in the *Cost of Capital Yearbook*. The authors have not seen a four-stage model in the literature, but it is conceivable.

11.d There are a dozen statistics for each stack, but sum beta is only one of them. There are six statistics for CAPM OLS betas, and six statistics for the Fama-French three-factor model.

12.d Ibbotson does not offer marketability or liquidity analysis.

CHAPTER 21 SOLUTIONS

1.b It has been shown that the market focuses on net cash flow.

2.d The correct focus is the target WACC for the project, reflecting the risk of the project, rather than the firm's overall WACC, which might be higher or lower than the WACC for the contemplated project.

3.c DCF is the logical link to basic fundamentals of value.

4.d To add to shareholder value the returns must be above the project's overall cost of capital, reflecting the risk of the project.

5.c The project's WACC over its estimated life is the correct focus for capital budgeting.

CHAPTER 22 SOLUTIONS

1.d RMA does not deal with cost of capital.

2.b ASC 820 (which supersedes FAS 157) says that reporting units should be valued under the standard of "fair value" (not to be confused with fair value in the context of shareholder disputes).

3.c Fair value focuses on the price at which the units could be sold.

4.c Goodwill impairment testing must be done at least annually and when there is a triggering event that calls into question the value of goodwill.

5.c Cost of capital is based on the risk of the subject investment. In some cases, it may be ameliorated by the parent firm's borrowing power, but it must be evaluated on its own business risks.

CHAPTER 23 SOLUTIONS

1.d ASC 820 (superseding FASB 157) says that fair value is an exit price.

2.c ASC 820 says that the type of market participants who would be most likely to maximize the value should be the ones considered.

3.b The pertinent cost of capital is not based by default on the market participants' cost of capital, but rather on their perspective on the risks and other assets of the subject entity.

4.   TRUE
     Synergies should be included only if several market participants could benefit from the synergies.

5.b Assembled workforce is not considered an identifiable intangible asset unless it is contractual.

CHAPTER 24 SOLUTIONS

1.c If more CFOs took this approach, there wouldn't be so many overpayments.
2.d Too many acquirers use their own cost of capital and project cash flows including the expected synergies, thus making a gift to the shareholders of the target companies.
3.c ASC 805, effective for fiscal years starting on or after December 15, 2008, requires measurement of contingency consideration when the deal closes and measurement afterward every reporting period until the contingency is resolved.
4.a One of the most frequent reasons for overpayment is underestimation of the cost of capital appropriate for the risk of the target.
5.b But accurate results from the DCF require diligent analysis of the prospective cash flows and an appropriate discount rate.

CHAPTER 25 SOLUTIONS

1.a Transactions between affiliated entities are subject to heavy scrutiny in many countries, especially those with relatively high corporate tax rates.
2.d Cost-based methods are rarely used because the underlying assumption of cost-based methods is that the cost drives the value.
3.d Taxing jurisdictions are interested in transfers of all kinds of property.
4.c Even the unlevered cost of equity capital generally underestimates the implied rate of return on overall intangible assets.
5.d The profit split method and relief from royalty are both income methods, but the comparable uncontrolled transaction method is a market approach method.

CHAPTER 26 SOLUTIONS

1.d EVA is defined as net operating profit after taxes, using CAPM with a WACC at the company's or division's target proportions of the capital components. A capital charge is deducted from NOPAT.
2.d In addition, another criterion is "is it likely to have a material impact on EVA?"
3.b The employees buy in-the-money options at their intrinsic value. For example, if the stock is $5.00 per share, the employees pay $1.00 for an option to buy a share at $4.00.

CHAPTER 27 SOLUTIONS

1.c The most popular way to reflect the DLOM is by a discrete discount for that factor at the end, but some people (notably venture capitalists) build the DLOM into the discount rate.
2.b The John Emory studies are pre-IPO studies.
3.c The other three listed are all restricted stock studies.

4.a A minority of practitioners take the position that there is no basis for a DLOM for controlling interests. DLOMs for controlling interests are generally lower than DLOMs for minority interests.

5.c Effective February 2008, the SEC reduced the required holding period for restricted stocks from 1 year to 6 months.

CHAPTER 28 SOLUTIONS

1.a All five studies presented show evidence that private companies sell, on the average, for less that public companies, related to various measures of profitability.

2.c The U.S. Tax Court has granted DLOMs for controlling interests up to 30%.

3.d Cash acquisitions had a significantly lower discount compared to acquisitions for stock.

4.d None of the studies suggested poorer management as a reason for the private company discount.

CHAPTER 29 SOLUTIONS

1.d All the organization forms listed are pass-through entities, and it is estimated that more than half of profit-making entities in the U.S. today are in one of these forms.

2.b Pass-through tax items retain their tax character, for example, capital gains or ordinary income.

3.a But the Court sided with the IRS expert who did not tax effect earnings.

4.c In one case the court stated succinctly, "Under an earnings valuation analysis, what is important to an investor is what the investor ultimately can keep in his pocket."

5.d One advantage of owning a pass-through entity is that there is no federal income tax at the entity level, although some states levy a state income tax.

CHAPTER 30 SOLUTIONS

1.c Typically, venture capital companies tend to invest at an earlier stage than private equity companies.

2.b PIPEs have become quite common in recent years.

3.c Of course, these are the expected rates for individual investments. The overall realized rates of return are much lower.

4.c One-tenth had IPOs, but 27% were acquired.

CHAPTER 31 SOLUTIONS

1.c It depends on whether the projected cash flows are what a minority or control owner could expect. The cost of capital is not significantly different for minority versus controlling interests.

2.c Control owners can distribute what otherwise might be profits as salaries or bonuses and provide other perks to themselves not available to minority owners.

3.c A minority owner cannot register a company's equity securities for a public offering.

4.d However, if b or c were the case, unless there was a pool of buyers with similar objectives, the resulting standard of value might be investment value rather than fair market value.

5.d Many are surprised to learn that, over the years, about 15% of the takeovers of public companies are at less than the prevailing market price.

CHAPTER 32 SOLUTIONS

1.b The excess-earnings method (also called the formula method and the treasury method) was originated as A.R.M. (Accounting Review Memorandum) 34 during Prohibition to establish the amounts the U.S. Government would reimburse brewers and distillers for their loss of goodwill.

2.b Rev. Ruling 68-609 is also called the formula method.

3.c RR 609 says "The 'formula' approach should <u>not</u> [emphasis supplied] be used if there is better evidence available from which the value of intangibles can be determined." It also says, "The above rates are used as examples . . ." and "The past earnings to which the formula is applied should fairly reflect the probable future earnings."

4.d RR 68-609 uses the term *earnings* without specifying what level of earnings it is applicable to. The Ruling is silent on which economic income variable to use. Many analysts do not use net cash flow, which is the variable assumed that the discount and capitalization rates developed by the build-up and CAPM apply to, so after reconciling the capitalization rates when comparing a value by the DCF method to a value by the excess earnings method, the analyst might also have to adjust the income variable used in the excess earnings method to net cash flow.

5. | | | |
    |---|---|---|
    | Tangible asset value | | $500,000 |
    | Less: Return on tangible assets: | | |
    | 8% × $500,000 | $40,000 | |
    | "Excess return" ($70,000 − $40,000) | $30,000 | |
    | Capitalized at 15% | | $200,000 |
    | Value of company by excess earnings method | | $700,000 |

6. | | |
    |---|---|
    | Weight of assets: $500,000/$700,000 = 71% at 8% | = .06 |
    | Weight of intangibles: $200,000/$700,000 = 29% at 15% | = .04 |
    | Implied cap rate by excess earnings method | = .10 |

7. | | |
    |---|---|
    | Risk-free rate | .04 |
    | Equity risk premium | .06 |
    | Size premium | .05 |

Specific company risk premium	.10
	.25
Less: growth rate	.05
Capitalization rate	.20

8. $$= \frac{\$70,000(1 + .05)}{.20}$$

$$= \frac{\$73,500}{.20}$$

$$= \$367,500$$

Would you pay $700,000 for this company as suggested by the excess earnings method? If you would, Pratt and Grabowski have a bridge to sell you.

What might be more reasonable in the excess earnings method would be to require 12% on the tangible assets (thereby using $60,000 of the $70,000 net cash flow) and leaving $10,000 excess earnings. A reasonable cap rate on excess earnings might be 33.3% (implying that the buyer would be willing to pay for three years of excess earnings), making the total value by the excess earnings method $530,000.

But by the capitalization method the company is only worth $367,500. Some companies just are not worth their net asset values.

CHAPTER 33 SOLUTIONS

1.c If there is not a reasonable constant relationship over time between net cash flow and the variables of interest, the procedure will produce meaningless results.

2.d Net cash flow to equity doesn't make any difference when we are converting a rate applicable to WACC to a rate applicable to EBITDA.

3.c In order to produce a valid result, the tax rate must be expected to prevail in the future. Like the cap rate on a noncallable perpetual preferred stock, in order for the cap rate to equal the discount rate the variable must be constant in perpetuity.

4. $c = k - g$

$\quad = .25 - .05$

$\quad = .20$

$c_{(pt)} = \dfrac{c}{l - t}$

$\quad = \dfrac{.20}{1 - .20}$

$\quad = \dfrac{.20}{.80}$

$\quad = .25(25\%)$

5. $k_{(pt)} = c_{(pt)} + g$

$\quad = .25 + .05$

$\quad = .30$

CHAPTER 34 SOLUTIONS

1.b Deferred taxes are not a cash item.

2.a Amortization, repayments or borrowings of long-term debt, and deferred taxes do not affect cash flow to invested capital.

3.c Most practitioners avoid making their own forecasts, although there are exceptions.

4.d b and c are important for forecasting both revenues and expenses and a is important for forecasting capital expenditures.

5.a Because of inflation, replacements will cost more than existing equipment.

Index